DESIGNING PARENTAL LEAVE POLICY

Sociology of Children and Families series

Series Editors:
Esther Dermott and **Debbie Watson**
University of Bristol, UK

The Sociology of Children and Families monograph series brings together the latest international research on children, childhood and families and pushes forward theory in sociology of childhood and family life. Books in the series cover major global issues affecting children and families.

Forthcoming in the series

A Child's Day:
Children's Time Use in the UK from 1975–2015
Killian Mullan, July 2020

Sharing Care:
Equal and Primary Caregiver Fathers and Early Years Parenting
Paul Hodkinson and **Rachel Brooks**, November 2021

Out now in the series

Social Research Matters:
A Life in Family Sociology
Julia Brannen, November 2019

Nanny Families:
Practices of Care by Nannies, Au Pairs, Parents and Children in Sweden
Sara Eldén and **Terese Anving**, July 2019

Find out more at
bristoluniversitypress.co.uk

DESIGNING PARENTAL LEAVE POLICY

The Norway Model and the Changing Face of Fatherhood

Berit Brandth and Elin Kvande

BRISTOL
UNIVERSITY
PRESS

First published in Great Britain in 2022 by

Bristol University Press
University of Bristol
1-9 Old Park Hill
Bristol
BS2 8BB
UK
t: +44 (0)117 954 5940
www.bristoluniversitypress.co.uk

British Library Cataloguing in Publication Data
A catalogue record for this book is available from the British Library

ISBN 978-1-5292-0158-1 paperback
ISBN 978-1-5292-0157-4 hardcover
ISBN 978-1-5292-0160-4 ePub
ISBN 978-1-5292-0159-8 ePdf

Cover design by blu inc, Bristol
Front cover image: Erin Drago/Stocksy

Contents

Contents.

1

Introduction

Rationale of the book

The starting point for this book is the Norwegian model of work and welfare, which, together with other Nordic countries, includes policies to support working mothers and fathers through an extensive parental leave system combined with high-quality daycare for children (Brandth et al, 2017). This reflects the dominant parenting norm of dual-earners and dual-carers (Sainsbury, 1999; Gornick and Meyers, 2009a), a norm promoted by scholars of welfare state regimes as a key to achieving gender equality (Esping-Andersen, 2002; Pascall, 2012). Parental leave and granting fathers parental leave rights remains a much-discussed topic in the Nordic gender equality debate. An earmarked right for fathers, the *father's quota* is a core component of the parental leave system, and the major focus of this book. It has existed for many years, it is popular and it is widely used.

Internationally, few elements of social policy have drawn such sustained attention as parental leave policies (Gornick, 2015). Many countries across the globe are currently in the process of introducing policies in this field, with others developing and refining already-existing policies. Despite global crisis and a politics of retrenchment, nations are continuing to develop this policy area, with only a few examples of cutbacks during the decade from 2004 to 2014 (Moss and Deven, 2015).

The annual report from the International Network of Leave Policies and Research (Blum et al, 2018) provides an overview of policies in the 43 countries represented by its members. It shows great variety in policy design and eligibility, reflecting diverse welfare regimes, economies and family cultures. This is illustrated by contributions in a special issue of the journal *Community, Work & Family* (2015), where a regime-type framework was used to illustrate countries' different policy trajectories. Moss and Deven (2015: 140) point out that most policy developments fit the notion of 'path dependency' as they do not seem to diverge far from an established policy. Many countries continue to reproduce maternalist presumptions at the expense of rights for fathers. Nevertheless, one common trend that stands out is a growing attention to fathers and an interest in fashioning leave policies that help increase fathers' involvement in childcare. Considering this recent and ongoing switch from maternity leave to other types of parental leave, leave policies for fathers seem generally to be in their infancy, although the Norwegian parental leave policy for fathers, the father's quota, has now reached a mature stage of 26 years.

Based on the annual report of the International Network of Leave Policies and Research, Haas and Hwang (2019) recently assembled a national overview of leave policies in Europe. They point out that fathers have been given the right to take parental leave in 30 of the 31 European countries included in the review, but that the rights vary widely. For instance, in 19 of the countries, fathers are granted an individual right to leave, but in only 6 are they offered well-paid leave (at two-thirds or more of their salary). Usage data shows that in only four countries do more than 75 per cent of fathers take the individual parental leave. Norway is one of these four countries (together with Iceland and Sweden from northern Europe, and Portugal). But compared to Iceland and Sweden, Norway currently has a longer father's quota, and it is more generously compensated. So, as a relatively rare case in point compared to other countries, the Norwegian situation is interesting. Why is it that fathers in Norway don't pass up the opportunity to take parental leave like fathers do in so many other countries? This is one of the primary questions to be dealt with by this book.

Concurrently with increased political interest in leave policy developments, research on fathers' use of parental leave has flourished. On the macro level, scholars have studied cross-country differences and similarities concerning leave policy characteristics (see, for example, Moss and Deven, 2006; O'Brien, 2009, 2013; Ray et al, 2010; Castro-Garcia and Pazos-Moran, 2016; Dearing, 2016; Karu and Tremblay, 2018). The focus has often been on comparing and ranking countries regarding institutional dimensions, gender division of leave, payment, duration and more. Widely debated questions concern how to design leave policies that are in line with evolving views about gender divisions of labour in paid and unpaid work. Several studies compare various clusters of countries (see the 2015 special issue of *Community, Work & Family*; Valarino et al, 2018), and there are also two-country comparisons where micro-level analyses are more prevalent (Almqvist, 2008; Gregory and Milner, 2011; Roosalu et al, 2016; Kaufman and Almqvist, 2017; Suwada, 2017). Studies of fathers and parental leave within single countries are abundant, and several edited volumes consist of single-country studies on specific topics (Kamerman and Moss, 2009; O'Brien and Wall, 2017; Moss et al, 2019). The chapters in this book are of this last kind, focusing on fathers in Norway and the way the welfare state has shaped practices and cultural meanings of fatherhood through parental leave policies.

Parental leave connects with many research topics, such as work–family balance, gender equality, childcare, masculinity and working life. Generally, the literature on fathering and fatherhood show a strong trend in affluent countries towards ideals and practices of more involved fatherhood (Hobson, 2002). In this respect, scholars have increasingly examined aspects of fathers' leave use. Relevant topics have been fathers' motivations to take leave (Almqvist and Dahlgren, 2013; Romero-Balsas et al, 2013), factors supporting or preventing leave use, such as social structure, working life and gender norms (Oechsle and Beaufaÿs, 2017), the impact of using leave on childcare, the division of housework (Lammi-Taskula, 2008; Haas and Hwang, 2008, 2019; Almqvist and Duvander, 2014) and masculinity (Schmidt et al, 2015). These studies (and many more) have reported positive effects on fathers' take-up of leave on parents sharing household tasks and fathers' involvement in childcare (see, for example, Østbakken et al, 2018). The longer the leave, the more lasting the effects are. Rehel (2014) points out that leave provides fathers with the necessary space to be active co-parents rather than helpers. Yet what fathers do during the leave and their lived experiences of taking leave are sparsely researched, but will be a main focus of this book.

The following chapters are based on three studies conducted decades apart: (1) before the individual, non-transferable leave for fathers was introduced (in the 1980s); (2) right after its introduction, when fathers were given four weeks (in the 1990s); and (3) when the leave given was 10 weeks (in the 2000s). We conducted all the studies, which are based on interviews with heterosexual fathers living together with the child's mother. They are, in various ways, concerned with exploring what fathers' take-up of leave means in terms of the father–child relation and fathers' caregiving practices in the three decades explored. Three separate qualitative studies from various decades are brought together and compared. Since the studies cover such a long time period, the chapters are able to pick up on changes towards the dual earner/dual carer model of which fathers' involvement in childcare is an important component. We suspect this will be interesting for countries in various stages of developing their parental leave policies for fathers.

The main aim of this book is to examine how the design of parental leave influences fathering practices, to show how the design impacts on employees with care responsibilities demanding parental leave from work. Furthermore, it aims to contribute knowledge on how men's care work changes men's gender identities and produces caring masculinities. Thus, our primary focus is on the father's quota and its importance for dual-caring, work–family balance and father–child relations. The main questions dealt with throughout are: How does the design of the father's quota impact on its usage and the content of fathers' caring practices? How has working life adapted to this regulation, and how do immigrant fathers relate to the laws and expectations directed towards fathers in Norway? How has the design of the father's quota influenced the normative perceptions of fathering in Norwegian society? These questions and more all concern aspects of gender equality in terms of the dual earner/dual carer model.

The following sections of this chapter describe the development of parental leave and the father's quota in Norway, its extensive use and popularity, and the hard political debates and conflicts that have been rendered visible around policy changes. The chapter ends with a review of the structure and chapters of the book.

Leave policy development in Norway: from motherhood and equal rights to fatherhood

Parental leave is the statutory right to paid absence from work after childbirth. Parents are given economic compensation for loss of wages during the leave period corresponding to full wages and up to a fairly high ceiling. This is called 'parental money' or 'benefit'. An important element in the leave scheme is that mothers and fathers earn the right to leave by having participated in working life and having had a taxable income prior to the leave – in order to be eligible for leave, both mothers and fathers must have been employed for six of the last ten months before birth. It is estimated that 13 per cent of fathers were ineligible for parental leave in 2011 (Kitterød et al, 2017). In addition to parental leave, there is a welfare leave of two weeks for fathers to be taken around the birth of the child, the so-called 'daddy days' or 'paternity leave'. Employers pay this leave after collective bargaining agreements between unions and employers' organizations.

Like most countries, Norwegian parental leave policy consists of several parts. As can be seen in Table 1.1, mothers and fathers have their own, individual leaves as well as a common period that they can share as they

Table 1.1: Development of paid leave 1909–2019 (number of weeks given)

Year and total number of weeks	Before birth	Maternity leave/mother's quota	Shared parental leave*	Father's quota	'Daddy days'
1909: 6		6			
1915: 8		6			
1946: 12		12			
1978: 18		6	12		2**
1987: 20		6	14		2
1988: 22		6	16		2
1989: 24/30*		6	18/22*		2
1990: 28/35		6	22/29		2
1991: 32/40	2	6	24/32		2
1993: 42/52	3	6	29/39	4	2
2005: 43/53	3	6	29/39	5	2
2006: 44/54	3	6	29/39	6	2
2009: 46/56	3	6	27/37	10	2
2011: 47/57	3	6	26/36	12	2
2013: 49/59	3	14	18/28	14	2
2014: 49/59	3	10	26/36	10	2
2018: 49/59	3	15	18/28	15	2
2019: 49/59	3	15/19*	16/18	15/19*	2

Notes: * 80% (instead of 100%) wage compensation increases the length of leave.
** Paid by the employer after collective agreements.

wish. In 2019, the total length of the leave was 49 weeks with 100 per cent pay or 59 weeks with 80 per cent pay. Mothers and fathers have 15 weeks each with non-transferable leave and 16 weeks that can be shared if they choose 100 per cent. The leave is thus currently divided into three equal parts.

Over the years, the parental leave policy has undergone significant shifts, and the different periods are marked with normal text, italics and bold in Table 1.1.

The nature of the earliest leave schemes, introduced in the first half of the 20th century, was to provide special protection for female workers from the demands of work, this being in the mother's interests as well as the child's. The leave was paid, as its goal was also to ensure economic security. Motherhood was the focus, and typically the leave was called 'maternity leave' or 'post-natal leave'. This maternity leave must be understood in terms of the male breadwinner model and one-income family that was dominant in the period of industrialization. The division of work between men and women was distinct, with women being expected to take care of the home and children and fathers having full responsibility for the family's income.

In Norway, the first breaks with the male breadwinner model appeared in the 1970s when values and norms concerning family and gender were set into play by a new women's movement. Influenced by ideas of equal rights, family policy intended to ensure mothers had the opportunity to combine participation in the labour market with giving birth and providing care, but also to enable men to provide care for their own children. Hence, what was totally new with the leave reform of 1978 was that most of the leave time could be shared between the parents. This meant moving away from the idea that leave was just for mothers, that is, it was a shift from maternity leave to parental leave. By granting fathers the right to share the leave, leave legislation in the 1970s signalled a new political view on men's responsibilities and participation in childcare. Both parents were subsequently given rights and obligations in relation to both the household and workplace.

In the 1980s and early 1990s, this model of parental leave continued to be developed, mostly by extending the length of the period available for parents to share. The idea of equal rights continued to be a strong rationale for extending parental leave. Although fathers were given the right to share the parental leave, this did not noticeably influence their use of the leave, and so the vision of equal parenthood did not receive much of a boost. The leave was relatively short during these years, but in 1989 parents became able to extend it by choosing 80 per cent instead of 100 per cent wage compensation, which implied one month more leave.

To further encourage fathers to take leave, the father's quota was introduced in 1993. This was an explicit political aim to strengthen father–child relations, but as a consequence of this, to also change the gendered division of work with respect to caring for small children. The father's quota is an individual right given to fathers and not to the family as a caregiving entity, which implies a break with the familistic character of the previous model. In addition to gender equality, individual autonomy became an overarching goal in the modernization of society in Norway (Ellingsæter, 2018). The father's quota was made non-transferable to the mother; if the father doesn't use it, it is forfeited. An additional rationale emerged with the father's quota – the child's need for a caring father: 'To strengthen the father's place in the child's life, it is important that he should take part in caregiving during the child's first year. Some of the parental leave should therefore be reserved for the father' (Stortingsmelding no 4,

1988–1989, p 32). The purpose of a father-specific quota was for the child to have better contact with the father, so the aim was not only to bolster equal rights, but also fatherhood more generally.

The father's quota introduced in 1993 was four weeks, and as seen from Table 1.1, in 12 succeeding years there were no changes to it. During this period a conservative government had prioritized other family political issues, first and foremost cash-for-care, but also the expansion in the number of kindergartens. However, in 2005 and 2006 the father's quota was extended by one week for both years, and in 2009, 2011 and 2013, with still more weeks. By 2009 it was extended by a whole month, and in 2013 it reached 14 weeks. All these extensions took place under a red–green government. When a conservative government gained power again in 2014 the quota was reduced to the advantage of shared parental leave, but in 2018 it was again increased to 15 weeks as a result of negotiations among liberal coalition parties, and in 2019 it became possible to lengthen the quota by choosing 80 per cent pay. This had only been possible for earlier shared parental leave. At the same time as the father's quota and mother's quota has been extended, the leave that can be shared has been reduced. The parental leave system now consists of three parts that are similar in length.

As can be seen from Table 1.1, another important change happened in 2013 when mothers were given a similar quota as fathers. By earmarking an equivalent number of weeks for both parents, the policy signalled the equal status of mothers and fathers. This is important, as it was expected that equivalent quotas would give a clearer signal that both parents had a right to the shareable part of the leave (Prop 64L, 2011–2012). In the political debate there has been great disagreement about the length of the shared leave in relation to the individual quotas, which can be seen in the changes highlighted in Table 1.1. The father's quota and mother's quota mean that the respective parent must take the leave weeks, or else they are forfeited. For mothers this has little practical meaning since very few take less than their quota, but a quota greatly influences fathers' use of the parental leave. To a large extent it is this earmarking (that the quota is not transferable to mothers) that explains its high take-up (Brandth and Kvande, 2003a). Several chapters in this book go on to explore the mechanisms behind this.

There have also been further changes that are not shown in Table 1.1, and one concerns eligibility. Until 2010, fathers did not have the legal right to the father's quota if the mother worked less than 50 per cent. Since then eligibility has been extended to include more groups of fathers such as those taking part in the introduction programme for immigrants to Norway, fathers receiving disability support and fathers who are self-employed; same-sex parents are also eligible. Nevertheless, eligibility rules are complicated. The father's right to leave is, for instance, dependent on both the mother's and father's participation in the labour force *before* the birth of the child. This means that parents who do not work and have not worked have not earned the right to parental leave. It also implies that the father's right to leave is neither completely independent nor individual. Their right to shared parental leave is, however, dependent on what both parents do *after* the birth. This means that fathers can take the shared leave independent of the mother's labour force participation as long as she starts work or studies when the father takes the leave (*aktivitetskrav*). This means that parental money (paid by the state) is a substitute for lost wages, and thus the welfare state is not at risk of paying for double care. Still, this principle is not implemented for the father's quota as it allows the mother to stay home on leave on a 50 per cent basis together with the father during his quota. These rules are currently being debated (2020), and may be next in line to be changed.

When the father's quota was introduced in the early 1990s many mothers were not ready to return to work after their leave, and some wanted to stay home longer, for instance, on unpaid leave while they waited for a place for their child in kindergarten (Vollset, 2011). For these parents the alternatives were either that the mother returned to work temporarily for one month during the quota, something that wasn't very practical, or that the father opted out of the quota to let the mother have continuous leave. This is why the law was changed the year after its introduction, to allow both parents to be able to stay at home at the same time during the quota. Chapter 5 deals with the differences in fathers' care practices dependent on the mother staying at home or not during his quota.

Another important change in the father's quota is the development towards greater flexibility. The quota cannot be transferred between the parents, and this means it appears inflexible. There are, however, many other types of flexibility in the its design. During the years that the father's quota has existed it has changed from being relatively short and having to be taken during the first year of the child's life to becoming longer with the option of postponing and spreading it over time until the child turns three years of age. The most prevalent types of time flexibility are stretching the leave by choosing reduced pay or combining the leave with part-time work and splitting it up into several blocks of time. Parents in many different situations use parental leave, and since the 1990s the need for flexibility has been related to family change and diversity, as well as a more flexible working life. How flexible leave is experienced and influences fathers' caregiving is the topic of Chapter 4.

The father's quota: use and attitudes

Fathers have had the opportunity to take paid parental leave in Norway since the end of the 1970s, but very few used their right to leave, which was only 18 weeks at the time (see Table 1.1). In the years following the introduction of the quota in 1993, the percentage of fathers using their leave rose from 4 to 45 per cent in 1994 and to 57 per cent in 1995 followed by a gradual increase to 85 per cent in 2000 (Brandth and Kvande, 2003a). Today, the father's quota is widely used by fathers in Norway, with over 90 per cent using all or part of it (Kitterød et al, 2017). Data from NAV (Norwegian Labour and Welfare Administration) confirms this: among fathers who had children in 2014 and who passed the three-year limit for uptake in 2017, only 7 per cent had not taken any leave (Schou, 2017). Fourteen per cent used less than the full quota, according to Kitterød et al (2017). Fathers who do not take their full quota are overrepresented among fathers with a low education, low or very high income, and among fathers born outside Norway. There are a variety of reasons behind non-use. Based on interviews with fathers who had not used the quota, Kitterød et al (2017) identify two main reasons. The first is the potential risk to their job, income and career, ranging from direct threats of being fired to worries about loss of goodwill. The second has to do with administrative troubles in relation to NAV.

The father's quota has been characterized as a success story because of the pronounced increase in fathers' leave use immediately following its introduction and after its expansions in length. Most fathers take exactly the days they are given (Fougner, 2012; Schou, 2017) – data from 2011 shows that 77 per cent of eligible fathers took the entire quota (Kitterød and Halrynjo, 2017). After the quota was reduced from 14 to 10 weeks in 2014, fathers consequently took shorter leave. This reduction in leave implied that 4 weeks were transferred to the shared parental leave period. Since mothers use the shared leave, their parental leave use increased accordingly (Schou, 2017). This 'natural experiment' demonstrates that fathers' leave use follows the father's quota regardless of its length. An increase in fathers' leave-taking would not have happened without the quota. This is illustrated by the fact that when the father's quota was reduced its usage was reduced accordingly. This was why the government decided to increase the father's quota again in 2018.

It is difficult to find comparable figures of leave use over time. Not only have the policies changed in eligibility, length and composition, studies have also defined their samples differently. Some include all fathers, some include employed fathers or fathers registered for parental benefit, while others define sub-samples of fathers, so numbers vary between studies. It has been estimated that about 20 per cent of fathers with a right to leave took more than the father's quota days when it amounted to six weeks (Grambo and Myklebø, 2009). In Kitterød and Halrynjo's (2017) study when the quota was 10 weeks, 25 per cent took longer leave than the quota. Fathers who take longer leave more often have a higher education and a middle income; they work in larger companies and in those with a greater gender balance. Mothers in these couples tend to have a high education and high income, and be born in Norway or another Nordic country (Kitterød et al, 2017). The effects of country of origin are mixed, with fathers originally from Eastern European countries taking the shortest leave.

Just a few years after parents could use the quota flexibly, it was extended from 6 to 10 weeks. Since then, fathers have more often tended to split the leave up or take it on a part-time basis (Fougner, 2012). This may be due to fathers worrying about staying away from work for long, or that it is more practical for the family that the father takes leave when the mother takes her holidays. Data show that it has become more common for the father to take parts of or the entire quota during the summer regardless of what month the child is born or how much leave the mother has used (Fougner, 2012). As shown in Chapter 4, flexible use has its downsides when it comes to fathers' caregiving. Some fathers, who had themselves used the option of taking part-time leave in combination with work, argue against flexible use. A high uptake does not necessarily mean that fathers use the leave as intended by the authorities, that is, to stay home from work and take main responsibility for childcare.

As can be deduced from the high take-up rates, the father's quota is popular. Fathers voiced no opposition when it was introduced; rather, the opposite. Through the Committee on Men's Role, fathers themselves were an important driving force behind the reform (Brandth and Kvande, 2009a). To take leave from work when you have become a father has become commonplace, and fathers hardly need to justify taking the quota – not to themselves, the mother or the employer (see Chapter 2).

Several studies have documented the popularity of the father's quota (Lappegård and Bringedal, 2013; Halrynjo and Kitterød, 2016; Hamre, 2017; Schou, 2017). In a survey conducted by Schou (2017), 89 per cent of the fathers and 83 per cent of the mothers supported it. Fathers' perception of the ideal length of the quota seems to change with its increasing length. In 2002, when the quota was 4 weeks, 50 per cent of the mothers and 50 per cent of the fathers thought that the ideal length was 4 weeks while 47 per cent thought it ought to be longer. In 2010, when the quota was 10 weeks, 80 per cent of the parents thought that it ought to be 10 weeks or longer (Lappegård and Bringedal, 2013). Parents seem to have quite similar attitudes that correspond with the existing policy. In Schou's (2017) survey parents were also asked their opinion on the ideal length of the quota – the average for fathers was 15 weeks and for mothers 13 weeks. This is a longer period than the quota was in 2017, but it is close to the length of the quota in 2020. It thus seems that the current, longer father's quota is more in accordance with people's opinions about the ideal length of the quota than when it was 4 weeks.

Political debates: conflict and consensus

Even if the Norwegian – and Nordic – family policy often stands as a model for other countries, this doesn't mean there are no conflicts about such policies within the country. The new direction in family policy that started in the 1970s led to long-lasting party political struggles over models of breadwinning and caregiving (Ellingsæter, 2018). This revealed a split among Norwegian political parties concerning family and childcare, a split that was particularly great between the political parties of the left contra the centre-right. Although all political parties had gender equality as a goal in the 1960s and 1970s, Labour governments introduced the reforms that came to characterize family policies in the next few decades. These implied greater autonomy for women in terms of income-generating work, and they met opposition from parties to the centre and right, which favoured policies of a more familistic character, such as supporting home-working mothers. Research has demonstrated that for many years Norway had a dualistic family policy with two different ideologies (Ellingsæter, 2003, 2018). Cash-for-care supports a traditional family-based care model, while parental leave and kindergartens accommodate the dual earner/dual carer model with gender-equal parenting.

One reason that parental leave nevertheless obtained cross-party support over the years is that it satisfied the family political aims of both wings of the political landscape (Håland, 2005). Parental leave satisfies both family-based care during the child's first year at the same time as it stimulates a return to working life for mothers. This mix between familistic and defamilistic elements was combined with different political views on the role of welfare state regulation of the family, and the borders between public and private solutions. In other words, this is a conflict between regulation and free choice.

From 1987 to 1993, the length of parental leave was extended every year until it reached 52 weeks with 80 per cent pay, without much disagreement between the parties. In this period, differences between the parties only appeared from time to time when they wanted to demonstrate disagreement in their reasons for supporting the initiative and its timing (Håland, 2001: 55). Agreement on the length of the parental leave reflected a long-term goal that most political parties had already accepted.

When the father's quota was debated in parliament (Storting) in 1992, most parties were in favour of the quota except for the Conservative and Progress Parties whose representatives argued against it. One of their main arguments was that it would hinder families' freedom of choice, families themselves being best able to decide which of the parents should take parental leave. The majority of the Norwegian parties, however, saw it as an acceptable exercise of mild pressure on fathers to participate more in childcare, maintaining that it would represent an important signal of men's responsibility. So, one dimension of disagreement between the parties in the father's quota debate concerned the question of choice, with an incipient conflict between a neoliberal ideology propounding freedom from state control and legislation that has been described as more 'paternalistic' (Brandth and Kvande, 2009a). This conflict was to become much stronger.

The parliamentary debates about the father's quota illustrate different perspectives on gender equality between the parties. For instance, the father's quota was supported by both Labour and Christian Democratic Parties, but on different grounds. The Labour Party saw the father's quota as an important step towards equal responsibility for work and home between mothers and fathers. The Christian Democratic Party, on the other hand, saw it as positive that the quota would give fathers a greater insight into women's care work in the home and thus come to value it more highly. This argument mirrored a maternalistic perspective on equal worth rather than a dual earner/dual carer view (Håland, 2001: 59). This illustrates that the father's quota is interpretatively flexible – it can be seen as a means to valorise work in the home traditionally done by women, but also to stimulate equal sharing.

Parental leave represents an arrangement where the ideal is parental care during the first year of the child's life without having to use any external caregiving. The relatively long period of paid leave thus allows for the family to have a mother at home and a father at work. All parties agreed that it was important to give parents more time with their children, and extended parental leave allowed for this. Moreover, all parties were in favour of supporting stronger father involvement and gender equality, and in 1993, reserving 4 weeks for fathers at the same time as the total leave was extended did not represent any competition with motherhood.

As long as the father's quota was 4 weeks, there was little debate about it. Rather, a publicly expressed pride over the large share of fathers using it was noticeable. This consensus continued during the expansions in leave in 2005 and 2006, but in 2009 and 2011, extended father-specific leave at the expense of the shared parental leave period was implied, and this set off an intense debate (see Ellingsæter, 2012). Since this redistribution of parental leave weeks between the father's quota and the shared leave (which mostly mothers use) had consequences for mothers' leave opportunities, it activated a maternalistic normative position in the debate. Inspired by the Icelandic model, the parties to the left aimed at a division of the leave into three equal parts, one for each of the parents and one to share. This struck another argument – that extension of the father's quota would reduce mothers' possibility for breastfeeding since, as it was claimed, the weeks left for mothers to use would be too few. This debate had actors other than representatives from political parties. Doctors and midwives used nutritional arguments against the extension of the father's quota. In this debate, ideas about breastfeeding, motherhood and children's health were used against the expansion of leave for fathers. The focus was on what fathers could *not* accomplish, and the struggle between ideas became a conflict between motherhood and fatherhood.

Another important difference in the debate after these extensions of the father's quota concerned state regulation contra free choice – positions that reflected a fundamental ideological difference between the political parties. When the red–green government proposed to divide the leave into three equal parts in 2010, the Conservative Party characterized the proposal as an encroachment on the possibility for families to organize their own lives. It was not against parental leave for fathers, but it opposed the quota. The two parties on the right, the Conservative and Progress Parties, added abolition of the quota to their platform and suggested the whole leave period should be a subject of choice between the parents. If so, this would represent a paradigmatic shift in the policy that had been prevailing in the last few decades (NOU, 2012: 15). When these two parties gained power in 2014, the father's quota was in real danger. However, since they represented a minority government and had to negotiate with the parties in the centre, the father's quota was saved – albeit shortened by a month (see Table 1.1).

The Conservative Party argued that they had regarded the father's quota as just a temporary measure, and that fathers in Norway, after having had a quota for 20 years, were ready to go on leave without this father-specific incentive. As it turned out in the following years, the fathers' use of leave dropped, illustrating that fathers take what is theirs and mothers what can be shared. In 2018, the father's quota was again extended to 15 weeks after a political compromise with the Liberal Party, which had then become part of the government. According to Ellingsæter (2016), these new party political constellations imply that the hybrid character of the Norwegian system, the mix between a gender-equal and a traditional family political model, has come to an end. This model, often presented under the guise of 'free choice' (Eydal et al, 2015), has given way to a gender equality discourse. The political parties have formed the parental leave system through conflicts and compromises, and the new core in family policies seems to be the gender-equal family. Neoliberal arguments of free choice seem to have been overruled by regulation.

How parental leave policies for fathers will develop in the future is hard to say. Although consensus and compromises have settled the political party debate for the moment, new party political constellations may change this. One key issue that seems to confront leave policy in Norway is presented in a recent white paper from the government (NOU 2017: 6). It suggests a leave scheme divided into two equal parts for mothers and fathers, and no longer an employment-related benefit based on certain eligibility qualifications. Rather, it suggests a reconceptualization of parental leave for it to become a universal social right for all parents who provide childcare.

Structure and content of the book

The chapters in this book are previously published articles and chapters that we have adapted to fit the context of this book. They are organized into three topical sections, focusing on leave design, fathers' caregiving, and relations to work.

The importance of leave design

Qualitative research linking leave design and outcomes is not extensive. However, on the macro level, many international studies have shown that parental leave designed as an individual non-transferable right results in a higher take-up by fathers than a right given to parents to share. Chapters 2 and 3 are concerned with understanding the mechanisms behind this pattern. In Chapter 2 we compare the meanings attributed to the two types of leave, and show how fathers' different senses of entitlement impact on their use. The cultural perspective of norms and understandings contributes to explain why the father's quota works so well.

One political debate concerning the father's quota has dealt with the question of parental choice vs state regulation. With this background, in Chapter 3, we explore how fathers from other European countries with different welfare state regulations regard the father's quota. A position as 'outsider-within' seems to enable these fathers to see how a statutory, earmarked and non-transferable quota works to their advantage when it comes to working life and their own experiences as able caregivers.

The last chapter in this section examines a different design element, namely fathers' option to use the father's quota flexibly. As the earmarked leave has become longer, fathers are more flexible with their timing of it. Chapter 4 deals with fathers' motivation for flexible use and the consequences of part-time and piecemeal use. Fathers report that part-time use combined with work creates problems of continuity and stress, both at work and at home, indicating that flexibility via part-time leave benefits neither working life nor caregiving.

Caregiving: fathering in transition

In Chapter 5 we jump back in time to before the father-specific quota was introduced. Fathers taking parental leave was rare at that time, and we expected a possible conflict between masculinity and childcare. Using an interactionist perspective, which is concerned with mothers and fathers negotiating their caregiving roles, we find that fathers who take leave assert their masculine identity using several strategies. One is insisting on their different style of care from mothers, and another is defining caregiving as an extension of masculine activities and giving it a meaning that corresponds with this.

Chapter 6 represents a gradual transition from the topic of leave design to caregiving, as it takes as its point of departure the opportunity (given by the rights to leave) for fathers to stay at home on leave alone or together with the mother. The chapter compares the two leave situations and their different consequences for a father's relation to the child and his development into an able caregiver. It shows that being home alone sensitizes a father's awareness of the child, which doesn't happen when the mother continues her presence in the home during the father's leave.

This finding is carried on into Chapter 7 that examines fathers on leave alone at a later date, when the leave has become longer. Comparing solo leave in two time contexts, it shows both similar and different results regarding the impact of solo leave on fathers' transformative experience. Although experiencing the leave as rewarding, fathers currently take more responsibility for housework, and call their leave experience 'hard work', expressing great respect for what mothers did previously during their leave.

Chapter 8 also bears relevance on masculinity as we explore how immigrant fathers to Norway frame taking parental leave. Parental leave for fathers, being rare or non-existent in their home countries, needs to be justified in an acceptable way to their family and friends in their homelands. Thus, in a transnational perspective, the leave is narrated into an account of the positive aspects of their life in a new country, and they fight against being defined as 'lesser' men because of having to take leave. The analysis confirms that staying at home with a child increases their capacity to provide emotional and practical care for their children. They justify their practices using the 'involved father frame', which may be variable in content but fits well with Norwegian culture.

Reconciling work and care

The third section has a greater focus on work–family balance and the way fathers and workplaces deal with the father's quota during and after its use. Chapter 9 directs attention to work–life reconciliation *after* the leave, asking what consequences the leave experience has for fathers' work involvement. A reduction in working hours is rarely an option for men, but the emotional and existential changes reported by the men having become fathers impacts on their boundary management strategies. These are used to reduce the time demands of work in order to benefit time with their children. Chapter 9 describes four such strategies.

Chapter 10 shows how fathers in various male-dominated work organizations relate to the obligation to take leave at a time when the father's quota was in its infancy. It underscores the importance of work context as well as personal agency and perceptions. Four different leave practices are described, and they show variations in how seriously the fathers and their work organizations relate to the new policy, and how they adapt to it. Some opposition is demonstrated, but there are clear indications that something is set in motion by the introduction of the father's quota.

How employed fathers experience their workplace's reactions to their use of leave is the topic of Chapter 11. Attention is directed towards the Norwegian model of working life based on cooperation and democratic work relations, which is an important institutional context for parental leave use. Contrary to literature that has been concerned to define workplaces as barriers to parental leave use, the analysis shows that fathers encounter few hindrances from employers and colleagues when they want to take leave. On the contrary, workplaces are supportive. In return, fathers seem to take their leave in a manner that does not create problems for the workplace.

Studies have shown that in some types of work such as management, men's parental leave use is very low. Chapter 12 looks into a group of middle managers in engineering and explores their experiences of taking leave on their career development. We use the concepts of 'availability' and 'irreplaceability', used earlier to analyze how the career logic works. By making themselves continuously available for their children while home on leave, the managers experience being irreplaceable in caregiving. They also experience being replaceable at work without it having any consequences for their career development. The chapter discusses how this might be a sign of a shift in the career logic.

PART I

The Importance of Leave Design

2

Fathers' Sense of Entitlement to Earmarked and Shared Parental Leave[1]

Introduction

Parental leave is one of the main policies to support working fathers and their ability to reconcile work and family. In Norway, as in many other European countries, parental leave consists of several parts, both individual and family-based rights (see Blum et al, 2017). As noted, shared parental leave is a family right available to both mothers and fathers, being gender-neutral in character. The father- and mother-specific quotas are earmarked, non-transferable rights and are thus inherently gendered. We investigated whether fathers' use of and understanding of these two types of leave differ.

In their analysis of what is needed to achieve 'strong gender equality' in family and working life, Brighthouse and Wright (2008) distinguish between policies that promote equality and those that enable it. As they see it, shared parental leave granted to the family enables parents to adopt egalitarian strategies, but puts no pressure on fathers to use them. Leave policies that promote equality are exemplified by paid leave granted to individual parents, which lapses if it is not used. Brighthouse and Wright find that type of leave necessary for breaking down the cultural barriers to gender equality in family and working life. Likewise,

[1] First published as B. Brandth and E. Kvande (2018) 'Fathers' sense of entitlement to earmarked and shared parental leave', *The Sociological Review*, 67(5): 1154–1169, https://doi.org/10.1177/0038026118809002 © the Author(s) (2018).

Morgan (2008) contends that shared leave is a 'partial reform' in the development towards gender equality. Partial reforms may be helpful to parents' work–life balance and bring some progress towards equality, but they may also reinforce a traditional division of labour between mothers and fathers. If the objective is greater equity in terms of the dual earner/ dual caregiver model, the father's quota represents a full embrace of this model (Morgan, 2008).

The international literature on specific policy provisions for parental leave is expanding (McKay and Doucet, 2010), particularly concerning fathers. Within research based on Nordic experiences, there is a consensus that parental leave rights given to individuals, rather than to families, are most likely to get fathers to take leave (Duvander and Lammi-Taskula, 2011; Haas and Rostgaard, 2011; Eydal et al, 2015). The father's quota in Nordic countries has been successful in involving fathers in taking care of their young children (Haas and Rostgaard, 2011; Brandth and Kvande, 2013a). These results are also found internationally (Gornick and Myers, 2009b; Moss and Kamerman, 2009; Miller, 2013). Fathers taking leave challenges the traditional gender norm that mothers are the primary caregivers of small children.

In contrast to individual, non-transferable rights for fathers, research from many countries without father-specific leave policies reports that fathers seldom take shared parental leave (Geisler and Kreyenfeld, 2011; Dearing, 2016; Kaufman, 2017). Explanations have included global economic instability (O'Brien, 2013), workplace conditions, job insecurity (Romero-Balsas et al, 2013), policy limitations such as inadequate payment (Moss and Kamerman, 2009), gender dynamics including prevailing ideas of masculinity and femininity (Schmidt et al, 2015; Valarino and Gauthier, 2016) and the moral obligations of motherhood and fatherhood (Lammi-Taskula, 2008). Mothers tend to take the leave that parents can divide however they wish, as men are not expected to take longer leave (Neuman and Meuser, 2017). Looking at what facilitates or hinders fathers from taking parental leave in Canada, McKay and Doucet (2010) point to three arguments: mothers' preferences, including breastfeeding; specific policy provisions, particularly the duration and non-transferability of parental leave; and ideological and social norms at workplaces and communities. In this analysis of how parental leave is understood in a Norwegian context, policy provisions and moral understandings of motherhood and fatherhood in workplaces are central issues.

To provide parental care in the home during the child's first year is a strong parenting norm in Norway. 'More time for children' translates into home-based care until the child is one year old. From the second year, when parental leave has ended, institutional care is accepted as the 'ideal' form of childcare while parents are at work (Ellingsæter, 2016). The father's quota gives male employees the right and obligation to provide home-based care. For fathers to opt out of the leave would thus go against this norm as the quota would be forfeited. Another principal aim of father-specific leave is to break away from the norm that men serve as breadwinners and women as caregivers. This also emphasizes children's right to care from both parents. Today, gender equality in terms of the dual earner/dual carer model is advocated by the political parties in Norway and practised by both parents taking parental leave (Ellingsæter, 2016).

The contemporary contexts for fathers to become caregivers are complex, contradictory and dependent on country-specific models of welfare policy, work–life traditions and legislative provisions. Policy provisions have consequences for societal ideas of men and women's capabilities and entitlements. Several of our publications have already explored the institutional and design characteristics of the father's quota in order to understand its high rate of use (Brandth and Kvande, 2001, 2009b, 2017). In this chapter we contrast and compare fathers' experiences with and attitudes concerning shared and earmarked parental leave further. How do the different policy characteristics and norms regarding parental care influence fathers' use of and understandings of the two types of parental leave?

Sense of entitlement

In exploring fathers' understandings of these two types of parental leave, we have chosen the concept of 'entitlement' as our theoretical lens. This is developed by Suzan Lewis (Lewis, 1997; Lewis and Smithson, 2001) to explain differences in expectations of support from the state or the employer for the reconciliation of work and family life. Lewis argues that 'for work-family needs to be translated into demands for and take up of supportive policies there has to be a sense of entitlement' (Lewis, 1997: 15). The concept stems from social justice theory and denotes beliefs or feelings about having rights to something based on what is understood as fair and equitable (Major, 1993; Lewis and Smithson, 2001). It may concern the right to a benefit specified by law or agreements if some required qualifications are met but, as Lewis and Lewis (1997) point out, a sense of entitlement may also reflect less objective considerations. Formal rights alone do not ensure that employees regard themselves, or are regarded by others, as entitled. Subjective meanings that parents attach to work–family policies also influence what they perceive as fair or unfair.

The sense of entitlement to work–family support is therefore highly context-dependent. It differs between countries and welfare states, which often have very different types of family policies and working life regulations. It also differs within countries between organizations, whose support for these policies varies. The Nordic welfare states, whose policies have shifted away from the male breadwinner/female caregiver model and instead expect all adults to be both breadwinners and carers, may lead to a different sense of entitlement than other countries whose policies are more asymmetrical.

According to the entitlement perspective, a sense of entitlement is also affected by wider social values. People make care decisions based on moral and socially negotiated views about proper behaviour. What parents may feel entitled to is embedded in normative understandings of appropriate parenthood. Entitlement is conditioned by conceptions of 'good motherhood' and 'fatherhood' as mothers and fathers consider others' assessments. Gender differences in parents' sense of entitlement result from societal norms regarding women's and men's roles within the family (Major, 1993). It has been pointed out that women and men experience a different sense of entitlement when it comes to work and family – fathers may lack a sense of entitlement regarding family support, while women may lack a sense of entitlement regarding career development, including pay (Lewis, 1997; Lewis and Smithson, 2001; Gatrell and Cooper, 2016), and thus they might feel a greater obligation to be carers.

The expectations in working life that employees should live up to the norm of the 'ideal worker' may limit the family support that organizations offer to men. In neoliberal economies, employment has been increasingly characterized by competitiveness, long hours, and a requirement that employees be available during the evening and on weekends, exacerbating the imbalance between paid work and family life. Policies, however, have the capacity to reduce this imbalance and empower employees. In this context, we must explore gendered moral rationales and social norms regarding work.

There is considerable evidence that fathers are becoming more involved in caring. Even though as a group fathers have a low sense of entitlement to work–family support, studies documenting a change in fathers' caregiving practices towards more involvement and responsibility have recently proliferated, showing a development that is paralleled by increased state support for men's rights to parental leave (Eydal and Rostgaard, 2016; O'Brien and Wall, 2017). There are strong reasons to believe that this development implies a nascent shift among fathers regarding their sense of entitlement to support for caregiving (Gatrell and Cooper,

2016). This shift is particularly relevant in the Nordic countries where achieving equality between men and women is an important goal, and where international observers have been impressed by how public policies seem to facilitate a more equal division of work and caregiving (Gornick and Meyers, 2009b).

The project investigated fathers' different senses of entitlement concerning individual and shared parental leave. We explore how fathers who have used parental leave understand their entitlement to leave by focusing on social comparisons with those they assume are similar to or different from themselves, including mothers, other fathers, and colleagues and managers at work.

Data

The analysis is based on a qualitative study in which 40 fathers who had taken parental leave were interviewed. About half the sample consisted of immigrant men. For the purpose of the analysis in this chapter, we analysed the data from 22 native-born fathers while interviews with the immigrant fathers are analysed in subsequent chapters. The interviews were conducted in late 2012/early 2013 and carried out during the second year after the child's birth. Thus, the fathers in the sample had rights to 10 and 12 weeks of individual leave and 27 or 26 weeks of shared leave if they chose 100 per cent compensation. The fathers were recruited by contact with various workplaces and then snowballing. The interviewees had become fathers after the father's quota was expanded to 10 weeks in 2009, and had thus experienced relatively long periods of leave. The length of the leave taken by the sample varied; most fathers had taken the father's quota of 10 or 12 weeks, but eight (36 per cent) had also taken all or part of the shared parental leave. Two of them had taken all the shared parental leave available, as the mothers were not eligible.

We endeavoured to find interviewees with varied social backgrounds. Half had a higher education (Master's level), while the other half either had a medium-level education at Bachelor's level (6) or no education beyond high school (5). The fathers had a wide range of occupations, including engineers, artisans, teachers, office workers, consultants, and administrative, healthcare and technical staff. They worked in organizations of various sizes and composition.

As Norwegian leave rights are employment-based, that is, accrued by the participation of both parents in working life, all the fathers and most mothers (except for three) were in paid employment prior to the birth of their child and had a right to parental leave. Private companies employed half of the fathers, but only one was self-employed, and one, a student, was temporarily employed. Except for this father, all worked full time. All the fathers lived together with the mother and the child. At the time of the interview, the child was between one and three years of age, and the child who triggered the interview could be the father's first, second or third child. Most fathers were in their thirties, although they ranged in age between 27 and 43.

Having presented the theoretical perspective, we discuss the empirical results in two sections. The first explores fathers' sense of entitlement to the father's quota, emphasizing workplace culture and norms. In the second we focus on fathers' sense of entitlement to shared parental leave when it is confronted with the moral obligations of motherhood and workplace norms.

Sense of entitlement to the father's quota

This analysis focuses first on the father's quota, which enjoys a high degree of support among fathers in Norway (Hamre, 2017).

The father's quota as an obligation

Studies on father's quota usage have pointed out that it has become a norm among men in Norway to take leave when they have become fathers (Naz, 2010; Halrynjo and Kitterød, 2016). Our findings support this claim.

"There was no doubt that I should take the father's quota", said Steinar, an engineer with two daughters. According to Ivar, "For fathers to have 12 weeks is quite natural in a way.... It has become incorporated." Their viewpoints illustrate that the father's quota is a matter of fact. Twenty-five years after it was introduced, taking leave seems to be taken for granted among fathers in Norway. That it is based in law, earmarked and non-transferable identifies this leave with fathers, and defines it as their right and 'property'.

It is also interpreted as an obligation and seen as a signal from the welfare state that fathers are expected to engage in taking care of small children. "Society reacts if you don't take it, right", Harold said. Lars, an engineer, claimed that the quota "feels like something you ought to ... that it's something you should take, really.... It feels like there's pressure on you to take it. That ... if you want to be a good parent, or a good father, then you have to take the daddy leave." Several fathers indicated that if they had not taken the father's quota, they would have to explain themselves to others.

A strong sense of entitlement to leave is supported by social norms of good fatherhood that these fathers seem to have incorporated into their identities. As the next section shows, fatherhood has also been incorporated into their practices as employees.

Employers' support of fathers' caregiving responsibilities

Many of the fathers in the sample strongly felt that having a quota given to them as employees was an unconditional strength in relation to work, and that it would have been much more difficult to gain support from employers if it were not for their legal right to the fathers' leave. "It makes your position stronger when the quota is based in law", said Geir. Kristoffer and many others believed that if the father's quota was not retained as a father-specific right, they would fail in their negotiations over leave with their employer. Since the father's quota is statutory, employers have little leeway to adopt discriminatory practices.

The fathers' sense of entitlement becomes explicit when Steinar reflects on how he would have had to argue in his previous job as a consulting engineer with a small company: "It was very intense with a call on us to work 80 hours a week and perform all we could with lots of pressure and bonuses. In this place, taking leave would have been frowned upon. But still, should you have to fight for your rights?" Moreover, the state rather than the employer pays the father's quota. Comparing his right to the father's quota with his right to paid holidays, Steinar said that if he did not take his "three months 'holiday' with pay", he would lose it. Entitlements to paid time off are acceptable in working life. To have to argue with his employer about his childcare responsibilities would not work as well, Steinar claimed.

None of the fathers in the study reported that they had experienced any serious problems with their current employers when planning to use their entitlement. Indeed, employers and colleagues seem to expect men to take the father's quota. Harold, a schoolteacher, said: "It was all right, and it was expected! It would have been more of an issue if I hadn't taken it. Public workplaces have to play by the rules." For fathers it seems inevitable that working life must adapt to the regulations of the welfare state. Christian, a senior advisor in the municipal administration, pointed out that even though the father's quota might sometimes represent challenges for workplaces, organizations do adapt to this legislation (see Chapter 11).

The father's quota has existed for more than a quarter of a century, which means that men who have advanced to management positions in organizations have taken leave themselves. This experience influences what is considered fair and feasible. Tore, a doctor in a large hospital, described how his leave-taking was received by his director, a 60-year-old chief physician: "He is updated on the father's quota.… He has had young children himself.… And I am not the first father to be in this situation." Steinar, too, explained that his bosses are fathers: "They are 54 and 62, and both were home with their children at a time when it was much less common than now. So they pushed me, saying 'Steinar, it is clear that you must stay home' and 'Are you sure you won't take a bit longer leave?' They said so even if it was bad for the job." Likewise, Sivert described his boss as very positive: "He understood me very well. I suppose he is 50 years, so he is very up to date." His boss was eager to help him find out about the regulations concerning the father's quota and the rest of the parental leave system. Sivert considered him a "modern" man who regarded fathers' involvement with children as important. Hans said:

> 'I think most employers today live in the modern world and understand that they must live up to that. This is how it is. They need employees who are happy with their job and have a good family life. Now, we see that both managers and middle managers in companies, 35 to 40 years old, experience the same tensions concerning career, childcare, parental leaves and work hours. I have a mate who is manager of marketing, only a few years older than me in a top job; he had four months daddy leave, so that says a lot.'

Fathers are more likely to take up family-friendly working practices if they can 'compare themselves with other fathers and realize that it is feasible to do so' (Lewis and Stumbitz, 2017: 230). The fathers we interviewed reported that as leave takers they did not stand out in any way. Hans, a communications advisor in a transport company, told us that at his workplace "many of my male colleagues had a child at about the same time as me, which was great! We were about three or four who had kids within a two- or three-month span. In addition, many employees here have small children." The norms that are produced by these practices make it easy for fathers to take leave and for organizations to plan for it. Dahl et al (2014), who studied the peer effect of father's quota usage, found that fathers are even more likely to take the quota if their colleagues did. The effect was greatest if a manager at a higher level in the organization had taken the fathers' leave.

Many of the fathers confidently portrayed the quota as *their* leave. In so doing, they conveyed a sense of entitlement and beliefs about what was right and fair. Ivar, an engineer with one daughter, took more leave than the father's quota. He was occasionally contacted by his workplace and asked to help out:

> 'I sometimes helped out [at work] when she slept, but I let them know that it had to be on my conditions, that I couldn't promise anything; I would only do it when I had the time, and I would register the hours I worked generously. If I worked one hour, I would register two or three.'

Ivar felt empowered by his right to leave. Hobson and Morgan (2002: 14) hold that family-friendly policies provide men with discursive resources with which they can make claims on their employers. Ivar communicated that it was he who was in control, and he was not afraid to insist on his priorities.

Entitled as caregivers

The father's role as a caregiver is important for their sense of entitlement. They communicated an identity as competent caregivers and attributed this to their time on leave when they had got to know the child well. They thought that children benefit from close contact with fathers, and that fathers are significant caregivers for children. Erlend said:

> 'It is quite unfair that only mothers are regarded as important for the children. Speaking as a man I think this is a new situation for gender equality.... I have been able to prove that I can be just as good a carer as the mother. I think it is super important! It increases men's self-confidence and society's confidence in men as caregivers.'

Regarding it as unfair that only mothers are given support as caregivers, these men see the father's quota as remedying this injustice. They justify their entitlement to leave as based on their ability to care for their small children and think that the father's quota contributes to their being seen as important parents. They feel entitled to both the joys and burdens of childcare, and stress that the father's quota represents an opportunity to develop an autonomous relationship with their children. "Being home on leave has in a way laid the foundation for the contact we [father and child] have today. A lot will happen later in life, but this is the basis," Didrik said.

The quota as a father-specific right simplifies negotiations with the mother. Sivert realized that this was the point of earmarking it: "This is why they designed it like that. If not, nothing would have come of it. Then the mother would have taken the whole leave." He thought that to many people it was still not obvious that the father would choose to stay home with the child. To avoid making parental leave only mothers' leave, he said it was important that things were not "made completely free".

Employed fathers view the father's quota as an entitlement, support from the state for them to be active caregivers. Over the years it has produced strong moral obligations for fathers to take the father's quota and for employers to accept this. This finding seems important in understanding the high use of the quota among fathers in Norway.

Fathers' sense of entitlement to shared parental leave

Do fathers feel equally entitled and obliged to take the leave that is given to mothers and fathers to share however they wish? As entitlement is embedded in cultural and moral understandings of appropriate fatherhood and motherhood, we first explore how fathers compare their sense of entitlement with mothers', and then turn to the feedback they receive from colleagues and employers, which shapes their understandings of shared leave.

Fathers' rights and mothers' entitlement

The fathers are fully aware that they have the right to more leave than the father's quota, but their sense of entitlement to shared parental leave is much weaker and quite ambivalent. David expressed it this way: "In my view the father has 10 weeks and the mother has the rest. But this is *not* how it is. Only, in my head it is." This statement juxtaposes legal rights and policy provisions with his subjective sense of what is fair and just. Several other fathers expressed a similar ambivalence. "We are equally valuable for the child", David said, "but the mother has better rights than the father in this whole process. Fathers are in a way only supporting players in the pregnancy – and birth – and confinement period. To share the leave equally would be unnatural."

These fathers know they can take more leave time than the quota provides, but they view the shared leave as the mother's entitlement. Many fathers said it was unlikely that they would take any leave if it was not father-specific. When asked how he regarded the shared leave, Lars stated: "I think about it as a … really as mothers' leave, actually." This attitude was also apparent in the plans this couple had for their next child, who was due quite soon: "For us it was never a question that I would have more than what I had to have. Now, the father's quota is quite long, really, in my opinion…. So for us it's quite natural…. Both of us, she and I, want her to have the largest portion of it." Max shared this way of thinking: "I view it as mother's leave, and I would never have been able to fight for more leave for myself. She insisted: 'I want the leave!' There was no opening for me to have more, and I didn't push for it, either." These stories reveal that even when parental leave is gender-neutral in character, it is often perceived as the mother's entitlement.

The main reasons why these fathers understand shared leave as mothers' entitlement more than their own concern mothers' need for rest after childbirth. Erlend explained that in their case, "Both mother and child were affected by a hard birth. So, it would be hopeless for me to take five months leave. Mother was not physically or mentally fit to start work. She needed nine months." A second reason they mentioned was breastfeeding. Christian elaborated: "Equal rights to parental leave is one thing, but I think there are some biological facts here that are difficult to neglect. All that has to do with giving birth and breastfeeding – I think it is a difficult matter." Steffen, a police officer, was eager to take part in providing childcare, but he felt that the mother was the most suitable person when the children were small. He explained: "She enjoys it, in a way. And then I don't see anything wrong with that…. I think that … there is something special between mother and child when kids are so young."

About a third of the men we interviewed, however, had used some shared parental leave. Didrik and Emil took all the shared leave because the mothers were students and not eligible. The fact that mothers' ineligibility influences fathers' parental leave use has also been pointed out in other countries (McKay and Doucet, 2010). Hans took most of the shared leave because the mother of his child wanted to return to work as soon as possible. These three men felt entitled by virtue of their competence as caregivers. Moreover, the child's entitlement to home-based care during its first year of life, which is a social norm in Norway, contributed to their sense of entitlement to a long leave.

The other five fathers who had taken some of the shared parental leave had negotiated with the mother. Sivert said that, "actually, she gave some of it to me. She wanted me to have it." Here he confirms that he understands shared leave as mothers' leave because the mother is in the position to give it to him. Others are more aware of their own entitlement to the shared leave and engaged in strong discussions with the mother about sharing. Steinar said:

'Really, I want as much leave time as possible with the kids, but we have to weigh that against how dependent the child is on being breastfed and how attached to the child the mother is. We have had intense discussions about how much time I am allowed to have in addition to the father's quota. Many speak about mummy's leave and daddy's leave, meaning daddy's leave is the quota and mummy's leave is everything else. I am allergic to that because it is a *parental* leave.... It's fairer to share fifty-fifty.'

Steinar referred to the general understanding that shared parental leave is a mother's right, and he wanted to educate people because many did not know that fathers were entitled to more. His feeling of entitlement is based on society's gender equality norms.

Fred and his wife are the only couple in the sample who shared the leave equally. He explained that, having had "a feminist mother", he never regarded the shared parental leave as only a women's entitlement, although he recognized that view was common. He had a strong motivation to stay at home with his child as long as possible and opted for equal sharing. They agreed on fifty-fifty sharing long before the baby was born. Fred said: "I took the initiative to share equally, and she supported it from a theoretical perspective. She hesitated a bit when we did the paperwork, but we felt we would both gain from it. Later, it was emotionally harder for her, but she saw the importance of my involvement." For this couple there was a correspondence between legal and subjective rights. Like Steinar's, Fred's sense of entitlement to an equal share in parenting was rooted in social norms of gender equality. In his case, his wife agreed, rather than appealing to traditional gender norms and the biological strains of giving birth and breastfeeding.

These examples underline the different views and ambivalences concerning fathers' entitlement to shared parental leave. Some comply with the norms of gendered parenting, while a few others actively oppose them. The men's legal rights and their subjective sense or moral obligations of motherhood and fatherhood are sometimes, but not always, in line with each other.

Workplace norms

Fathers' sense of entitlement is heavily influenced by workplace cultures and norms of the 'ideal worker'. While men's entitlement to the father's quota is supported in the workplace, to what extent does shared parental leave comply with the norms of the 'ideal worker'?

There is some ambivalence when it comes to attitudes in the workplace towards shared parental leave. Geir, who worked in a very demanding organization, said that his workplace encouraged use of the father's quota, "but not more than that! None of my bosses said 'you just have to take more if you feel like it'. So, 10 weeks were taken for granted, but no one suggested more, and I felt it was not natural at that workplace." He had to adjust his sense of entitlement to the cultural values of his workplace. He continued: "I don't think they would have refused me if I asked for more than the 10 weeks, but it wouldn't be very popular." He feared that he might lose his bonuses and be assigned to customers who were not considered 'attractive'. As the other fathers also pointed out, it is a different matter telling an employer when fathers want more time under the optional shared leave.

Although Sivert had personally taken a larger portion of the parental leave, he observed that taking more than the quota would be frowned upon, particularly among his colleagues. His workmates took exactly what they felt they were entitled to, which is to say, the father's quota: "The people I know, they only take just what they have to. Not an hour more!" Sivert's story is an example of a father who challenged expectations as to how parental leave should be shared between the mother and the father. His choice provides an insight into his workmates' attitudes on this issue. Sivert worked as an electrician in a male-dominated construction industry. With his second child he stretched his leave over a long period of time, by using both the father's quota and shared parental leave on a part-time basis, alternating with the mother. His wife preferred this arrangement, as she wanted to go back to work on a part-time basis a little earlier than if she had taken all the sharable leave. For the two of them, this was an "easy choice". But his colleagues found his use of shared parental leave strange, confronting him with their dominant ideals of masculinity at work: "So they said to me many times: 'Quite the little woman, aren't you?'" They mocked Sivert for his caregiving. At Sivert's workplace, fathers were not regarded as entitled to the shared parental leave.

Colleagues in many places seemed to regard the longer shared leave as more targeted at women and therefore gendered. Comparing fathers to employed mothers, Geir felt: "When women say they are going on leave, employers think that she bore the child, so it's not mandatory for her to go to work, but if a man says that he will have half a year's leave, they would probably say: 'Can't your wife take it?' Something like that." Sivert countered his colleagues' comments that he was doing "women's work": "Nah, I told them: Why shouldn't I be doing that? At least I know my kids. I really get to know them well!" His co-workers' reactions reveal that in some sectors fathers are not expected to use the parental leave that can be shared with their spouse.

Two of the fathers we interviewed who used considerable amounts of shared leave, Emil and Fred, had very tolerant employers. Emil's vocational training was in the construction trade and he worked as a house painter. He was home on leave with his youngest for the full 12 months because the mother was a student. When asked whether he had problems at work when he had decided to take such a long leave period, he said: "No, I.... It was easy, because the boss simply had to accept it. That's the way it is, really. He would just have to accept fewer work contracts then. He had to!" Emil stated that he did not feel guilty, although no one was hired to replace him: "It's not so simple in the house painting trade, you know, because you don't know what you get. You can't just hire somebody, really. It's hard to find good people, because they are probably doing well where they're working already. That's the way it is...." At Emil's workplace, his employer had to accept and adapt to the fact that men have caregiving obligations and are entitled to long periods of leave.

Fred, an architect with one daughter, worked in a very small firm with three middle-aged women as colleagues: "They are very understanding, and they are well-educated women who have had their challenges with gender equality. Career-wise, leave is not negative for me." Fred was the partner with technological competence, which could have been a problem during his leave, but he thought that it had gone well, partly thanks to his ability to be flexible:

> 'They called and asked for assistance sometimes. We agreed on that. It is okay, but I told them to limit it as much as possible, and they are very good at it, I think. They called mostly in the beginning of my leave as there were matters they had forgotten to ask me about, but lately they have been good at refraining from calling. It's important to me, because I don't want to think too much about my job when I'm home on leave.'

Emil and Fred both worked in small businesses, which are considered particularly vulnerable when fathers take leave from work (Bygren and Duvander, 2006). Both were irreplaceable. Yet, even though we might expect very different ideals of masculinity in these two industries, both Emil's and Fred's employers supported their long periods of leave and found solutions to their absences. This may be a sign of a new social contract that considers male employees as caregivers at home as well as contributors at work.

Conclusions

The study reported on here examined the sense of entitlement to parental leave from the state among fathers who have taken parental leave in Norway, which has generous parental leave rights based on a goal of gender equality with mothers and fathers sharing childcare and employment.

The sense of entitlement as a concept denotes beliefs and feelings about rights based on the broader social ideology of gender equality and parenting norms as well as the more local cultures and norms in workplaces (Lewis and Smithson, 2001). The father's quota seems to be firmly embedded in workplace practices and cultures in a way that can sustain active fatherhood and contributes to increased gender equality in childcare. That the father's quota has become internalized as an entitlement indicates a certain shift in masculinity (Brandth and Kvande, 2018). Brighthouse and Wright (2008) seem correct in claiming that individual parental leave rights tend to promote gender equality. The father's quota, which is earmarked and non-transferable, is understood as 'owned' by fathers, which renders negotiations with employers as well as mothers unnecessary. Their sense of entitlement to this leave influenced social comparisons and perceptions of the feasibility of letting men work in ways that are compatible with family life. It is interesting that fathers also see themselves as entitled on the basis of their own competence as caregivers. The more they are involved in the nurturing and care of their own children, the more self-confidence they seem to gain.

Fathers have, at most, a tentative and ambivalent sense of entitlement regarding shared parental leave. The general societal norms constitute shared leave as primarily a mother's entitlement – not the least because of their felt obligations to be carers. These norms, which are also dominant among managers and colleagues, affect fathers' own understanding and actions. The strain on women's bodies caused by pregnancy, birth and breastfeeding strongly influences men's feelings about what is just and fair. Yet these results are ambiguous rather than unqualified. Some fathers stress that this leave is parental, and not maternal, and insist on their own entitlement. Gender equality norms and comparisons both with the mother and colleagues suggests ongoing processes of change. Despite the negative attitudes that prevail in many workplaces, some fathers use their individual sense of entitlement to take advantage of this policy, and their decisions are supported by employers who find ways to handle their long absences without the fathers losing their status as essential employees. Our findings support Brighthouse and Wright's (2008) claim that such policies enable equality, rather than reproducing and reinforcing gendered prescriptions.

By comparing fathers' sense of entitlement to these two types of leave, the analysis adds to previous research that has explained why statutory, earmarked and non-transferable leave works better than shared rights when it comes to fathers taking parental leave. Fathers' uptake of leave is one manifestation of the norm of equal parenting, and the leave has given fathers valuable caring experiences and competences they would otherwise not have had (Brandth and Kvande, 2018). To more fully understand how the norm of gender-equal parenting works would require further examination of the content of fathers' leave practices. This question is, however, beyond the analysis in this chapter.

The current liberal–conservative Norwegian government seems to believe in the qualities of the father's quota as it has recently (2018) expanded it at the expense of shared leave. Notwithstanding, our analysis has shown that legal rights alone are insufficient to create a sense of entitlement. Rights do not exist in a contextual vacuum, and entitlements are constructed on the basis of social and normative comparisons on the local as well as the national level (Lewis and Smithson, 2001). Norms and rationalities that underlie how families work are important parts of the context. If welfare states seek to promote fathers' involvement in caring for young children, they must recognize that parents' reactions to policies are mediated by normative conceptions, including what is considered 'good' mothering and fathering. There are no universal norms that mandate the same response to similar policies in all social groups and in all countries. We have studied white, heterosexual fathers in a Norwegian context. Comparative research to inform policy-making and employers would be welcome.

3

Decomposing Policy Design: An Outsider-Within Perspective on the Father's Quota[1]

Introduction

This chapter examines migrant fathers' experiences with the Norwegian father's quota. There has been an increase in migration to Norway, particularly of migrant workers from countries of the former Eastern Europe and Sweden, but also from countries in Southern Europe, such as Italy and Spain (SSB, 2014). This is why it is interesting to look into how immigrants who have become fathers in Norway experience a 'father-friendly welfare state'. Family policy intervenes in what is often seen as private family life. The fathers in this chapter all come from countries where welfare and caregiving services come under the aegis of the family to a larger extent, and where, compared to Norway, a smaller proportion of mothers of small children are employed outside the home.

We concentrate on migrant workers from Central and Southern Europe who, in this study, are the highly qualified people who migrate to find jobs that match their qualifications. They represent the so-called 'global nomads' (Bauman, 1998) and the move of young Europeans within the European Union (EU) (Bagnoli, 2007). These fathers have become part of the Norwegian welfare state regime through participating in working life and having children in Norway, although they are also participants

[1] Adapted from E. Kvande and B. Brandth (2017) 'Individualized, non-transferable parental leave for European fathers: Migrant perspectives', *Community, Work & Family*, 20(1): 19–34. Reprinted with permission from Taylor & Francis.

in the contexts represented by their homelands. They have all stayed at home on father's leave. We are interested in how these fathers encounter the Norwegian leave system, and whether their perspective can help us understand how the father's quota works as a means of increasing gender equality in working life and care work. As they are positioned between different care regimes, this enables them to reflect on differences and similarities in social policy in the different countries. The research questions addressed in this chapter are: (1) How do the migrant fathers experience the design elements of the Norwegian father's quota? (2) What are the mechanisms behind these elements that promote more gender-equal fathering practices in caring and employment?

The chapter starts by describing the institutions of the welfare state and caring work in the family in the immigrants' homelands and also in Norway. The theoretical concepts of 'outsider-within' and 'institutional actor' are presented. Based on comparative research on care regimes, the concept of individualization processes is used in order to discuss variation and change in family policies in the different European countries, with a special focus on parental leave systems.

Familistic and defamilistic care regimes

In international comparative research on welfare states, Esping-Andersen's (1990) three types of welfare states have been seminal. Typologies, however, tend to become static descriptions and do not capture the variations and the changes that might be taking place in the different sectors of the different welfare states (Sumer, 2009; Boje and Ejrnæs, 2013). In response to Esping-Andersen's work, a substantial amount of gender-critical analysis has brought the issue of the gendered division of paid and unpaid labour to the foreground (Sainsbury, 1994, 1999; Daly and Rake, 2003). As a result, the centrality of care work is now widely acknowledged (Sumer, 2009). By analyzing how care is organized in different European countries, Anttonen and Sipilä (1996) identified different care regimes. Since the focus in this chapter is on institutions that can support changes in fathers' participation in childcare, we will use the concept of a care regime.

In the Northern care regimes, the care responsibility is shared between employers, the welfare state, mothers and fathers. These principles have been described as the cornerstones of a 'universal caregiver model' (Fraser, 1994; Gornick and Meyers, 2009a). When distinguishing between different welfare states, Esping-Andersen (2009) uses the concepts of 'familistic' and 'defamilistic'. In order to create a care regime based on the universal caregiver approach, as in the Nordic countries, the principle of defamilization is built into the design of family policy through parental leave and early childhood education and care institutions. This is different in other European countries that have a more familistic tradition, which implies that families have sole responsibility for the care needed. They can, however, buy care services in the market, and parental leave policies are gradually being introduced (Kamerman and Moss, 2009).

There are, of course, variations between these countries. In spite of this, the main distinction is between the Nordic defamilistic care regimes with a generous welfare state contribution and other care regimes with different combinations of family and market with little or no state contribution. In the Nordic care regimes (Anttonen and Sipilä, 1996), the processes of defamilization (Leitner, 2003; Ostner, 2004) of care have been promoted through public subsidies of parental leave and early childhood education and care institutions. The countries (which the fathers in this study come from) belong to care regimes where the principle of familization has had priority (Ferrera, 1996; Bonoli, 1997; Kammer et al, 2012), either through policies that directly support family-based care or by what has been labelled as 'familialism by default', indicating the lack of public policies in this field (Leitner, 2003; Saraceno, 2004).

This is, however, currently in the process of transformation due to changes in the role of women and the 2008 economic crisis (Cais and Folguera, 2013). According to Romero-Balsas, Muntalnyola-Sura and Rogero-García (2013: 678), the European trend of change regarding parenting policies is 'slowly reaching the Mediterranean countries'. Other comparative studies of family policies focus on 'hybridization processes' (Strohmeier, 2002) when analysing changes in family policies. Based on the extensive research literature on family policy regimes, Kaufman (2002: 419) finds a trend towards 'implicit' family policy that is labelled 'Scandinavization'. This implies that family policy is increasingly 'individualized', focusing on individual family members, especially when gender issues are on the agenda (Matzke and Ostner, 2010). Similarly, Daly (2011) suggests applying the concept of 'individualization processes' in order to capture variations and change in family policies which implies a shift away from policy assumptions based on the male breadwinner/female carer model, and instead expecting all adults to be both breadwinners and carers.

This chapter is based on a larger study that includes interviews with 18 immigrant fathers living in one of the larger Norwegian cities. For this analysis, we selected 12 immigrant fathers whose background is from countries with a familistic care regime and weak parental leave rights for fathers. The interviewed fathers have resided and worked in Norway from

3 to 17 years. All 12 are middle class and most have a university education at Master's or doctoral level, and work in the knowledge industry in Norway. Their wives are also well educated and employed. They know the parental leave system in their own countries through the experiences of friends and family, and are able to make comparisons. First, we ask how the fathers assess the design elements in the parental leave system from their 'outsider-within' position.

'Outsiders-within' as institutional actors

The institutions of care regimes provide a vital context for understanding fathers' practices. The focus in this chapter is on the regulations and norms that are part of the institutional anchoring of the welfare state and the family in Norway, as well as in the countries of origin of the informants, representing institutional contexts that differ in many ways from the Nordic ones. The fathers in this chapter are considered 'institutional actors' whose practices are based on experiences from two different institutional contexts, represented by their homeland and by Norway. They are between two institutional contexts, which may prove to be a useful contribution to comparative research because they have experienced how two different welfare state regimes work. They have an 'outsider's view' as well as an 'insider's view', which makes it interesting to focus on their experiences with the Norwegian welfare state's caregiving programmes.

A prominent proponent of this type of 'outsider-within' approach, Collins (1986) has described how the standpoints of black feminist researchers can enrich sociological research. Bringing an 'outsider-within' position into the centre of the analysis may uncover perceptions of reality that might otherwise have been hidden. Merton (1929) analyzed the potential contribution of insider and outsider positions to sociology, as did Simmel (1921) in his work on 'the stranger' whose vision might represent a special 'objectivity'. The combination of nearness and remoteness produces the ability of the stranger to see patterns that may be more difficult for those who are immersed in the situation. Insiders share a taken-for-granted knowledge, labelled 'thinking as usual' (Schutz, 1944). By applying this 'outsider-within' perspective the focus is on how being an institutional actor positioned between two different care regimes might make the father see the important institutional characteristics of the different care regimes.

The term 'institutional work' (Lawrence and Suddaby, 2006) refers to the practices undertaken by actors who contribute to building, maintaining, changing or challenging institutional regimes. Following Smith (2005) who points to the importance of working from people's experiences if we are to discover how the organization of local and everyday experiences is connected to and shaped by institutions, we believe that the everyday experiences of these migrant fathers can help us explore the institution of the father's quota in Norway.

Research on immigrant fathers' use of parental leave in the Nordic countries seems to be a growing topic (Kvande and Brandth, 2013; Mussino and Duvander, 2016; Skevik Grødem, 2017; Tervola et al, 2017; Bjørnholt and Stefansen, 2019; Mussino et al, 2018). Tervola et al (2017), for example, point to immigrant-specific policy hindrances, and claim that these are prone to diminish with the immigrants' duration of stay, which indicates an adaption to the leave use pattern of native-born fathers. In their comparison of parental leave use in Finland and Sweden, they explain immigrant fathers' higher uptake in Sweden with policy features such as flexibility and earmarking. Immigrants' use of welfare benefits targeted at families may be problematic, because such policies embody normative expectations of women's employment and gender-equal sharing of care work that other social policies do not (Skevik Grødem, 2017).

The concern that immigrants may not share the gender-equality values that are behind parental leave policies but cling to traditional roles is the point of departure in Bjørnholt and Stefansen's (2019) analysis of Polish work migrants to Norway. Expecting more traditional family models among immigrants than parents in the host country, they find that both immigrants and Norwegian-born fathers adapt to the gender-equalizing family policy regime in Norway, the dual earner/dual carer model. There are, however, variations in how the two groups live with their adaptions to these policies. For the Norwegian parents the policies are part of a normative order that creates a strain and frustration if they do not manage to live up to the dominant norms. The Polish parents experience the Norwegian family policies as an opportunity, enabling them to create a new future. With their home country in mind, they use the welfare state entitlements in a 'pragmatic and eclectic way' (Bjørnholt and Stefansen, 2019: 302) to shape more gender-equal family practices in Norway. In a cross-national research study of immigrant work–family orientations in 30 countries, Breidahl and Larsen (2016) find that immigrants in general adjust to changing circumstances and adapt to the prevailing gender norms in the host country relatively quickly. Their new orientations are highly structured by the cultural and institutional context in the country of settlement.

There has, however, been little research on fathers from Central and Southern Europe migrating to Nordic welfare state regimes and their use of parental leave for fathers. We will explore how migrant fathers from these European countries perceive the Norwegian father's quota, and what this implies for policies that aim to increase gender symmetry in caregiving and working life. In so doing, we address the request put forward by Ray et al (2010: 199), in which they point out that surprisingly little research has been carried out that links the design of leave policies to their outcomes, something that has left a gap in the cross-national literature on leave policies.

Understanding the design elements of the father's quota

As emphasized above, it is an essential design characteristic of the father's quota that it is given to the fathers and not to the family. In this part we explore how the migrant fathers make sense of the various design elements of their individualized parental leave rights.

Statutory universal right: job security

The father's quota is a tax-financed legal right given by the welfare state to all eligible fathers in working life. The universalistic nature of the quota stands in contrast to rights given by the work organization or by collective agreements that would lead to different leave rights between fathers. It is against this background that the fathers in the study give a particular focus to the quota being based on law regulations. Johannes, originally from Austria, explained:

> 'I can easily envision that there are jobs where it's not so simple to just say, "Yes, I'll take half of the parental leave: if there are no state regulations." Because it's a different situation if you say, "I'll take the father's quota." If the man must take it or leave it, then it's very difficult for your employer to say, "No, you cannot take it," which, incidentally, I can envision happening. Or 100 per cent happen, because it's a market-oriented society.'

In this quote, Johannes recognized that as the quota is a welfare state regulation, this secured the right of fathers to take parental leave. He saw the advantage of having a 'pre-negotiated' right in which the father did not have to negotiate with the employer, but which was decided by a third party, the welfare state. It might not be equally easy for fathers to take optional, shared parental leave in all parts of working life. Considering the uneven power balance between employer and employee, this would most likely lead to the employer determining the possibility for the employee to take leave.

A statutory father's quota with job security being given to all eligible fathers is perceived as being particularly important. Daniel is one of two fathers from Spain in the sample. He is an academic, married to a woman from the Netherlands who is also an academic and working in Norway. They have lived in Norway for seven years, and both their children of 4 years and 17 months were born in Norway. He was home on father's quota leave for 10 weeks with the last child. When he first heard about the father's quota, one of his main concerns was what effect it would have on his career prospects:

> 'I knew we were not supposed to have problems at work, but I was a little concerned whether that was actually true. Because sometimes things look good on paper, but it may … it may be that you get some problems. But I had no problems, and I felt really privileged I could have leave.'

He emphasized the fact that the father's quota is an established right in working life. He spoke from the position of an 'outsider-within', wondering whether this was actually an accepted practice or just a paper provision. Like many of the fathers, he was excited about the system that he had not heard about before, and was delighted to have this opportunity. His outsider perspective made him reflect on how the father's quota worked: "In Spain, when I talk with my friends they tell me that if you take out a lot of leave it may have consequences, that you may actually lose your job."

The fathers reflected on how the statutory universalistic principle created respect in working life. This promoted its use by the fathers, as they could take leave without fear of losing their jobs. The right is connected to being an employee and a father, and not something they can obtain by negotiating with the employer, thus making it a right for all eligible fathers.

Generosity: enabling fathers' leave-taking through full wage compensation

Making the father's quota a statutory right constructs it as universal, but it does not ensure that a majority of eligible fathers will use it. In their discussion of incentives for men's take-up of parental leave rights, Ray et al (2010) focus on the importance of generosity in terms of length and wage compensation.

Daniel from Spain pointed to the importance of this design element. Referring to the father's quota, he said: "We're very lucky to have such an opportunity, that we can have such a long leave with pay. That's so good about Norway. Everybody thinks it's fantastic and very good." He saw this as a privilege and a practice which was not opposed by his partner nor his family in Spain: "They thought that we were so lucky. Anybody … family in Spain and also in the Netherlands, they're very like … they think it's fantastic."

The differences between care policies in his homeland and Norway were important when Johannes and his wife decided to remain in Norway. When asked how it would be to move to Austria if they wanted to have a third child, he stated: "If I were to make a comparison I would earn more in Austria than in Norway, a higher total amount. But life is a compromise; you get other benefits." He continued: "I feel I get other things. I get welfare, and the leave programme is a fine system. In Norway you can take leave for almost a year with 100 per cent of your pay." Since his wages are fully compensated for, it is possible for him to stay at home and look after his children without losing economically because the system provides both time and money. Even if he could have earned more in his homeland, he saw that there were other advantages. In particular, he pointed to the full pay coverage for an entire year, and as a relatively highly paid employee, he seemed rather surprised that he would not lose more of his income when taking leave. He continued: "You stay home for a year, don't have to think about money, 100 per cent focus on the children, and then you're back in your job, and this is only possible because your child is in daycare. Everything is set up for you. That's so nice."

Here, again, he underscored the importance of the long parental leave with full pay, and also mentioned daycare coverage, which ensured that as a family they would "have a good life", as he put it. The effect is that both parents could be earners and carers. As he noted, the system was not only set up for you, parental leave was also accepted and used by fathers. Regarding how his Austrian friends in the same situation would have acted, Johannes said that, "they don't exist". He knew of no situation where the man had stayed at home: "And then I felt that I'll show you!" He was very proud that when given the opportunity he had used the father's quota and managed childcare well. Hence, he clearly departed from the care regime in his homeland, and wished to break with the dominant norms to show that it was possible for fathers to take leave.

We see here again how the 'outsider-within' position enters into his assessment of the father's quota.

Likewise, Adam, who is married to a Norwegian woman and has two children, experienced the leave as a privilege. Referring to family and friends' reactions in England, he said: "I talk to a lot of my friends, and they all have kids and they are all like: 'What?' My sister is like, 'Do you still not work?'" They think it is strange that a man can stay off from work to care for children, and frame staying home to care for children as a feminine practice:

> 'My friends would also think it is odd and not something that a man should do. Many of them have wives at home that do not go to work. They are housewives. Some of my friends work 14 hours a day, and they don't come home for weeks [working away]. So therefore it was kind of the woman's job.'

Despite being devalued as someone who did 'women's work', the fathers felt lucky to have been given the right to parental leave. Ian, originally from the US, felt as if he had won the lottery. His friends couldn't believe it, and when Simon from the Netherlands first heard of the father's quota, he exclaimed "Wohooo!" It was just too good to be true that the father was given his own leave. He considered the opportunity to stay home from work for 10 weeks with full pay as rather extravagant and a luxury, not least when he thought about the costs involved. Comparing the Italian and Norwegian systems, Fabio related that his parents would certainly have offered to help in caring for the baby if he had lived in Italy:

> 'But this is because welfare in Italy is only a word. Because there is no state scheme, or perhaps there is actually, but it's not as strong as in Norway. So much of the economy in Italy is based on family and not on the individual. This means that parents help their children, and the grandparents help the children.... The same happens with grandchildren.'

He illustrated how informal family-based care was dominant in his homeland. Being a participant in two different care regimes he was able to make comparisons based not only on his own experiences, but also on his sister's. If parents with small children want to use daycare, it is market-based and expensive. This was different from his experiences with long paid parental leave and subsidized daycare in Norway, and was also why it would be difficult for his family to move back to Italy: "Because both of us believe that it's much better the way it is here. And ... how we would have organized ourselves I don't know, we would have been dependent on my parents, probably, or on my sisters.... She [wife] wants to keep her job, and I want her to stay in her job." They would have been dependent on grandparents when it came to caring for the children, and it would have been difficult for both of them to continue in a working life. He preferred a care regime designed to support gender equality and a dual earner/dual carer model.

These fathers explicitly used their 'outsider-within' position to reflect on the importance of the wage compensation and length of the leave that enabled them to stay at home and look after their children. They illustrated how this made it possible for them to use the individualized rights that they were entitled to.

Earmarking: empowering employees as fathers

As its name indicates, the father's quota is earmarked for fathers, and it is also not transferable to mothers. The two principles work together in the system – if fathers don't make use of the quota, it is forfeited. This puts pressure on the fathers to use it, as by declining to do so, it causes a much shorter leave for parents to care for their children at home. The fathers tend to see these two principles as one, or as strongly connected, with Daniel (from Spain) saying: "I believe that it is the fact that it is reserved for fathers that makes people in Norway respect it, because this is just the way it is, right? You have to take the leave, so there's no discussion about it." Andreas from Germany had some similar thoughts about the leave being 'compulsory' when comparing it with what was available in his homeland:

> 'I don't quite know how it is in Norway, but in Germany it is obvious that if it isn't compulsory and you don't have to do it, it is much easier to pressure an employee to do as much as possible at work.'

He assessed the compulsory nature of the father's quota as an advantage, hence empowering the employee in relation to the employer. Most fathers did not see the earmarked father's quota as an inappropriate intervention by the welfare state into the freedom of choice for families: "No, I perceive this as positive ... well done, rightly so. I don't experience less personal freedom. The intervention has been done in such a way that I see it as positive", Fabio from Italy said. The value of the earmarked father's quota was that it had given him time to establish a close relationship with his child, so he considered the father's quota as an opportunity. Douglas from England explained:

> 'Even if it had been absolutely compulsory so that I would be arrested if I didn't take it, I still don't think that I would have a problem with that [the design]. I never knew that such a thing existed ... that it was possible.'

The fathers also appreciated the fact that the earmarked father's quota did not have to be negotiated with the mother. If parental leave for fathers had been defined as an optional instead of non-transferable entitlement, negotiations with the mother would have been more likely. Fabio read the non-transferability and its possible implications in a similar way: "I think it's important that we have some time reserved for the father, and which lapses if it isn't used. I think this will give fathers not the option, but more the obligation to take leave." If there was no obligation like this, he envisioned that the mother would take the entire leave. Hence, he saw how the earmarked leave created room for him to care for his child. Being an individual, earmarked, non-transferable right, the father's quota might also have an effect on gender equality in working life, according to Fabio:

> 'The obligation to take leave ensures that there is no difference according to your employer. With no obligation to take the father's quota, then it'll be the mother who stays home with the child, and then an employer will be more sceptical to hiring a young woman who might become a mother ... it will lead to differential treatment if there's no father's quota.'

He saw earmarking as a contribution that might help employers stop thinking differently about female and male employees, because it would define men as both employees and caregivers in the same way as women. Connecting care responsibility to their role as employees contributes to change in the 'abstract worker norm' (Acker, 1990). Thus, the earmarking is perceived to have an equalizing effect in working life by empowering employees as fathers and supporting the development of a dual earner/ dual carer model in working life.

The 'outsider-within' perspective is illustrated when Fabio was asked what his Italian family thought of him being home alone with the child after the mother had returned to work. In Italy, leave is reserved for the mother, which is reflected by the female gendering of the word for this leave: *maternita*. He stated that:

'It was ... well, a somewhat mixed reaction. It was a bit like I felt bullied by friends. That it was like absurd that I was taking leave. In Italian it is called *maternita*, so it was like "Ha, ha, ha, are you taking *maternita*?" It was a bit ... not really serious bullying, but it felt a little bit like it. And then there were others who were very positive and said there should be more of that in Italy too.'

This refers to the light humorous bullying he was subjected to by his Italian friends and family; in particular, the older generation found the father's quota very odd.

Conclusions

Research on parental leave has documented which design elements are most effective when it comes to promoting more gender-equal fathering practices in caring and employment (Ray et al, 2010). Comparative research between Sweden and Finland has found earmarking of the leave for fathers effective for immigrants (Tervola et al, 2017; Mussino et al, 2018). Studies have not, however, explored the way these elements gain meaning in everyday life situations of work and care for fathers. In this chapter, we have investigated this issue by means of interviews with middle-class immigrant fathers from various European countries to Norway. The 'outsider-within' perspective represented by immigrants' experiences helps us explore and understand why certain policy characteristics work.

The results highlight the importance of the design elements of *statutory* and *universal*, *earmarking* and *non-transferability*, and *generosity* in the parental leave system in order to encourage fathers to engage in childcare and therefore enhance more egalitarian practices between women and men at the workplace and in care work at home. The migrant fathers in our study were positive about and used the parental leave despite being from a country where fathers' parental leave for two months or more was not the norm. They are, however, all middle-class fathers, and research finds that fathers belonging to this class tend to have more gender-egalitarian views (Brandth and Kvande, 2016a). The fathers aligned their practice to institutional benefit structures. Their position as 'outsiders-within' makes them think institutionally. Because the father's quota does not exist in their homelands, they may be able to see more clearly how and why its design worked. While Norwegian fathers take it for granted because it has existed for almost a generation (25 years), the migrant fathers coming from outside seem to experience and understand the meaning of this type of policy.

The father's quota being a statutory, generous, earmarked and non-transferable leave is perceived as important because employers play by the law, and as seen from their perspective as outsiders-within, the fathers in this study were quite surprised that leave for fathers was so well accepted in working life. Being a statutory right paid by the state and not dependent on an employer's good will constructs the leave as a universal right. The generous income replacement ensures that the fathers do not face losing out financially by taking parental leave. They observe that this contributes to the broad acceptance and use of the father's quota in Norway. And furthermore, during the leave period, they do not have to give up their identity as 'breadwinners' – as it is economically possible for them to use the leave, they thrive as carers, and seem proud to have immersed themselves in a new phase in life as fathers.

The principle of earmarking and non-transferability is not understood as infringing on their free choice, as might have been expected. Despite the pressure these principles put on fathers, the quota is understood as a great possibility for fathers to care for their children. Moreover, the slight compulsion of non-transferability is emphasized as important since it connects fathers' care responsibility to their role as employees. Thus, it is perceived as having an equalizing effect in working life. Both male and female employees are constructed as potential parents who will take parental leave. This earmarking empowers employees as fathers, and in turn this promotes the development of a dual earner/dual carer model in working life. This means fathers becoming encumbered workers in line with mothers, and thus giving women better opportunities in the world of work because care responsibility is no longer seen as just the responsibility of mothers. It is in comparison with the care regimes of their homelands that this insight becomes perceptible to them.

Our results highlight the enthusiasm that most of the fathers express from having been home on leave caring for their child. This enthusiasm is nurtured by the privilege they feel has been granted to them and what they get in terms of getting close to their child and becoming confident carers. The joy they talk about and the competence they have gained is put into perspective when they meet with their families and friends in their homelands.

These results can be seen as supporting the tendency to convergence between care regimes (Bettio and Plantenga, 2004), not in the actual care policies, but in the attitudes towards parental leave held by the fathers from these countries. European societies' attitudinal studies find that a majority of women and men want to give priority to a better work–life balance (Hobson and Fahlen, 2009). Our findings may be useful in the ongoing discussions in policy-making, with a focus on incentives to draw men towards life courses with more care responsibility.

4

Flexible Use of
the Father's Quota:
Problems and Possibilities[1]

Introduction

This chapter deals with how fathers make use of the flexibility provided by the parental leave scheme in Norway. The public debate on the father's quota in recent decades has involved the weighing of earmarking (which reduces choice) against parents' freedom to choose for themselves how to divide the leave between them (Ellingsæter, 2012). It is strange that the debate has overlooked the type of choice that is already embedded in the father's quota, which concerns flexible timing of the leave and provides fathers with many options and choices. As the father's quota combines earmarking and flexibility, it is within ideologies of regulation as well as the neoliberal ideas based on freedom of choice (Brandth and Kvande, 2017).

The option given to parents to use the leave flexibly is often lauded by policy documents as well as research reports. It is viewed as an opportunity for mothers and fathers to control the timing of their leave-taking, and as having the potential to increase the use of the leave, particularly by fathers.

---

[1] This chapter is compiled from: B. Brandth and E. Kvande (2016) 'Fathers and flexible parental leave', *Work, Employment & Society*, copyright © the Authors (2016), reprinted with permission of Sage Publications Ltd, and from: B. Brandth and E. Kvande (2019) 'Flexibility: Some consequences for fathers' caregiving', in P. Moss, A.-Z. Koslowski and A. Duvander (eds) *Parental leave and beyond*, Bristol: Policy Press. Reprinted with permission.

Leave policies differ greatly between countries, reflecting many different political values, goals and designs, and many countries offer flexible use of parental leave to a smaller or greater degree (see Blum et al, 2018). All the Nordic countries offer flexibility in their leave designs, but not the same options (Duvander et al, 2019).

When the father's quota was introduced, the weeks had to be taken during the child's first year. This fairly rigid design proved to be effective as fathers very soon adapted it as part of their work–family practice (Brandth and Kvande, 2001). The quota has been lengthened over the years, and measures have been introduced to make more fathers eligible (for instance, by juxtaposing employment with a disability pension and introduction programmes for immigrants) and to encourage them to take leave. One such regulation meant to encourage fathers is increased time flexibility. As the neoliberalist ideology of choice made an increasingly strong mark in politics, authorities introduced flexibility into the leave design. According to a parliamentary proposal (Ot prp nr 104, 2004–2005: 28), the most important rationale for a flexible father's quota was 'to make it simpler to combine work and childcare'. Flexible leave was intended to help achieve the broader goals of the father's quota: dual earning/dual caring and closer father–child relations. Even though Norway prioritized home-based care for the first year of the child's life, the leave can be spread over a period of three years. Like flexible work, flexibility in leave design seems to be taken for granted as a positive solution for combining work with childcare. However, flexible leave may have other effects, such as getting more fathers to take leave. Another aspect concerns the content of the leave, examined in this chapter – how flexible leave affects fathers' ability to take on childcare.

As noted, flexible leave design takes a number of forms. In this chapter, the focus is on *time flexibility*, taking the father's quota as part-time leave combined with part-time work, or splitting it up into smaller blocks of time to be taken over a longer period. The different forms of flexibility may affect fathers differently, so in this chapter we explore fathers' part-time leave and piecemeal use of the father's quota, asking two questions: (1) What are their motives for choosing flexible leave? (2) How do the two flexible solutions influence fathering?

Research on flexible leave design

While much research has been concerned with the effects of parental leave use, particularly its length, research on the effects of flexibility in the parental leave design for mothers and fathers is still rather scarce.

Some exceptions are Brandth and Kvande (2013b, 2016b), Smeby (2013), Duvander (2013) and Boyer (2017).

Shared parental leave has been flexible in Norway since 1994, with the so-called 'time account scheme' allowing for part-time and piecemeal use. The father's quota was, however, excluded from this. The scheme was meant to enable families to tailor the leave to their own special situation, and to make it easier for employed parents to manage the time squeeze of combining work and family. Since it reduced the period of total absence from work, it was argued that it would make it particularly attractive for men to use the leave (NOU 1993: 12). A study found that flexible use was hardly used by mothers or fathers (Holter and Brandth, 2005) – only 2.2 per cent of mothers, the main users of the shared parental leave, used the leave flexibly. These mothers had a university education and a career, and wanted to return to work as soon as possible, even if it was part-time. The study pointed out that this practice represented a break with the moral obligations of parenting in Norway, which is for parents to care for the child at home during the child's first year. It also showed that use of flexible leave for parents with a career demanded competent planning as the borderline between work and home became blurred. Parents tended to work more than they had agreed, and the study concluded that employers benefited more from flexible leave than parents. Smeby (2013) has called this take-up pattern a 'work-oriented' leave practice in contrast to an 'equality-oriented' practice where fathers take their leave all in one go. Another take-up pattern described by Smeby (2013) is 'family-oriented'. When the father times his leave so that the mother is at home at the same time, the mother's main responsibility for the child is not interrupted, and the father becomes her support person. These results show that the take-up pattern affects the content of the leave. Bergqvist and Saxonberg (2017) point out that flexibility in the Swedish parental leave system negatively affects gender equality since it allows fathers to simply prolong their summer holiday over a number of years, rather than taking the main responsibility for their children over a longer period of time.

Flexible leave may be a useful work–family balancing tool in some contexts. A French study describes the effects of flexible parental leave in terms of one day a week in the child's three first years (Boyer, 2017). Since it is rare that French fathers take on parental duties in terms of parental leave, the fathers themselves positively assess part-time leave as giving them 'a good mix' of work and time with the children. However, the study concludes that part-time leave does not change the cultural norm of mother-child primacy where fathers are not fully acceptable as nurturers (Boyer, 2017: 203), and thus it is not effective as a gender equality tool. If the standard reference situation is that fathers receive no leave, they may assess it differently than in a country where leave is normally taken full time (see Valarino, 2017).

This chapter is based on interviews with 20 fathers who have taken the father's quota on a part-time or piecemeal basis. Thirteen fathers had used part-time leave combined with work while seven split the quota into blocks of time of various lengths. Flexible use means many different ways of using the leave, so in this sample the leave is more spread out over the child's first three years. Some of the fathers on part-time leave had a well-organized system alternating between work and leave every other day or taking leave for one day a week while working for four days. The part-time leave could also be more fluidly organized, the fathers agreeing with the employer on, for instance, a certain division between work and care, but not on which days or what tasks that would amount to the percentage agreed on. There were also fathers in the sample who used it to shorten the work day. Regarding piecemeal leave, its most common usage was to take one block of leave relatively early during the first year as a family holiday, and a second and third block later. We ask: What are the reasons for choosing to use flexible leave? What are the consequences for a father's care practice?

Why choose flexible leave?

As noted, the father's quota has developed to become a matter of fact among fathers in Norway. "A man must take the leave. There is no question about it", Paul said, perhaps stating the obvious. What is not so obvious is in what ways to take the leave. With the opportunities for flexibility, there are many options. Fathers have various motives for choosing flexible use, and often it is a combination of motives. In this section we will describe three main motives.

In pursuit of the optimal arrangement

"We're talking about 50 days that I can actually take as I choose", said Harold, expressing how pleased he felt at the thought of all his options. The many choices create great expectations among fathers, but also pressure to make sure the best choice is made. There are many considerations and adaptations, and in terms of time, the fathers adapt the quota according to their own and their partner's shift work, part-time work, holidays and their employer's wishes.

Flexible use of the leave must be agreed with the employer in advance, but such agreements can also be modified along the way, and employers are generally cooperative in granting flexible leave. Several of the interviewees told how their employer gave them carte blanche. "The boss was willing to accept what was best for me, so I was left to do as I wanted", Ben stated.

Since the individual father chooses how to take the leave, he is responsible for adapting the leave to his work, and the flexibility demands careful planning. Olav, a police officer married to a nurse, stated:

'I was quite lucky to have a very flexible employer then, so we [Olav and wife] just sat down and counted days. We looked at the calendar and selected days, and then she spoke to her employer, and she was allowed to choose which shifts she wanted to work, and then, well, we just sat down and worked out a plan together, in fact a six-month plan.'

Even if it was not always easy to plan, Olav pointed out that part-time use of the father's quota was quite common at his place of work. This was because "it's shift work, so you get things spread out much more." Leave days are planned to fit the shift schedule.

As seen, detailed customizing of the leave is possible, and the goal is to obtain the ultimate combination package, which must satisfy many wishes. The demands placed on the 'package' primarily come from the fathers and not from the employer. What we therefore see is an individualization of the choices, where the onus of choosing is on the father's shoulders.

Flexible use of the leave opens up the possibility for strategic planning. "Oh my God, how you two speculate!" was what Sigurd and Anna heard from their colleagues. This was because they decided to take weeks with 'red days' marked in the calendar (Norway has a number of holidays in May) as their holiday weeks. The optimal choice for them was to defer their leave because of holidays, when they would be off work anyway. Thus, they saved both money and days, and were able to stretch their leave out for longer.

"We did it bit by bit", said Christian, "Neither of us can boast of having a master plan fully prepared from day one, you know." They started with the baby's date of birth, the number of leave days and the date for starting in kindergarten, and then they tried to draw up a schedule consisting of work, paid leave, holidays and unpaid leave. Needs would continue to surface during this period that would require new choices and adjustments. Thus, flexible use of the leave may be complicated to plan because so many choices could be made. "One gets the impression that it's very easy to go for flexibility all over the place, but when you get down to it it's very complicated – when you start to use the flexible solutions", Sigurd said. Flexibility introduces new sorts of stress. He believed that the government should instead recommend a standard solution so that flexible use would be the exception: "There is always this and that. So ... the idea of flexibility is a bit artificial, and they could have made it easier for the user by recommending a standard solution, and then rather customize the leave only in special cases."

Logic suggests that having options allows people to select precisely what makes them happiest, but as some studies show, abundant choice often makes for misery. With such a great degree of flexibility in the father's quota, it is possible that parents feel this is a tyranny of planning – or a 'tyranny of choice' (Schwartz, 2004).

Work motivates flexible use

The most prominent reason given for flexible use has to do with work. Some of the fathers said that they could not be completely absent from work, such as Magnus and Lars, both self-employed business owners. Lars, the co-owner of a house painting company, pointed out that it was impossible to take 12 weeks of continuous leave: "I can't be off that long. It's simply impossible", he said, "I have to be there." His solution for being able to use the father's quota was first to take three weeks of it as holiday together with the mother, and the rest combined with work without having a regular schedule for this. Some days he would take his daughter with him to work; other days he would work from home. He stated that the leave could be well organized: "You can, for example, take leave for two or three weeks, and then you can work. Then you can take another two or three weeks, and then you can do one or two days a week for a period of time. It actually depends...." He recommends both flexibility in terms of deferred leave due to full-time work and part-time leave combined with work.

Magnus combined the father's quota with part-time work during his entire leave period: as a freelancer in advertising it was important to maintain customer contact and to accept assignments. As with Lars, Magnus could not be completely absent from his work for continuous period of time, and part-time leave use was his solution. He worked 20 per cent every Friday:

> 'If I had not been able to carry on working I would have had to just give them [the customers] away. So I feel the

flexibility is important, because I simply could not take three whole months, really. I know people who are working as stockbrokers, and they cannot take leave just like that. Then they would have to take their kid to work with them, and then they probably have trouble making the best deals. I think flexibility is good, otherwise it [the leave] would simply be lost. You need the flexibility to keep your job. I'm very glad we have the flexibility.'

Ben was in a similar situation. Even if he was not operating his own business (he worked for a bank selling financial products) he would risk losing many deals if he was absent for an extended period of time. For him, the vital issue was adapting the leave rules to his work: "What happens is that legislation and needs determine our choices, but I also need to keep the plates spinning at work", he states. His solution, when they had their second child, was part-time leave for about a four-month period.

It can also be difficult to be away for a longer period of time if you have just started in a new job. This was the case for Harald, who changed to a new job during the year of leave and consequently needed to catch up. After taking three weeks of the father's quota as a holiday with the mother, he later used the remainder of the quota as part-time leave so that he could be at work and learn the ropes of his new duties.

The fathers' motives behind opting for a part-time father's quota may also involve adapting to the mother's work, particularly if the mother works shifts or part time. Gustav, for example, took his whole father's quota part time because his wife was a nurse and worked shifts so that when she returned to her job after the leave, he took his father's quota on the days she worked. Arne also praised the possibility of flexible use of the leave because his wife was working irregular hours as a freelance musician playing concerts and going on tour. The situation for Julio and his wife was that she needed to go back to work after having had 10 months of leave, and chose to work part time from the start. He did not want to lose contact with his workplace during full-time leave. Hence, alternating days of part-time leave and work was the solution for both of them when he was starting his father's quota period. Eivind also took his father's quota (10 weeks) as part-time work so that he worked 50 per cent for 20 weeks. During this period, the mother worked part time as she did not want to return to full-time work immediately. It is thus a motive for choosing part-time leave that the mother would like to have a gradual transition from leave to work. Part-time use of the father's quota may soften the transition to work for the mother.

Reluctance to provide childcare

One last type of motivation for flexible use of leave that fathers express is a reluctance to have continuous full-time leave with responsibility for the child. Flexible timing reduces their unwillingness to stay at home to provide care. The reluctance concerns both the length of the leave and the young age of the child. "The length is a problem. It's simply too long", John felt. "Really, when I was thinking about leave, I couldn't envision staying at home for 10 weeks with the kids. It's simply too much", Jean stated. Both Jean and John are examples of fathers who would not have taken any parental leave if it had not been for the quota. Their solution to deal with leave they thought was too long was part-time leave – one day of leave per week was what Jean felt he would be able to manage. Describing his reluctance the following way we see that it also has to do with the age of the child: "When the child is so young, there's not that much you can do, I feel. But I thought that it was a very good idea to do it ... working 80 per cent over one year." Ben, who had stayed home with his first-born, described his motivation based on previous experiences in a similar way:

> 'Being home with a one-year-old, that's ... it's really, yes, I'll be quite honest; it was terribly hard! It was the dark winter, and it was exhausting. When the kids are so small, you really communicate in a different way than you normally do. So compared with now, now I'm starting to reach another, how to say it, a new communication level with him. He's starting to talk, and we're doing things together.'

His previous experience was a strongly motivating factor for deciding to take his father's quota as part-time leave with their second child. For first-time fathers the demanding and externally unvalued work of nurturing and caring often comes as a shock (Miller, 2011), and may be the underlying reason for this choice.

Some of the other fathers also considered a postponement of the leave if they were to have children a second time. "I might want to have my leave when my child is a little bit older, really", Gustav stated, "For my part at least, when your child is a little bit older, there's a little more, how to say it, response with it, like, so I feel this is more rewarding for my part, really." It is interesting to note that he treated the father's quota as something that should also be rewarding for him; the child's need for care was not his only concern. This idea, that it could be more rewarding to take parental leave when the children are older, is a main reason some fathers in the study wanted to postpone it.

In sum, their intentions were good. They envisioned that combining care work and employment would run smoothly, and that managing both would be easy if they chose part-time leave combined with part-time work.

Consequences for fathering

This section examines what the fathers say about the *consequences* of flexible leave for their care practices.

Part-time leave: interrupted caregiving

As noted, fathers who chose part-time leave combined with work did so because they believed it would work well in their situation – they would be able to attend to work at the same time as taking leave. In retrospect, however, many fathers who chose part-time leave were dissatisfied with their choice for several reasons. It often created stressful situations and they felt that taking the father's quote in this part-time way didn't work well when trying to combine childcare and work. Gustav, a graduate engineer, who took his whole quota on a part-time basis, stated:

> 'I did not envision that there would be so much stress because I was actually also at work at the same time. So, this is a thing I … I don't think I would do this again. It wasn't really leave because I never got into it as a routine. Then it wasn't really work either, because I couldn't go to work every day. So, it became very … it was really two things that both were sort of half-way. And that was really not a good solution.'

Gustav took his leave days when his wife, a nurse, worked her daytime shift. Although it seemed like a good solution, neither work nor care benefited from the part-time leave as his job affected his focus on childcare and vice versa. Since this was his first child, he felt it was particularly important to be able to establish a good routine, which was something part-time leave hindered: "That you establish a routine every day, if you get up and do this and that, then I think it would be easier. Then I think there's less work too. For example, clothing and that stuff, and that she has, like … that you make it flow." It was this flow that he missed. He did not experience any 'slow time', in which the child's needs directed how time was spent, and where not too many other things had to take place at the same time. He believed that being able to totally disregard his job during the period of leave would have been much better, "because it's a little bit like this, there are phone calls and mail." Ben, a financial advisor in a bank, stayed home on leave for two or three days a week with his second child. He related how it worked for him:

> 'Monday I went to work, Tuesday I was home, Wednesday I went to work again, and like this.... You felt that when you were at work, you were always lagging behind. You would bring some of this grind home with you, and then you're home and the baby is crying and then you need to feed it. It was more of a hassle for me than not, so if I were to do it again ... but let's be clear, we're not having any more babies! But if I were to do it again, I would have chosen to take out the full leave in one go; could have made some plans, perhaps travelled to see grandparents, done more trivial things together. You don't have that option in an off-on situation.'

He described quite well how making himself available for work caused many interruptions:

> 'It simply didn't work; it was a horrible lesson to learn. Really, having such a part-time set-up.... In my job, customers call early and late, mail pops in, inquiries come in. They don't know when I'm on father's leave or not. If I had been able to tell them that I'll be back on this or that date [full-time leave], they could have related to that. But the point is that they also called when I was home with the baby. I muted the phone eventually, and then I saw 13 unanswered calls and there were texts. So this was far too poorly organized by me. I must admit that my boss at work told me to do what was best for me, so I had free rein to do as I wanted. But as it turned out this was not a success.'

It was only in retrospect that he saw that he had made a poor choice when opting for part-time leave, and had to accept the consequences of his choice. From Gustav's and Ben's experiences, it is clear that part-time leave needs strict organization. What Ben recommended to others was:

> '... to put the job entirely on the sidelines! Even if you're in sales, you just have to say that this is how it is during this period of time! Just put everything else aside and say to yourself:

"Now you're taking your father's quota for so and so many weeks and nothing else." That's my hot tip.'

In the words of a father currently on leave with his nine-month-old son who was interviewed by one of the larger Norwegian newspapers: 'This is a period where you have the time to be 100 per cent with the children. The rest of our lives means much work and stress, but this time is reserved for us. I think it's wholesome!' (quoted in *Aftenposten*, 2013: 5).

Many fathers on a part-time father's quota described that it felt as if they were working full time while additionally having a one-year old to care for. "I needed to switch off and on all the time", said Jean, a research scientist, who was on leave of one day a week. "You can't work normally, so it was stress…. It might be my job, because I'm doing research, and then you're working more than the hours you spend sitting in your office. So you must be strong and not check your email when you're home. It wasn't easy", he said.

Julio, an engineer working in telecommuting, who also took his father's quota as part-time leave, stated: "The plan, or idea, was that I shouldn't lose so much contact with the job, but it didn't work out in practice." Part-time use of the father's quota meant that the leave was not used to get mentally involved in the day-to-day chores with children and home. The chaotic life they were describing attempting to handle both work and care weakened fathers' chances of establishing autonomous care routines. 'Multitasking', by combining part-time care with part-time work, did not supply the continuous 'slow time' that favours childcare. As a result, part-time use of the father's quota confirmed the mother's position as the primary caregiver in the family, as she needed to be available as ground crew.

Consequences of piecemeal and postponed leave

Some of the fathers involved in the study who had used flexible leave were quite pleased with their choice after the leave period was over. This was particularly for those who had divided the father's quota into several weeks and taken it after the baby's first year.

One of the fathers was Arne, a cultural worker. Since he was the father of three children, he had used the father's quota three times. His last time, when the quota had been expanded to 10 weeks, he had split it in two parts. He stated: "My experience is that it is nice to have father's leave and stay home, so that's what I will remember…. I would really have liked to have had longer leave, but this is about finding a good solution with my wife." With all their experience, this couple found that leave in two parts worked well for them since it gave him two continuous periods of five weeks, each of which was not interrupted by work. He said:

> 'As a man I have been used to prioritize myself, career, studies and such, so this is a completely different role.... When she [youngest daughter] is awake you can't do anything else than mind her, and that is the purpose, of course. So I felt privileged. You get a different form of contact with the child when you don't compete with the mother. Feeding and nursing the baby are clearly the mother's advantage. So in that way, it is lovely that she is not there as you get a better contact then.'

Although he took piecemeal leave, the length of the two blocks of leave resulted in the type of father–child relation that is described as happening during continuous, fairly long periods of leave (Brandth and Kvande, 2003a). Another father, Steinar, a consultant engineer, who first had a period of full-time leave and then part-time leave for a second period, was also fairly pleased with his choice, but he was the most positive in describing full-time leave:

> 'I would say that the first period, when I had this nice daddy-on-leave feeling where I was at home alone and had the ongoing run of the household with Emilia. And this was ... it was just like I had envisioned. Bliss, really! It was very nice and time to spare and calm and lots of nice things.'

It seems relatively common among fathers who took leave in separate blocks to define one part of the father's quota as a holiday spent together with the mother and child. After the quota was extended to 10 weeks, it exceeded the weeks the mother might have of holiday, and consequently she had more leave left after her holidays. Some fathers take the rest of the leave as part time, but others, like Ivar, took it in one block. He and his wife organized the parental leave so that his wife took the first six months, and then a three-week holiday break together with Ivar, who used his father's quota. After this 'holiday break', the wife went back to work and Ivar took the rest of his father's quota plus the remaining three months of shared parental leave. His choice is an example of how the father's quota is split up and partly defined as holiday, but it is also an example of a father who took longer leave than the father's quota and was home alone with the child for a relatively long period of time.

It is not customary to see the whole father's quota as a holiday, but this applied to David. After David's wife had taken leave for five months, David took five weeks father's quota plus four weeks of his saved summer holiday. In this period his wife was also home. David planned to repeat this practice next summer. He explained: "So I will do it like this next year as well. Nine weeks' holiday, two years in a row! I haven't had that since I left school, ha, ha." David worked in a private consultancy firm, and nine weeks' absence during the summer seemed possible for the firm to manage:

> 'Before I left I said that I am going to have nine weeks' holiday, and I was laughed at a bit at work. Holiday, like! Ha, ha. Honestly, I did have nine weeks' holiday. We were together as a family for nine weeks and shared the caring. So, it had been more of a drudgery to mind the child if I had been alone than it is when we are two and can share it and take it a bit as it comes.'

We see from this that David describes his daily caring during this period as being shared with his wife. Sharing as they see fit is quite different – and less an obligation for fathers – from what would have been the case if he had had the responsibility alone. Timing the leave to coincide with mothers' holidays doesn't strengthen fathers' own care competence and responsibility compared to being alone, however. The common leave period parents spend together without work obligations was experienced by the fathers in Smeby's (2013) study as 'a golden period'. To be two parents together sharing the daily tasks became a relaxed time, a longed-for break with no stress. However, according to Smeby, even if a family-oriented leave is experienced as positive for the family, it doesn't challenge the father to take actual responsibility, and thus the full gender-equality potential of the father's quota is not realized.

As noted, the idea that it could be more rewarding to take parental leave when children are a bit older was a main reason why some fathers in the sample postponed their leave. This was the case with Dag, an executive advisor, who decided to take the leave when his son was older. He negotiated with his wife, who would have preferred him to have longer periods of leave during the child's first year, but Dag steadfastly insisted that he "take it in periods until he [their son] turns three", the longest period of leave he ever took being four days in a row. He believed that the relationship between father and son would benefit from having some common experiences they would both appreciate:

'It means more for the future development between me and my son that I do something that he is able to understand, remember and enjoy. And then I thought that enjoying things together must be something he thinks is exciting and fun, thus he must learn what an excavator is first! Otherwise, we cannot go together and look at construction sites. Because I knew for certain that we would be stopping to look at construction sites. He must be old enough first, then I'll take father's leave. Now he thinks this is great fun!'

Dag and his son often took a drive to look at construction sites, which is a typically masculine site, and felt it had given him richer experiences with his son than if he had stayed at home minding him. Infant care did not qualify as a meaningful father–son experience to him:

'I did it, I took some Fridays and walked him in the stroller while he was sleeping and burping and drinking milk from a bottle. But I felt that this didn't give me the same, because I could have done this on Saturday and Sunday as well. But now I feel that it is much more rewarding to be with him because now he is much more interested in being with his father, now it's not just about feeding him.'

For Dag, the father's quota became days off with his son and not ongoing daily care. He constructed a different type of fathering as he attached more importance to fun and games with his three-year-old child. These findings confirm research about men participating in the more enjoyable aspects of childrearing, leaving ongoing, primary responsibility for children to mothers (Klinth and Johansson, 2010). Fathers' ability to choose the character of their involvement shapes their fathering, and in such cases taking leave doesn't seem to represent any real shift towards fathers taking greater responsibility for childcare. Flexible leave therefore increases the risk that leave policies will only partially dismantle the gendered division of care responsibility.

Conclusions

This chapter has explored part-time and piecemeal leave, the alternative to taking all of the leave in one go, which was the main option in the first 14 years after the introduction of the quota. Full-time leave is thus the alternative, and fathers' standard reference situation. In other countries where flexible leave is introduced from the start and men's family involvement is less well established, this may be different; flexible use of leave is preferable to no use of leave.

Fathers' motives for and experiences of the flexible father's quota might tell us something about how today's father's quota works. There are many options, and making the best choice possible is seen as stressful. Flexible use appears to have become a way of dealing with a long father's quota and minimizing absence from work. It is generally chosen so the father can continue working. Fathers preferring part-time to full-time leave may illustrate men's reluctance to stay away from work even when they are on the much-accepted mandatory father's quota. Institutionalizing the opportunity to work during the leave discursively defines fathers as people who cannot be separated from work. Reluctance to take on child-minding for an infant also appears as a legitimate motivation for flexible leave.

Although the flexibility of the leave is indispensable for fathers in some occupations, part-time leave is a double-edged sword because it often ends up with work subtly controlling the situation. Our results show that taking leave on a part-time basis combined with part-time work has negative effects on fathering. Choosing this as an alternative implies making themselves available for work, something that often creates stressful situations and interruptions. The boundaries between work and childcare become blurred and prevent men from getting fully immersed with their children. Part-time use of the quota assumes that the mother is available, and thus it tends to confirm her as the primary caregiver. Consequently, there is no clear change in the main responsibility for caring. To work during the leave is, therefore, not a guaranteed way of increasing fathers' involvement.

The analysis presented in this chapter indicates that flexibility as part-time leave may even work counter to the aim of making men more competent carers. It doesn't provide fathers with the continuous time needed to bond with a baby, and it hinders the establishment of autonomous care routines. Many fathers on flexible leave seem to experience double stress because they feel they are not living up to the expectations of either work or caring. Thus, this evidence does not confirm the assumption of policy-makers that flexibility will make it simpler for fathers to combine work and care.

Piecemeal leave seems to have two different types of effect on fathering. When a block of time is taken by fathers as a holiday together with the mother, the opportunity to take responsibility and increase their care competence is limited. This resonates with studies comparing what effects staying at home alone with the baby or staying at home together with the mother has for fathering. Minding and being continuously responsible for a toddler is different than merely giving the mother some relief. However, when the blocks of leave are fairly long and the mother is at work, the situation for fathering is different. In such situations, the effect of staying at home on leave alone corresponds to what previous studies have found about the effects of continuous, solo fathering (see Chapters 6 and 7).

We have also seen that flexible leave is an appreciated option for fathers who are reluctant to take on childcare, either because they think the leave is too long or the child too young. Thus, flexibility supports the idea of the choice-making father who has the privilege of making his own choices when it comes to work and care. One motive for taking leave when the child is older is that fathers might see it as more rewarding for themselves.

The aim of this chapter has been to get an insight into an important issue in leave policy: how flexibility as a design element in parental leave may affect fathering. The experience of Norwegian fathers suggests that offering a part-time leave option and the possibility of taking leave over a long period may stall progress towards dual-caring and gender-equal practices. Part-time leave over three years is an option that weakens the effects of non-transferability in leave design. This lesson may be important for the EU, whose proposed directive envisages spreading leave-taking over 12 years, as well as individual countries developing their parental leave systems. Considering the objectives of the measure, these results emphasize the importance of making explicit the gendered meanings of flexibility and being careful about adopting the enticing arguments of flexible arrangements to rationalize a practice that may have unintended effects. Flexible arrangements may be more significant for the symbolic level of shared parenting than for the level of actual fathering practice. The results indicate the need to consider the effects of flexibility when assessing the much-commended Nordic leave systems. It is important to note, however, that the period over which leave-taking may be spread is relatively short in the Nordic countries, and that there may even be a trend to reduce the period – Sweden has just done so, and a recent white paper on family policies in Norway suggests the leave must be taken within two years instead of three (NOU 2017: 6).

PART II

Caregiving: Fathers in Transition

5

Masculinity and Childcare[1]

Introduction

In gender studies, research on men and masculinities has been an important research field, and in family sociology the study of fathers is now an important area of focus. The aim of this chapter is to combine these two strands of research by focusing on fathering and the masculine content and performance in childcare. In doing so, we study a group of Norwegian men who availed themselves of parental leave before it was made father-specific. Fathers who stay at home on leave caring for a baby while the mother goes back to work constituted a very small group before the non-transferable father's quota was introduced.

An important contribution to the research on men and masculinities is David Morgan's book *Discovering men* (1992) in which he addresses the importance of work in men's lives. Work is assumed to be a major basis of masculine identity. He suggests that a strategy for studying men and masculinity is to study situations where masculinity is put on the line. He pinpoints two situations where masculinity is challenged, namely when men are unemployed and when men enter female occupations. Another strategic point for studying what might be labelled a challenge to masculinity is when men temporarily leave the work arena and enter the home in order to assume the main responsibility for a child.

In research on men from a gender perspective, one concern has been to examine the changes in masculinity and to ascertain which values

[1] First published as B. Brandth and E. Kvande (1998) 'Masculinity and child care: The reconstruction of fathering', *The Sociological Review*, 46(2): 293–313 © Editorial Board of the *Sociological Review* (1998). Republished with permission from Sage Publications Ltd.

other than strength and power, which have traditionally characterized the relationship between men and women, can now be observed as masculine ideals. In developing this interest, researchers have called for a masculine concept of care and have looked for ways of understanding it (Connell, 1987; Kimmel, 1987; Segal, 1988).

The changing nature and meaning of fatherhood, and the conduct and interaction of fathers with their children are two of the many central foci of contemporary research on fathers. In a review article on fatherhood, Marsiglio (1993) suggests the direction future research should take. Two of his recommendations bear special relevance to our study: (1) the relationship between men's work identity and father identity, and (2) the diverging perspectives of mothers and fathers and the need for reports from mothers to understand fatherhood. In this chapter we will analyze the gendered meaning and content of fathering by using an interactionist perspective where both the fathers' work identity and their relations to their wives are taken into consideration. Our interest is in seeing how these men include childcare in their construction of masculinity.

Fathers in transition

While a focus on mothers long dominated research on the parent–child relationship, the study of fathers has become a popular and expanding field of research. Early research focused on the influence of the father on his child's development (Lamb, 1976). Later, the experience of fathers and their attempts to change their experiences became the locus of interest. A central topic in much of the research and debates since the 1990s has been the interest and belief in the changing nature of fatherhood, the so-called 'new father' image (Pleck et al, 1985; Lewis and O'Brien, 1987; Pleck, 1987). However, this enthusiasm for the nurturing father, highly involved in housework and care, might have caused research on the 'new father' to be too uncritical and positive in its analysis of fatherhood (Pollock and Sutton, 1985; Drakich, 1989; LaRossa, 1992). One reason for this is the underestimation of the gender-relational perspective in research on fatherhood.

In several published volumes on fatherhood, articles have shown the diverse adaptions of fathers (Hansen and Bozett, 1985; Lewis and Sussman, 1985/86; Hood, 1993; Marsiglio, 1995). Fathering differs in relation to social circumstances such as family structure, occupation, ethnic group, work orientation of wives and stages in the life cycle. The need for a theory capable of encompassing the complex interplay of influences underlying variation and change has been strongly voiced (Pedersen,

1985: 438). Research on fathers has maintained its momentum, and both empirical and theoretical advances have been made that can satisfy much of the need for theory that was called for in the more pre-paradigmatic phase. In exploring and linking different themes of fatherhood, symbolic interactionism and the social constructivist-inspired theories have proven to be relevant and fertile (Stryker, 1987; Daly, 1993; Marsiglio, 1993). Rather than analyzing the identity of fathers as a *product* shaped by early socialization, emphasis is given more to identity as an ongoing *process* of social construction (Backett, 1987; Risman, 1987; Daly, 1993). Fatherhood is constantly being shaped and reshaped according to cultural context, work and family relations.

Constructing masculinities

Until recently, research on fatherhood had not been influenced to any large degree by the expanding body of theoretical research on masculinities. Inspired by feminist analyses, some male scholars have written critically about men and masculinity (Connell, 1985, 1987, 1995; Kaufman, 1987; Brittan, 1989; Kimmel and Messner, 1992; Morgan, 1992; Brod and Kaufman, 1994). These studies seek to make men and masculinity explicit and to focus on men's power (Segal, 1990). According to these theories, femininity and masculinity are not fixed and static roles that people have, but dynamic relational processes. Masculinity and femininity are constantly being reconstructed in a context of unequal, but shifting, power relations (Segal, 1990; Messner, 1993). There is also a strong focus on diversity, which is reflected in the concept of 'multiple masculinities' (Carrigan et al, 1985; Brittan, 1989; Morgan, 1992; Hearn and Collinson, 1994). The different forms of masculinity are not fixed, but continually shifting according to cultural and historical context. In spite of this focus on contingency and diversity, several researchers maintain that gendered power relations persist (Kimmel, 1987; Brittan, 1989).

In analyzing changing masculinities, Segal (1990) takes power as the central dynamic in the construction of femininities and masculinities. She views men's dominance and women's subordination as a historically grounded relational system, in which women continually contest men's power. The fact that women often contest men's power, and that some men oppress other men, creates possibilities for change.

Connell (1985, 1987) distinguishes between the culturally dominant forms of masculinity or 'hegemonic masculinity' and 'subordinated' or 'marginalized' forms. By hegemonic he means the dominant cultural ideal of masculinity, which need not correspond with the actual personalities of the majority of men. Hegemonic masculinity is constructed in relation to femininities, and in relation to subordinated masculinities. Although Connell uses the term 'hegemonic masculinity' in the singular, others have interpreted this to suggest that there is a core of dominant masculinity that is reflected in different variants (Wajcman, 1991). In contemporary Western society, hegemonic masculinity is strongly associated with income-generating work, and income-generating work is considered a central source of masculine identity. Concerning the construction of new father identities, an interesting issue is in what ways fathering expresses masculinity and how it relates to hegemonic masculinity. Is involved fathering a side-track – a subordinated form – or is it integrated into hegemonic forms of masculinity?

Analytic perspective of interaction

In our analyses of masculinity and childcare we apply an interactionist perspective in order to avoid undertaking an analysis of men and masculinity that excludes women and femininity (Hearn and Collinson, 1994). By using an interactionist perspective, we understand both gender differences and similarities as something mothers and fathers 'do' in interaction primarily with each other. Thus, masculinity (and femininity) are formed and maintained in everyday negotiations about childcare, housework and employment. Negotiations and the context in which it takes place give an insight into what significance and meanings fathers attach to their parenting and what implications it may have for their masculine identity.

As mentioned, power differences are constructed interactionally. However, status based on the different material resources that men bring to the relationship is also important for the outcome of the negotiations. On the one hand, we might expect that the general social inequality in gender status and gender ideology might continue to dominate the shaping of fathers' practices, giving the activities of fathers the highest status. On the other hand, childcare and housework is gendered feminine, and this might work in disfavour of men wanting to cross this gender boundary to establish their own ways of caregiving. In this study, however, the interviewed spouses had the same level of education, income and occupational status. By sharing the leave, they regarded themselves as practising equal parenting. This might lead to quite different outcomes as to whose model will dominate.

The fact that the spouses are structurally equal is relevant for the interactional construction of fatherhood and masculinity, both when a father interacts with a mother, and in a father's interaction with other men. The main question addressed here is how the fathers in our study construct their masculine caregiving identities. First, how does their own father as a role model influence their ongoing construction of fatherhood? Second, what is the relationship between fathering and mothering? Do the fathers create their own masculine form of caring or do mothers represent the dominant model of childcare? How does it influence the practice of gender equality? The third set of questions concerns the relationship between different masculinities. Are men who actively participate in childcare representatives of a subordinate form of masculinity, or do caregiving activities represent an extension of hegemonic masculinity?

Data and sample

In this chapter, we look at masculinity constructed by fathers who have shared the parental leave period with the mother, thus opting to stay at home and assume the main responsibility for a child during part of the first year of the child's life. When this study was conducted, the parental leave rights were much less generous than today, allowing 20 weeks at 100 per cent and 32 weeks without pay. After the first six weeks, the parents, both now and then, were allowed to share the rest of the weeks, but except for two weeks of paternity leave the fathers had no parental leave reserved for them.

A survey sent to all men in the municipality of Trondheim, who became fathers in 1987, showed that 3.6 per cent of the fathers in the sample shared paid or unpaid leave. In-depth interviews were conducted with all the couples this year who shared the parental leave period. This amounted to seven couples who shared the paid leave and three couples who shared unpaid leave. Both the mother and father in this group had a high labour market position and strong earning power, which was a characteristic of couples sharing parental leave at the time (Brandth and Kvande, 1992).

As is evident, couples sharing parental leave in 1987 comprised a very small group. Thus, the emphasis in this chapter is on positive examples – a minority of involved fathers. We believe that men who break common conventions might give us useful information about the processes that shape future fatherhood.

Fatherhood: from distance to closeness

Masculinity and fathering have been connected in various ways in different historical eras. Traditionally, power, authority and status were associated with the paternal role, especially with the father as patriarch (Seidler, 1988). Being a father has also been associated with such masculine qualities as virility and potency, and in the golden age of the nuclear family fatherhood meant being a good provider, which again was strongly associated with masculine honour. Thus a real man was a good provider for his wife and children. Being a good father rested on income-generating work, which meant activities away from home. In the context of modern family life it interesting to see what role the provider image plays when fathers combine masculinity and fatherhood.

Let us first examine how the fathers in our study defined the 'ideal' father. When asked to describe their ideal father, the role as provider was not emphasized. They did not define a good father as a good breadwinner. This suggests that the provider role has become secondary as an identity basis for these fathers. Nevertheless, there are ambivalences here as some stress that a good father represents material security and safety, which then serves as a basis for everything else. Further, these fathers all had good jobs and high earnings, indicating that they are important, if not the main, breadwinners of their families.

The fathers were striving to find out what it meant to be a good father. They lacked role models: their own fathers had not been much involved in family and care work. One of them said:

> 'I'm not really sure that I have an ideal at all. I didn't have very good contact with my own father, and I have often thought that I don't want to become like him. I suppose my ideal is to have good contact with my children and be there for them.'

In light of the changing patterns of work, with more mothers in the workforce, the expected distribution of parenting responsibilities is different for today's generations, making the models provided by their fathers inadequate. As their own fathers had emphasized work at the cost of time spent with their children, they were very distant fathers, and as such, they did not work very well as role models for their sons. Several other studies have made similar findings (Daly, 1993; Holter and Aarseth, 1993; Christian, 1994). Their fathers mainly served as a negative model that they had no desire to emulate; they did not want their children to have the kind of distant father they had had themselves.

It would be wrong to say, however, that the previous generation of fathers is completely without influence in the shaping of today's fatherhood. For instance, their lack of father contact made our interviewees emphasize the importance of just this element of intimacy in their own praxis as fathers. The following quotations express their main ideal of fathering:

74

'Being a good father does not just mean being an adult person who is there for security. It means being a close person for them.'

'Being a father today demands that you are genuinely concerned about your children and interested in following their development.'

'Being a father means giving them closeness and contact and showing them that you are fond of them.'

The most important aspect of a good father is thus to have close contact with the child – which contrasts with earlier images of the father. The kind of father they would like to be is a good carer for their children. Such an ideal has many of the same elements as the ideal mother: closeness, care and intimacy. This indicates that father images are constructed by combining traditional masculine and feminine elements in a new way. Their models are fragmented and, as Daly suggests (1993), they have to take a more piecemeal approach to the construction of fatherhood. We now take a closer look at what elements of parenting the fathers pick up from mothers.

Fatherhood in relation to motherhood

In this section we will consider how the fathers shape their masculine form of childcare by exploring the interaction between fathers and mothers. The couples in this study are, as we have shown, quite equal concerning occupational status, and this is a structural precondition for the men's involvement. We are interested to see what effects this has on their negotiations concerning childcare and housework. The spouses are also very committed to constructing an equitable sharing of parental work between themselves, and in some ways, this commitment must influence the gendered power relations. The question in this section is to what extent mothering represents a model for fathering when it comes to caregiving. Or, do the fathers construct their own way of caring?

Masculine construction of intimacy

In research on friendships between men, it has been claimed that men's forms of intimacy are seldom of the face-to-face variety that women are identified with; rather, they have more of a side-by-side nature, such as when men participate in joint activities (Sherrod, 1987). We see this element in the father's way of providing care, where friendship with the child is important. This is expressed by doing things together such as going for walks in the woods, both when the child is a baby and when the child is a little older. Going for walks is a typical side-by-side activity – being together and doing something together. Several of the fathers stated that when they spent time with the children, they went for walks in the woods and into town with them more than the mothers, and they feel it is good for the children to be together with adults of both sexes. "Women who stay home with lots of kids look tired, worn out and irritated. They have no energy left to play with their children, to read to them or to go for walks with them", one of them said. When we asked the parents if there were any differences in the way they spent time with the children, one of the mothers said:

> 'They [fathers] are maybe more active. Yeah, I might have them [the children] on my lap more often and stuff like that. More of the cosy stuff. He takes Tonje on ski trips. He carries her in the backpack and they go up into the mountains. I know it's a very big thing to do and Tonje really likes it, too. It is probably a great experience for her to have. I like to do stuff like that too. But I think I have to take care of the other stuff first, you know, make sure that everything is in order at home.'

The mother accepts and praises the father's outings with the child. She is proud of him, and gives his activities together with the child a higher rating than her own activities. Ivar Frønes (1989) has described the transition from 'the housewife family' to 'the symmetrical, administrating family' and the consequences this has had for parents and children. Children cannot go to their organized activities on their own as much as they used to. They have to have their parents' collaboration, and must be driven there. Small children can no longer be let out to play, but must be looked after. The local neighbourhood is not always a natural playground and the world is not felt to be as safe as it once was. In addition to its importance in giving emotional closeness, the family has also acquired new functions. For example, modern family ideology puts more emphasis on families' stimulation function – that the parents' input is decisive for the child's development and future. At the same time there is one aspect of Norwegian child culture that has been maintained. This is the outdoors ideal, the image of the 'outdoors child', where fresh air and physical games are considered healthy (Frønes, 1989). This is the landscape in which the fathers are finding their place. Childcare, or rather, 'parental work', has been expanded and changed in many ways. Much of what parents and children do together today takes place outside – away from the home and in the public arena. In this sense we can ascertain that the father who has exercised his right to parental leave has found his own platform in care work, and we may call the content of his childcare 'masculine care'.

Negotiating independence and empathy

Masculinity is often associated with independence. Bjerrum Nielsen and Rudberg (1989) refer to studies which indicate that the father promotes the independence of both girls and boys. Many of the fathers in our study felt that the mothers could be too close to, and worry too much about, the child, and that this, in turn, could affect a child's ability to be independent. Many fathers were concerned that the mother's constant worrying about the child could lead to overprotected children unable to exercise much independence. They felt that it was important that the child should not be 'pampered' too much, nor be too dependent on the parents. As opposed to the mother, the father did not worry as much. The fathers felt that the over-involvement of mothers was something that separated fathering from mothering. One father who compared himself with the mother put it this way:

> 'My wife has a guilty conscience because she spends too little time with the kids. I don't feel this because having a job, and the basis it gives to develop, the kids benefit from that too. I do not have a guilty conscience because the kids have to be in daycare 40 hours a week, but it bothers my wife.'

A constant characteristic of the fathers we interviewed was that they felt they did enough. "Fathers work a lot *and* are a lot together with their children", one of the fathers said. They felt that their involvement in their job did not lead to neglect of their children. Fathers are able to set clear boundaries between themselves and their children – everything is mostly practical and okay. Mothers, on the other hand, were said to have a more emphatic relationship with children, where worry and a guilty conscience for not spending more time with a child were always present. Mothers often agreed that they worried too much, and that the father's way was more straightforward. Mothers would have liked to get rid of their worries, but found it hard. They experienced conflict between a father's way of reasoning and what they felt and acted according to.

Extracts from the interviews with John and Greta may illustrate this. John said:

> 'We are different personality types. She is very conscientious. I'm lazier, more phlegmatic. She is on the alert all the time when it comes to children – also other people's children; she foresees dangerous situations. If she sees a child playing close to a staircase, she interrupts a conversation with adults and goes to sit down in the staircase to prevent the child from falling down. When I watch a football game, I watch a football game – don't interrupt that. I also think one should allow oneself to read the paper and let the children play on the side. One needs not stimulate them or pay them attention all the time – it makes them egocentric. But I still think I am a responsible father.... For instance, I don't think about the child when I am at work, but she does. I think I know when the child is well. It is my wife who has approached my style, I think.'

Greta agreed with John in that she is too worried. In answer to our question about to whom the children turned for comfort, she said:

> 'It's me, unfortunately. That goes for both the children, and it disappoints me because that was one of the reasons we were so keen on him staying home this first period. I was going back to work, and had to be relieved, but it hasn't been too much of that. The reason is that I am too involved. When he is tired, he just retreats. He is good at that.... I don't want to let go. It is now I have small children, it is now they need me the most, and it is now I must be there for them. The less my husband is available to them, the more I must be. We are very aware of this, and what we say is that I must relax more, and he must involve himself more.'

Greta illustrates a dilemma in these kinds of negotiations. On the one hand, she accepts his explanation that she is too conscientious and involved. On the other hand, she also says that her degree of involvement is necessary because her husband's involvement is insufficient; he is too relaxed and doesn't worry enough. As the children need strong parental involvement, the dilemma is that if the mother involves herself too much, their aspiration of equal parental practice will suffer, but if she involves herself less, the children will suffer. From the above quote we see that for her, equal parenting means equal emotional involvement. She felt she had lost the fight for equity when she was the one who must comfort the most. Mothers and fathers have ongoing discussions about what form the childcare should take. Greta assesses John's way of teaching the child independence and the outgoing activities he contributes to be good and important. One of the mothers had the following to say:

> 'Men have something to give the children. At least with the gender-role pattern we have grown up with. Men have some qualities, which I could have wished I had – which can have a positive effect on the children. They are outgoing, curious and interested in the world around them. I have two girls. If I were to be home with the kids … whether I wanted to or not, I would teach them a load of girl things.'

As noted, these couples are similar concerning education and position in the labour market. This, together with the fact that the fathers are unusual because they share the parental leave with the mother, leads clearly to what Hochschild (1989) has labelled an 'economy of gratitude'. Hochschild develops this concept in her book *The second shift* in which she analyses how family interactions over time tend to generate family myths such as 'we share housework and childcare equally', which actually covers a very inequitable family division of labour. Some women who perform a 'second shift' of work while their husbands enjoy 'the fat end of the leisure gap' still repeat the myth of equality because of their unequal position in an 'economy of gratitude' (Hochschild, 1989). This mechanism is clearly at work with our couples where the fathers have changed places with the mothers and have thereby become the 'avant garde' fathers to whom the mothers feel grateful. Even though motherhood is usually taken to be the standard reference for childcare, we find that mothers give the father's way of doing things higher status than their own. Parallel to this positive evaluation of the father, we find a corresponding devaluing of the female aspect, or what this mother called 'girl things'. Several mothers told us that they tried to learn from their husbands, and tried to emulate their way of being together with the children. The context in which this takes place is the economy of gratitude. There is therefore a clear tendency that in the name of equality the mother gives masculine care higher status than her own maternal practice.

What about the housework?

Today's parents organize and plan their children's lives, and the modern family uses more time and energy on their children than ever before

(Frønes, 1989: 45; Hays, 1996). This is confirmed by time use studies. These show that in spite of the fact that mothers have increased their participation in the labour force since the 1990s, overall, the parents do not spend less time together with the children; rather, both the mother and father spend more time alone with the children (Kitterød and Lømo, 1996). However, the time spent on housework has been reduced as it is considered less important. There are many indications that housework suffers because of the two-career family's lack of time.

Much research has shown that the distribution of housework between women and men in the family is very imbalanced. Still, there is reason to be curious about the fathers who take parental leave and share the care of the children to such a high degree. Do they also do more housework than the other fathers? Our previous analysis has shown that the mothers do far more housework, but that the fathers who have taken parental leave share most tasks more equally with the mother than fathers who did not take parental leave (Brandth and Kvande, 1991). However, tasks that deal with the child are shared much more equally between the mother and father than housework, a finding that is confirmed with the Norwegian time use studies (Kitterød and Lømo, 1996). Housework is a constant source of conflict and an ongoing topic of negotiation with the mother. The mothers expected that the fathers would also undertake housework and keep the home in order in the same way they did when they had parental leave. What they experienced was that the husband did no more than usual: "His housework in the period he was at home went okay. He did the housework he otherwise would have done" (and that is not much), one of the mothers said. Another mother had this to say:

> 'When he was home with paid leave, I threatened to move out. You wouldn't believe the way the house looked! After three weeks it looked like a real battle zone. But then it improved. I'm pretty flexible and I don't have to have everything picture-perfect, especially not at this time. But, it didn't take more than three weeks before I was about to give up.'

Conflicts as drastic as this were rare occurrences. Most couples were a little more careful with what they said, and pointed out that in this area there was a great difference between fathers' and mothers' leave. Even if they agreed that the person staying home should have the main responsibility for housework, it generally turned out that mothers, rather than fathers, did it. One mother explained this difference by saying that her husband was not so good at it and that she couldn't let things go. Her husband declared that he was not the 'housewife' type. The mother was generally careful not to make too heavy demands in this area. She felt she should be satisfied that her husband looked after the child. She strived to get him to do more housework, but rarely succeeded. He did little housework when he had leave, and he did even less afterwards. She lowered her demands or gave up.

This means that housework is not necessarily included with the fathers' conceptions of parental leave and with their commitment to look after the child. As Fassinger (1993) finds in her study, fathers are much more likely than mothers to feel that housekeeping is not a paternal responsibility. Because they do not like housework, they easily dismiss such tasks. On the other hand, housework has always been important for conceptions of femininity. Even though the mothers in our study were career women, and had acquired an additional basis for their identities as women, they saw housework and care work as naturally belonging together. For mothers, says Fassinger (1993), housework is tied to self-esteem, while it has no impact on the men's sense of self. When the fathers took parental leave and thus assumed the main responsibility for childcare, housework was not a part of this. There are no gains for masculinity in doing housework. Negotiations about housework are an important part of the gendering processes of their everyday life. That care work is easily combined with masculinity with these men, but not housework, is a way in which they mark a distance to mothering and reinforce women's secondary status and their own dominance.

Combination of hegemonic masculinity and caring

The last issue we intend to address in this chapter is the construction of fathering in relation to hegemonic masculinity and its strong connection to work. In what ways does fathers' use of parental leave involve a break with hegemonic masculinity? Or is a strong work identity a precondition for a happy integration of fathering and masculinity? As pointed out in an earlier section, the father takes his child 'out into the world'. Perhaps this is a case where the father, who traditionally has stronger ties to the world outside the home, takes the child out into the world when he comes into the home on parental leave or is an active father. This is also reflected in the way he uses the time during his parental leave. The fathers who were comfortable being home on parental leave were those who did it their way. In other words, they had found their own, masculine way of using the time. They managed to control the time themselves, virtually based on their own needs. They had continued contact with their job during their entire leave period, and took the child on walks, visits and to their workplace. They did not feel the child required too much effort and when the child was sleeping, they used the time for whatever they had planned. When asked to describe a typical day, one of them said:

> 'I read the newspaper. Then I went for a long walk. I brought things with me from work that I was going to read at home. I knew what I was getting into, and I had good contact with my job. There is always something to do.'

Another of the men described his parental leave period in the following way:

> 'I really enjoyed being home. That was because of the way I set it up. Just one month after I started my leave, we moved into a new house. So the first month was quite hectic. I took her with me up to the house to see how the carpenters were doing, then we went home and cleaned the house, and then we went to the daycare centre [to pick up the older sister].... Or we visited people. I have both my parents and parents-in-law in the city. I also went to my workplace a lot. That's mostly what I did.'

When the fathers had parental leave, they did many things they would have done anyway. The difference is that they brought their child with them. They fed them, changed nappies and put the child to bed, but when they were not busy with those things, they took the child outdoors with them. This way of combining childcare and masculine activities is clearly seen in our interviews with the fathers taking paternal leave. When asked if caring conflicted with his idea of what a man is supposed to do, one of the fathers who was an engineer said:

> 'No, I didn't feel that it was a problem. That's probably because of my age [30] and because my wife was sure I'd manage this. Then there's the point about education: as I had that [an engineering degree], I didn't need to prove I was macho.'

Staying at home looking after a small baby did not endanger their masculine identity. They seemed to have a secure and relaxed relationship with their own masculinity. Perhaps this security is a precondition for taking parental leave? Part of it is anchored in their strong work identity. They have a job that means a lot to them, and they will continue in their jobs; there is no doubt about that.

Several of the fathers were graduate engineers, a profession that has been described as an archetypical masculine culture (Cockburn, 1985). This means that taking parental leave and caring for children did not affect their main arena; in fact, childcare seemed to be an attribute to their lifestyle, an extension of the masculine sphere (Brod, 1987). The new man will not win any more victories in the old public arenas, according to Bengtsson and Frykman (1987), but rather through his efforts in everyday contact with his closest family. Care and intimacy with children can be seen as new territories to be conquered.

The fact that childcare had been accepted as a facet of masculinity was also seen in the reactions of those around the fathers. Fathers who had taken leave were admired both by their colleagues and by their friends. It was considered 'cool' to be able to look after small children. One of the wives put it this way: "I think it's a bit sad to see helpless men – faced with children that is – men who are not able to handle them, or dare to try." Being hopelessly clumsy with children is not considered particularly masculine. Being able to master a new challenge, even if it is childcare, is, however, regarded as an important masculine attribute. But there were also some fathers who did not tackle the situation especially well when they stayed at home on parental leave. They had planned to get much more done while they were home, for example, redecorating or renovating an apartment. They were plagued by constant interruptions so that they couldn't plan to do anything. "There is no point starting to paint and carrying on and think that you can make the kids disappear with a magic wand", as one put it. These fathers had few words to describe the content of their normal day. Not too much happened. When the baby slept, they also slept. Some described the passivity they experienced: "I would never have believed it could be like this, that I would be so lacking in drive as I was." These fathers had also believed that they would be able to manage their own activities while they were at home, but instead they found out that there was no spare time for this. Nor did they manage to fill the short intervals with minor cleaning tasks and other housework, like the mothers did. In other words, they did not manage to do things their way, like most of the other fathers did, and they encountered problems when they were going to do things like the mother did. This group of fathers, which was a minority, did not yet have the same strong foothold in their working life. Thus, it seems that a strong connection to hegemonic masculine activities may be a precondition for being able to construct a successful integration of masculinity and fathering.

Conclusions

In this analysis, we have focused on the changing nature and meaning of fathering. Our interest has been to see how men include childcare in their construction of masculinity. In this process, the fathers in our study are beginning to put together the elements of fathering in a new way. Their own fathers influence this process by serving as a 'negative' model to a large extent. The distant breadwinner model of fathering does not seem to satisfy contemporary demands on fathers in Norway. However, distancing the provider model while at the same time valuing work and being important providers of their families indicates an ambivalent identity.

Further ambivalence is seen when fathering is constructed in relation to mothering. The fathers who have used their rights to parental leave want to develop a close relationship with their children, thus borrowing elements from mothering. However, our data indicate that fathers have their own platform in care work, which they see as different from the way mothers construct their caregiving in these families. We have tentatively conceptualized the content of fathers' childcare as 'masculine care'. An important element in a father's way of providing care seems to be becoming friends with the child, expressed by being together and doing things together. Another element in 'masculine care', as we have observed it, is teaching the child independence. Independence seems to be constructed in relation to the way the mothers exercise closeness and intimacy with the child. The couples in our study are all committed to equality. There is, however, a clear tendency that the mothers, in spite of this, give masculine care higher status than their own practice.

When the father takes parental leave, there seems to be a redefinition and redistribution of work in the home concerning who does what task, and what is good childcare and 'good enough' housework. This restructuring process is also a negotiation process about what gender should mean. We see it as a gender-producing process. The differences between masculinity and femininity are marked by the fact that most of the men do not do housework to any great extent. This is due to the fact that to care for the child is why they took parental leave. They see themselves as active fathers, not as housewives. The fact that the majority of men exclude housework and are allowed to be fathers in their own premises displays their power of influential strength and reveals their relative domination in the relationship. The couples in this study have an intention of equality – a genderless order. But the result is gendered just the same. Relations of inequality and dominance are produced as they negotiate their domestic labour.

A final question in this chapter has been the relationship between fathering and hegemonic masculinity. Most fathers in our study represent hegemonic masculinity as they have strong ties to the labour market and as their identities are strongly rooted in income-generating work. Those with ambivalent feelings towards their work express greater problems managing the parental leave period. Dominant men have the influence to change hegemonic masculinity to include new elements, in this case, childcare. This is the most promising result as masculinity is in need of change in a more nurturing direction. Whether masculine dominance is also reproduced in other contexts when fathers take on caring roles is a question that needs further investigation. In the meantime, what greater father involvement in family matters might do to the equity between men and women in close relationships is an open question.

6

Home Alone on Leave or with the Mother Present[1]

Introduction

The development of parental leave policies as a system to strengthen parent–child relationships was the most important area of expansion in the Norwegian welfare state during the 1990s. In this decade, the schemes were extended, and earmarked rights were granted to fathers. Since one important intention behind granting special rights to fathers was to encourage their contact with and care for children, the welfare state was acting on behalf of young children by getting fathers to take responsibility for daily caregiving. The parental leave schemes are complex, as they have to consider various factors. In this chapter, based on our first interview study, the focus is on the father's quota, which was four weeks at the time of the study. We examine two ways in which the father's quota could be taken: either alone with the child while the mother went back to full-time work, or with the mother present on either a part-time or full-time basis.

Being responsible for infant or toddler care is perhaps one of the most radical breaks with traditional father roles, and may have long-term implications for the values and practices of fathers. Previous research has focused on the consequences of parental leave for the adults (mothers, fathers and parents), especially the extent to which the parental leave schemes have changed the participation patterns of fathers and resulted in a more equal division of family and work time between mothers and

---

[1] First printed in A.-M. Jensen and L. McKee (eds) (2002) *Children and the changing family: Between transformation and negotiation*, London: RoutledgeFalmer. Permission to republish granted by the Taylor & Francis group.

fathers. What type of changes this represents for children has been much less in focus, not least because of the methodological challenges involved and the difficulties in assessing such results over time. Thus, there is still a lack of parental leave research that takes a child's perspective, seeing children as actors in their own lives. In this chapter, the fathers' narratives are in focus, but we are primarily interested in how young children influence fathers' care practices through interaction with their fathers in the two different situations.

Theoretical approach

The topic of men and childcare is filled with preconceptions and myths. Care is readily perceived as an ability women have and that men do not have to the same extent. In this chapter we do not examine men's caring abilities or their personality that makes them either adept at exercising care; rather, we are interested in how they *practise* care for their children (Morgan, 1996). Thus, we ask how they act, not how they *are* as people.

Research on fathers and care has generally focused on how the care practices of the father have been shaped by the mother. Due to her activities in the labour market, the mother has opened the door to the father's entitlement to paid parental leave, and her negotiating strength is considered decisive for the father's degree of participation in the family (Brandth and Kvande, 1989, 1991, 1998). It has been pointed out that the mother's model power, that is, her standards for care and housework, is also required of the father's efforts (Holter and Aarseth, 1993). Whether explicit or not, in research studying a father's care in light of a mother's care, the perspective is relational. This means that what a father does is understood as a social product that is continuously defined and negotiated with the mother. In addition to studying the care practices of fathers in an interaction perspective, research has also focused on a father's care as a masculine practice, and whether childcare conflicts with or corresponds to masculine identity projects (see Chapter 5).

A less used perspective in father research is how the interaction with children influences *the care practices of fathers*. In this chapter, we focus on the relationship between fathers and children, and look for children's influence on how their fathers practise care. Theoretically, this implies that we see children as active agents who contribute to the production of the adult world and their own place in it. Seeing children as social agents contrasts with traditional socialization theory in which the notion is that children are formed by forces external to themselves in order to adapt to society (Corsaro, 1997). As in this analysis we deal with very young children, their creative influence might be limited. Indeed, their births are the source of the parental leave, but children cannot directly decide whether or not their fathers use the quota, or the ways they choose to use it. Nonetheless, in interacting with their fathers, they still exercise some influence, and in this chapter we will bring aspects of their influence on a father's care practices into focus.

Regarding care as a relational practice means that care can be learned and developed if and when the situation so invites or demands. This, in turn, means that we do not consider care ability as something fixed, but rather as a potential that may be formed and developed differently depending on the relations and situations in which it is practised. Hence, we see care as situationally dependent. In this way care also becomes more ambiguous and more open to variations. Seeing care as relational also enables us to study how children influence the father's practice.

One aspect of caregiving is *the practice of time*. In his book *Øyeblikkets tyranni* [*The tyranny of the moment*] Hylland Eriksen (2001) describes how *slow time* may be connected to safety, predictability, joy, cosiness, growth and maturation, with a special emphasis on the last two. This is a perception of time that differs from the one that applies in the working life of fathers and in life in general, where time is more a matter of division and fragmentation, framed by the demand for a high tempo. The consequence may be that it is more difficult to create narratives, sequences, development and maturation.

The questions we ask in this chapter concern the contexts that provide the child with the opportunity to influence the father's practice. Two contexts are studied: (1) when fathers care for their children alone during parental leave and (2) when the mother is also at home during his leave. How do these contexts influence the interaction established between a father and his child – where the child becomes an actor? What is the content of the practices the child influences?

Data, sample and contexts

The analysis is based on data from a larger study on fathers' use of the parental leave schemes. The study included a questionnaire that was sent to all men who became fathers in the period May 1994 to April 1995 in two municipalities in central Norway. A total of 2,194 questionnaires were mailed, and the response rate was 62 per cent. From this same sample we interviewed 30 couples who used the parental leave system in various ways. The interviews were conducted in 1997 and took place when the child was from 18 months to two years old.

We interviewed both the mothers and fathers. Thus, it is the parents who provided information for the study. Information from the toddlers is not available, and for the purposes of this chapter, we are only able to present their perspective indirectly.

We use data from the questionnaire to provide an overview of the two main types of father practices investigated, and the social background of the users. We distinguish between those fathers who did not stay home alone, that is, whose partners were at home when the father used the father's quota, and those whose partners went back to work full time. For 53 per cent of the sample, the mother went back to work on a full-time basis while the father stayed at home on leave. For the remaining 47 per cent, 15 returned to part-time work, 9 continued their leave on an unpaid basis, 9 had their holidays and 9 were out of work. The 5 per cent who do not fall under these categories ('other') are primarily students, on sick leave or mothers practising a variety of combined solutions. When we take a closer look at the mothers, we find social differences between them. The mothers with higher education, income and job status are those who return to full-time work when the fathers use their quota. These fathers are given the opportunity to care for the child alone during the day – thus young children in families with a high social status have a better chance of developing a relationship with their fathers in this way. In families where children are not cared for by their father alone, the mother's work status is lower, and within the couple, lower than the father's. This pattern is also distinct in the interview material.

To investigate the question of how children may influence fathers' care practices, we will focus on these two contexts. In the debate on how parental rights should be designed, an important argument was that fathers ought to experience what it is like to have the main responsibility for childcare when the mother goes back to work. It was first decided that a necessary premise was that the mothers had to return to work before the father would be able to use the quota. However, when objections to this were raised, the government changed this initial condition so that fathers could use the quota regardless of what the mother did after she finished her leave. In other words, the mother could stay home on a full- or part-time basis when the father was practising his quota. In this chapter we distinguish between those who had the sole care of their child under the father's quota and those who did not. We assume that using the father's quota alone, or taking it while the mother was also home, are two entirely different contexts with different opportunities for the father to be influenced by the child.

A second aspect shaping father's quota usage is that it can be shortened, for example, to two or three weeks instead of a month. The latter option is particularly relevant if the mother has worked part-time and has thus not earned full birth benefits. If the mother has been employed in a 50 per cent position, she will only have earned 50 per cent birth benefits, and consequently the father will also be granted only 50 per cent (although note that the eligibility criterion was abolished in 2010). An alternative for the father is to take two weeks with full birth benefits instead of four at 50 per cent. Another aspect of the context that is of significance for children's influence is if the father has been completely away from work during the father's quota period or at work part time alternating with the mother's part-time schedule. This will constitute an important framing condition for shaping the fathers' care practices.

In our analysis we have therefore chosen to distinguish analytically between, on the one hand, those fathers who were responsible for the child alone and who were also home full time for four consecutive weeks, and on the other hand, those who were home together with the mother and who were not completely off work during the father's quota period. These two contexts become a critical point for studying the change in the father–child relationship that was one of the project's intentions. We will compare the processes that arise when the father had the leave alone and full time and when the mother was home at the same time and the father had part-time leave.

Home alone

It is not only considered important for children that their fathers are home on leave, but the ways in which they are home also influences their care practices. We shall thus first consider those fathers who were completely off work for four weeks or more and who were 'home alone', that is, the mother was not home at the same time. What we want to know is what care practices develop and how the child influences these practices.

On the slow-time track!

A common characteristic of the stories of these fathers is their experience that care work means using time – time permeates fathers' narratives about care. The point is not only that they have understood that it is vital to spend time with their children (many fathers would agree with them on this), but also that these fathers have actually given time to their children. They have spent time caring for their children and thus obtained other perceptions of care. This is something they have done themselves – they have given their children time by taking leave. Hence, they have gained the experience that spending time with their children is important. This is time that is defined as being present for their children. When we consider what they do with their children while on leave, it is obvious that they are on the track of what we may call 'slow time' (Hylland Eriksen, 2001) – this means that the time is not spent running from one thing to another, to squeeze as much as possible into the shortest possible time. Nor is there that much that has to be done; rather, the children's needs are the centre of focus. Hence, it is the child who makes the time slow.

These fathers experience that time acquires another meaning; they understand that care is about time. The fathers' descriptions of how their day-to-day lives were spent while on leave provide us with material that can help us understand this. So what was a typical day during the period of leave like? One of the fathers described the following:

> 'The four weeks? It was to get up early. They wake up quite early, and that's more or less okay. They wake around seven, and they rise and shine, so like in the weekends, they can loaf around in their pyjamas. Avoids the stress of getting changed, there's more than enough of that at other times. Then there's breakfast before the morning routines, and then get dressed and if the weather's nice, then outside. And then we would be outside in the playground or in the forest, and then perhaps go to the store for some shopping, and then home to start dinner, and then mummy would be home, and then dinner and children's TV and then good night. Typical day.'

We see here how the father describes a day that is not filled with numerous events and things to do. Basically, there are very few things on the agenda. Time is spent doing such things as getting dressed, brushing teeth and going to the shop. 'Sunday time' was introduced in the sense that the children were allowed to "loaf around in their pyjamas". There is no impression here of a busy everyday; rather the slow rhythm of care decides. The children get the father up in the morning and control his time. Their activities give him another 'perception of slow time'.

The fact that the needs of the children regulate the use of time can also be seen in the next description. This is a father who has taken both the father's quota and shared the leave with the mother. He has now chosen to work nights as a social worker so that he can be home in the daytime with his three daughters, who are all under school age. Here he gives us a description of how days are regulated by the children's activities and the time they need to eat:

'She [the mother] gets up in the morning and gets them ready. I stay in bed a little longer, but then I get up and start breakfast for all of us. She goes to work and we eat. I clean and do the dishes. Then we usually play and read a book. In the middle of the day we have lunch, meals will usually take 45 minutes to an hour, depending on how impossible the middle one is [laughter]. Occasionally I have to feed her one small piece at the time. Then the two oldest ones go out to play, often with the neighbour kids. They'll run up to get the mail…. I'll go out and check them every half hour or so. The smallest girl usually sleeps from one o'clock and until her mother comes back from work. She'll come along outside in the morning, usually with me. I'll be busy outside with various activities such as some carpentry or…. There's not much time for my own activities, it's mostly family work.'

Again, we see that the children's time to sleep and eat regulates time. No strictly regulated time is described; rather, flexible time that can be stretched according to need. This is a perception of time that is different from the one that applies in the working life of the fathers and in life in general, where time is more a matter of division and fragmentation, all inside the framework of the demand for a high tempo. This is what Hylland Eriksen (2001) describes as 'the tyranny of the moment', which may render it more difficult to create development and maturation. Fragmented experiences will dominate our lives.

Need-oriented care practice

These fathers have given their children time by taking their father's quota and leave, and feel that it is important to use time with the children. As described above, they develop a care practice that is characterized by slow time controlled by the needs of the child. Thus, there is also a development of competence as the fathers get to know their children by having the main responsibility and spending a great deal of time with them. It is easier for them to develop an understanding of the child's needs. Arnfinn tells us about having responsibilities and using time:

'For my part I believe that there is a whole, like, both with the 14 days initially, and then the four weeks and my reduced hours at work in total that has given me a relationship with my children, in a way that the four weeks are part of a whole. Now, four weeks are not that much, but anyway you get enough time that you manage to understand that it is difficult and demanding to be the person who has the total responsibility, that's what you notice during this period. But you do get quite close to your kids during that time.'

And:

'Sure, I believe the fact that you have so much time with your kids, you virtually learn how to read how they tell you stuff which you maybe would have lost if you didn't have so much time. Because if you go to work and come home in the evening, the kids may be in a phase where they are tired and grumpy, and the father is also tired and grouchy, and you get this impression ... and then you don't want to do anything with them. I think there is something there. But if you spend a whole day with them, then you, like, see the totality of the days that they have too, and understand why they might be cross and crabby.'

He points out that having the total responsibility is what makes him see how demanding care work is, and that he feels how close he gets to his children. He also claims that he has a learning experience when he points out that he is learning to 'read' his children. By spending a great deal of time with them, the day-to-day affairs of his children become a whole, making it easier for him to understand why, for example, they are grumpy and cross. He then avoids being the type of father who comes home from work and disciplines his children. Again, we see how the children influence the father's care practice in this situation.

Another informant has had both the father's quota and stayed home one day per week in the subsequent period of time with his children. He also talks how having the sole responsibility helps him to see both how care is time-consuming and that he is gaining competence in seeing and understanding his child. He relates the following when we ask him about the importance of the leave for him:

'You get so much time together with the kids, and that in itself is positive, I think. The chance of following them from day to day and seeing how they behave and how they are doing in a day. And then you also gain insight into how demanding it is to have responsibility for children. That's really demanding, I must say. Actually, it's much more demanding at times than being at work, I would claim. Because there's something going on all the time, and you're on guard all the time, so there's a rhythm to having responsibility for children that is quite demanding. Seeing that this is the way it is has value in itself.'

From qualitative to quantitative time

These fathers practise what we have chosen to call 'slow time'. Their experiences also help them to understand that care is about *using a great deal of time* with the children. Fathers describe that the children have initiated a process in them where the focus is on quantitative time. They have experienced that care cannot be carried out in quality time, and a number of them have grown strongly critical of all mention of qualitative time. Rather, they have realized that you must be there for the child. This emerges through their responses to various questions, both regarding what they believe a good father must be and when we ask what they feel they are especially good at with their children.

Egil has found that it is important to be responsible alone, as this helps him to see things in another way. He really experienced having sole responsibility when his wife got a job that meant she had to stay in Stockholm for long periods of time. Here is his idea of what a 'good' father is:

> 'I think it is to spend a great deal of time with children, and not necessarily to have to do everything under the sun. I *have much more faith in quantity than in quality*, spending much time on your kids, being with them and just being outdoors with them so they see you. Allowing them to help and mess up the kitchen and run around, that's what I think. Both a good mother and a good father, there's no difference really between what a good mother and a good father is, simply the fact that they are there and they can be asked things and that they see that at least one of them is there generally all the time.'

Egil also illustrates that those fathers who have experienced the major importance of time focus on quantitative time:

> 'A good father is one who has time and who can spend his time with the kids, that is, I strongly believe that *we are not just talking about quality, but also about quantity*, and the fact that you are there. I really think this is important. They speak about

quality and how it isn't really important how much you're together, but that it's important that when you're with them that you're really with them, but I believe that it is important for kids to have a father who actually is there. And that you do things with your kids.'

The outcome is that he has combined quantity of time with quality of time:

'But there is always this, how we are concerned with how the kids should be close to both parents. This is essential for us, and we are always aware of this. And we have also seen results of this. Particularly our oldest kid, he's been daddy's boy ever since he was a baby. When he was 10 months old he refused to let his mother change his diapers, it was daddy, daddy all the time, so he was very.... He's only started to warm up to his mother again during the last couple of years. Yes I sat with him on my lap every afternoon, and that was something we both loved, so he had lots of contact with his daddy, he was daddy's boy. However, this has changed, it's not like that anymore. But I think it was because he was so much with me, from the start.'

This is contrasted with his own father when we ask if he himself had a father role model:

'My father worked a lot, and when he came home, we would often be in bed. What I mean is, I did see him a lot, but he didn't spend much of his time with us and wasn't close to us. He never changed diapers, or dressed us, and I've spent lots of time doing that sort of thing. I've changed diapers and bathed them since they were infants, both of them. I think it's important, really, to have that kind of contact.'

When we ask those fathers who have been home and have had the main responsibility for their children about what, in their opinion, makes a good father, many of them answer that a good father must spend time with his children. This is something they have done themselves – they have given their children time by taking leave from their job. Thus, they have gained the realization that spending time with their children is important. Giving children quantitative time becomes the ideal. When asked what a father should not be, one of the fathers says: "He should....

I don't believe in just giving kids things and gifts, I believe more in giving kids time and attention." He is also one of the fathers in our sample who allowed this idea to have consequences for his use of time, in that he declined to pursue a career at the expense of his children.

Home, but not alone

In this section we will look at the father–child interaction when the father takes his leave on a part-time basis and the mother is also at home. How does this situation influence father–child interactions?

Visiting in the mother's domain

The reason these mothers stay at home at the same time as the fathers is because they value childcare more than their jobs. After they had children, these mothers adapted their working hours to the family. Some work part time, some extend their leave past the first year (unpaid) and some quit their jobs indefinitely. For these mothers, who we generally find in unskilled jobs, being a mother gives them greater meaning, satisfaction and self-confidence than their jobs, and this is vital for their identity. In such families there will apparently be little momentum in the restructuring of the father's practices – it goes without saying that for them, the mother should stay at home. Parental leave is interpreted as a 'reward' for her. One of the fathers put it this way: "She's the one who has carried the baby, and then she should…. It would have been wrong if I had been the one to enjoy the benefits. She had the drawbacks before [morning sickness etc], and then I should have the time off later. No way. That would be wrong."

It is generally thought that children have a special relationship with their mothers during the first year of the child's life (Ahrne and Roman 1997), most of all because of breastfeeding. The fathers see breastfeeding as a natural part of the relationship between the mother and the child in the first year, taking this as a sign that their own role is limited while the child is so young. "It seems most natural to me that she's at home. She gave birth to the baby and all, and she breastfed the baby until it was more than a year old", says one of the fathers. This appears as traditional, making it more difficult to discern any change processes. Emphasizing the bodily closeness between mother and child may be understood as an excuse for not taking more leave, but there is also an aspect of taking care of the mother. The fathers see a body that needs repair, and interpret the leave as compensation or a reward for the strain of pregnancy and birth.

Thus, this leave practice may be understood as part of the discourse on motherhood that has been important in Norway when it comes to fathers' parental leave rights.

The father as a supporting player

The children in these families had the mothers as their main care person, and when the father's quota was due, normally towards the end of the first year, the mother had the main responsibility for almost a year. The child and mother developed a close, bodily relationship through nursing, they established daily routines together, and got to know each other by being together on a full-time basis. When the father started his leave, the father virtually came into the picture like a 'visitor'. One of the fathers describes the situation: "Because she was home and had been home and knew everything and had the routines, I just continued the same routines. I did a bit more with the kids, but basically, it was all on her terms."

The effect of the mother having stayed home on leave and continuing to be home when the father was taking his father's quota emerges clearly when these fathers describe what they did while they were at home. They can't remember all that much. They describe it as being like the weekends. They participate a little more in the daily chores than if they had not taken leave, but are unable to take full responsibility and are unable to 'test their mettle' alone with the child. Thus, they are unable to develop the self-confidence they would have come by if they had sole responsibility. Nor can they tell the same stories about the demanding job that care work is. A young child generates a lot of routine work, and the role of these fathers is to be a supporting player for the mothers.

Being attentive

In contrast to the fathers who are home alone with their children, these fathers do not argue that the most important thing is to give the child quantity time. Rather, the term they use is to 'give the children attention', a term they use to designate their perception of their father project. To be attentive concerns the use of time. "I believe they should have much attention *all the time*", one of them says, specifying: "The first thing I do when I get home then, is that the first kid I meet gets a hug and a kiss." "All the time", as he says, doesn't mean setting a priority between the job and the home. It is the time when he is at home that should be for the children. The attention is expressed by his giving the children a hug when he meets them as he walks in the door from work. Anders, who appears to be a busy and stressed man, describes 'attention' as follows:

> 'A good father, that's somebody who gives his kids attention, and who gives them attention when they demand it, and who is concerned with what they're doing, who is concerned with them *then and there* and like, well let's call it concentration. Like somebody who can bring them up, who gives them a defined framework, or perhaps clear limitations for what they should, and may or may not do. That you create some kind of framework so they know what they may or may not do, and who can answer questions and....'

As we see here, there are a number of aspects to being a father that he finds important. In addition to upbringing, he wants to give them attention "when they demand it – then and there." However, what kind of time is he speaking about? He continues thus:

> 'I think we give them attention all the time, *because the time is so short.* As I said, I get home at five thirty and then there is dinner, and there is very little time before they go to bed, so they have like, well we try to see some news, right, headlines, but they are around us all the time. We do cuddle with them a lot, see, put them on the lap and horse around, so they probably have one hundred per cent attention when we're there.'

The attention he gives his children concerns the time counting from when he comes home until his children go to bed. Then they receive full attention, but he also says that during this period the family will prepare and eat their dinner, and they will watch the news on TV. Perhaps the children also watch children's TV. Thus, there is no development of the cyclic, slow time where the tasks with the children determine how the time is spent. Rather, the time spent with the children is high-tempo time because many things have to be squeezed into the brief time available in the late afternoon and early evening.

Here the question of time refers to whether the children are in focus during the available time, that is, after working hours, and not necessarily that the children get more time. The children must be adapted to the available time, not the other way around, where work is adapted to the children. For some of these fathers the competition between work and children is hard when it comes to time. However, the ideal of giving children attention has yet another aspect that concerns how work shapes the fathers' care. Being a good father means giving the children attention after work *even if they are tired*. Even though the job is arduous, good parents always need to pay attention to their children. If the mother has been home with them during the day, afternoons become particularly important for the father:

> 'The question is also how tired you are, how patient. Immediately after dinner it is nice to relax a little and be quiet and then it may be that … you simply can't manage always. And when she has them all day, then I try to take them as much as possible in the evening, be together with them as much as possible, I really feel that that's right.'

What these statements tell us is that not only do work demands structure their time and consume their time, work requirements also drain them of the energy that is necessary to be a good father and make something of the afternoons with their children. They attempt to compensate for this through extra mobilization.

"Can't you see he's thirsty?"

As mentioned, the fathers who had been home alone developed a need-oriented care practice precisely because they spent much time together with the child. Those fathers who had not had the responsibility for the child alone are also able to see that spending a lot of time with their children was important. For example, they understand that the mother's extended period of leave is important for her contact with the children. Magnar makes a major point of the fact that the children are more closely tied to the mother, they communicate better with her, and she knows their signals better because she is at home with them all day. He says:

> 'It's easier for her to "read" them because they spend so much time with her.… She has had time to become thoroughly familiar with them for better or worse. Needless to say, I know their good and bad sides too, but not in the same way, really. She's able to interpret the children way before I can. I need more information to determine what.… Of course she has been with them in the day, and.… This is what it's about, I think this is the cause.'

Magnar compares himself to his wife who will be on leave for the second year running: "She'll say, 'Can't you see he's thirsty', but I can't see this because I am not with him 24 hours a day", he says. The children thus are more easily drawn to those they spend the most time with, he believes.

Nevertheless, Magnar feels that his son got to know him better during the quota period, even if it was only part time. Others point to the same conclusion, that the father's quota constitutes a break with going to work every day, thus allowing children to become familiar with their father. The fact that the mother is at home at the same time is less important when the quota means the father can avoid coming home from work and feeling too tired to give children the attention needed from a good father.

More fun with older children

The fact that the mother has had the dominant position in the care arena at least during the first year has led many fathers to move their father project a little further along the time scale. It is when they start speaking about their children when they have grown older that they get excited, feeling they can master childcare and are better able to cope. "It's more challenging and that sort of thing when they're older. It's more enjoyable and more important", one of them says. It is obvious that these fathers feel more confident in the father's role for slightly older children. When the children are able to start kicking a ball or doing other 'fun things', the father's role acquires more meaning for them. Therefore, when they talk about their father's project, it is care of the slightly older children that is in focus.

Because they emphasize their role as fathers in relation to slightly older children, the playing father has a prominent place in their narratives about how they perform their care. Children prefer their father for rough types of play, and fathers feel that they gain importance through this. They feel that they are better able to display their good sides as fathers when the children have grown older. As one of them says: "We'll throw some snowballs and stuff, see? We'll balance on the rail and jump down and do a somersault, right?" What many of these fathers like to do together with their children takes place outdoors:

> 'What I like most is to take my kids fishing. It's not all that often, but taking them outside into the forest.... They're quite curious and ... teach them stuff, that's the most fun. But we do many other things too. It's fun to play with Lego and things like that too.'

Another father tells us how much his first child, a boy of four, enjoys being outside and that one of the parents has to come too, this usually being the father. Thus, father and son can be found in the sandbox and on the football field. Being outside is an aspect of the 'daddy role' where the environment gives him positive feedback: "But I really enjoy being outside, like. I like doing small things and keeping my children happy, pushing them when they're sitting on the swing, you know, things like that."

Playing, taking short hikes and other outdoor activities have been considered a type of care that typically concerns doing something side-by-side. This is a form of intimacy that is often practised among men, one that could be said to be the traditional way for men to be together. One of those keenest to hike in the woods with his children says:

> 'It's really important for me to tell them that I love them and ... be nice to them and hug them too. Physical contact is important to me. Yes, I think it's very important for the kids to feel that they have somebody who loves them and that they feel they can rely on you.'

As this illustrates, even if they are not letting go of what they find important, that is, to do things together, they add that it is important to enjoy each other's company and let the children know how much they love them.

Conclusions

In this chapter it has been our aim to analyse what affect the father's quota has had on the relationship between fathers and their children. Our primary goal has been to focus on how the child influences the care practices of fathers. This implies that we see children as active agents who contribute to the production of the adult world and their own place in it. In turn, this helps us to say something about the consequences the new leave rights have had for children.

Our analysis examined two different contexts. We asked whether the influence of children on a father's behaviour was less observable when mothers were present. Therefore, we distinguished between the fathers who had responsibility alone for the child during the father's quota period and those who had not. We found that when fathers were 'home alone', that is, they used the father's quota and an extended period of leave while the mother went back to work, completely different processes would arise than when the mother was at home at the same time. When the father is completely off from work and has the main responsibility for the child alone, the children make him aware of what we have called 'slow time', where the child's needs determine the content of time. In this situation, the father develops a need-oriented care practice because he learns to read the child and thus develop his care competence. Consequently, the child's agency is allowed to influence the father's care practices.

When the mother is at home at the same time, this type of process is not initiated. The father also continues his paid work part time. In such a situation, the mother's main responsibility for the child is not interrupted and the father acquires the role of supporting player for the mother. In these cases, the mother continues her close relationship with the child, reading and translating the child's needs for the father. Consequently, the child has no independent influence on the father's care practices. It is the mother and not the child who interacts with the father. The father will therefore not get to know his child in the same way, and care practices based on knowing the child well are not developed. Hence, he feels more at home with the older children.

We see that the two different contexts result in quite different conditions for the development of fathers' care practices. When a father takes complete leave from his work and has the main responsibility for the child while the mother goes back to work, an interaction is established between children and fathers where the child more clearly becomes an actor who influences the care given by the father. When the father does not take this break from his job and the mother does not go back to paid work, the care the father gives develops much more in interaction with the mother. If we return to one of the intentions of the father's quota, which was to strengthen the contact between child and father, we see that this primarily occurs in the context we have called 'home alone'.

The introduction of the father's quota in the Norwegian parental leave legislation came about as a result of the intention to encourage fathers' contact with and care for their children. Another objective was to share the benefits and burdens of working life and family life between men and women. Our analyses emphasize that the father's quota may also be seen from a child's perspective. It reveals that if it is used according to the intention of making fathers into caregivers, it can contribute to the welfare of young children.

7

Fathers Experiencing Solo Leave: Changes and Continuities[1]

Introduction

This chapter explores men's actual practices of caring when they stay home alone on parental leave. While the avoidance of care has traditionally been seen as a feature of 'being a man', fathering has undergone many changes since the 1980s. Researchers seem to agree that change has taken place, although not on the magnitude of the change, as there is a great variety in relation to the circumstances of fathering. Parental leave offers an opportunity for fathers to spend time having responsibility for their children, but the leave may be taken in various ways. In Chapter 6 we saw that time spent caring for children by fathers alone is qualitatively different from time when the mother is also present.

Being home alone on leave means taking daily responsibility for the child, which helps facilitate a move from being the mother's helper to being a more equal co-parent. Such results confirm what Radin and Russell (1983) reported many years earlier, namely that being in charge of the children alone seems to be the 'cutting edge' with respect to fathers' positive feelings of involvement and competence. Interestingly, Radin and Russell also reported that solo fathering was important when it came to feelings of overload and distress. In their study the proportion of fathers who took care of their children when the mother was not home was low, but several later studies have noted that fathers are more likely than mothers to spend time with the children in the presence of the other parent (Kitterød, 2003; Craig, 2006).

To date, studies comparing the effects of fathers' solo leave with leave when the mother is also present are scarce, but those that exist give clear indications that caring alone over a period of time has the greatest effect on the development of father involvement and gender equality (Wall, 2014; Bünning, 2015; Ranson, 2015; O'Brien and Wall, 2017). The care practices of fathers on parental leave alone may also have a lot in common with 'stay-at-home fathers'. Research on stay-at-home fathering has provided knowledge about fathers who have taken on the responsibility of childcare (Doucet, 2006), but while this group is out of work for a variety of reasons, fathers on parental leave are returning to work. Moreover, stay-at-home fathers constitute a small group, whereas parental leave is common practice for fathers in Norway.

The fathers in this chapter have recently been home alone with their toddlers, and they represent the second generation of Norwegian fathers who have used the earmarked leave 20 years after its introduction. The first generation of fathers who experienced this leave was the subject of a study published in 2003 (Brandth and Kvande, 2003a). These fathers used the father's quota when it was four weeks, while the second generation of fathers has experienced a much longer period of leave, because the leave period was extended to 10 and then 12 weeks when they were interviewed. In this chapter we ask how these fathers do fathering alone. How does being home alone for a longer period of time impact on their caring practices? Can we observe any changes compared to the experiences and practices of the first generation of leave-taking fathers? The answers to these questions of similarities and difference between the two studies may give us an indication of the effects of father-specific parental leave and thus the development towards a more caring masculinity and greater gender equality.

In the 2003 study (see Chapter 6), we compared the fathers who were home alone with the group of fathers who were on leave while the mother was also present. In this chapter, the analysis is concentrated solely on the fathers from our latest study who have been home alone with their children. The design is comparative in the sense that it analyses the experiences of fathers using the longer father's quota in the light of the experiences of the fathers who were home alone many years earlier when the leave was much shorter, as described in Chapter 6. We expect that the length of their solo leave will influence their fathering practices.

Doing fathering: undoing fathering practices

In studying fathering through men's practices – what fathers do when they are home on leave – we are inspired by the 'doing gender' perspective (West and Zimmerman, 1987), in which gender is theorized as situated practice, something said and done. Gender is understood as practices and processes constructed in situations instead of existing a priori (West and Zimmerman, 1987). This perspective also points out that gender is relevant in all social situations as well as in social structures. The 'doing gender' perspective has been criticized for focusing too much on the persistence of gender differences (Deutsch, 2007). With the notion of 'undoing gender', Deutsch points to situations becoming sites of resistance in which gender might be undone or gender differences reduced. Recognizing that fathers are entering a highly mothered context when caring for small children, the fathers can be understood as 'doing' or 'undoing' gender. Applying the doing approach to the understanding of fathering we will use the concepts of 'doing fathering' and 'undoing fathering' practices. This reflects a very open understanding, in which the focus is on activities and practices.

Fathering practices are a situationally local matter (Acker, 1997: x). Practices can be similar from one location to the next, but still be affected by the specific context in which they take place; practices are therefore local, situational and changeable. The daily doings and sometimes undoing of fathering occur within material and ideological constraints that set limits or provide possibilities. For example, the boundaries of gender segregation, themselves continually constructed and reconstructed, limit the practices of particular women and men at particular times. Since 'different cultures, and different periods of history, construct gender differently' (Connell, 2000: 10), masculinities and fathering practices must be understood as multiple and dynamic. The father's quota in the Norwegian parental leave system represents a policy measure aimed at changing the gender-segregated field of caring for small children. This chapter focuses on men's fathering practices. It regards fathering as formed and changing in historical moments, following shifts in policies and practices.

In our previous study from the early years after the father's quota was introduced, the meaning of fatherhood was defined as 'joy' (Brandth and Kvande, 2003a: 137). The interviewed fathers told about a boundless love for the child that had added a new dimension to their emotional life (see Chapter 9). Although the experience of becoming a father and caring for their child was often described in a sober language, feelings of joy and delight were a common theme, and could, for instance, be embodied as 'tears of joy' when the child learned to walk or talk. The fathers were, however, very determined that their primary task when on leave was to take care of the child. Ascribing meaning to the leave, the father–child relationship was front and centre, while housework was not understood as part of the deal for fathers on the father's quota leave (see also Chapter 5). Our previous study reported conflict and tension between the parents with respect to housework. Moreover, there were many ways in which fathers sought to adjust: outsourcing, reducing and downgrading the standard of housework. There was, however, a slow acceptance with some fathers that doing housework was part of being home on leave (Brandth and Kvande, 2003a). Norwegian time use studies measure how much time fathers use on family and work, and how this has changed over the last few decades. Recent time use data material documents that today most fathers of small children do housework on a daily basis, and that this is a change during the period that the father's quota has existed (Kitterød, 2013). It will therefore be interesting to explore what the fathers report when on leave alone for a longer period of time.

The analysis in this chapter is based on 12 interviews with heterosexual fathers from our most recent study. The fathers were singled out from the larger sample of fathers who had used the parental leave scheme in various ways. The fathers are living and working in Norway, were employed full-time, and were home alone on leave with the father's quota for a minimum of eight weeks. Half the sample had a higher education, and the occupational variation is quite broad. Their leave length ranged between 8 and 40 weeks. The variation in leave length is caused by some fathers using more than the father's quota weeks (the shared leave) and some less, while the father's quota length itself also varied during the interview period. The empirical analysis is organized as follows. First, we look at how staying home alone for a long period of time doing care work is experienced. Do we find the same unconditional delight as in our first study when the quota was only four weeks? Second, do they integrate caring with doing housework, or do they concentrate on the care?

Care work as hard work

One distinct difference from the previous study is that the fathers tended to describe childcare as 'hard work'. They talked about it as challenging and tiresome (as well as wonderful). In our first study, the positive and thrilling aspects of being able to spend time with their young children dominated the fathers' stories. However, staying home alone for a period of two months or more seems to give the fathers greater insight into care work as 'real' work. With the extension of the father's quota to two-and-a-half months, the fathers may have raised their expectations as to what they wanted to accomplish while they were home on leave. While staying at home for four weeks (for fathers in the first study) might be experienced as 'visiting', they were now taking the main responsibility for the child and the housework during their leave, and learning that childcare required a reorganization of priorities to focus on the child. In short, the fathers experienced that caring for a baby was very time-consuming, more so than they had expected. Many of them also compared care work to their own world of work when having physically demanding jobs, and even claimed that they became more tired from being home.

When these fathers were home alone with their young children experiencing how exhausting it could be to have the primary responsibility for doing care work, they acquired a new understanding of the amount of work that mothers have to do. They talked about this as an eye-opening experience. "Before I had children I thought that this would be a 'piece of cake', and I couldn't see why people made such a fuss about running a house", Steinar said. He thought it would be an easy task, but experienced otherwise. Being home alone for a longer period, the fathers learned what house (and care) work meant in terms of effort. This experience helped couples to develop equal parenting practices.

Adam is a 32-year-old electrician married to Siri. He stayed at home alone for 15 weeks, and described his experience of being home alone and having the main responsibility for doing the care work in the following way:

> 'It's a big responsibility too. You have to put them first. Before we had kids, you only had to think about yourself. Whereas now you have to think every day okay, there's someone else you have to think about. And that's the way it was when I was on leave, your shoulders were always kind of like this [raises his shoulders] because you had to, you had responsibility for this little person. And as soon as mommy came home I could relax, and I didn't feel that until after maybe eight weeks. And we talked about it, and Siri was like "Now you understand what it was like for me for a year". I was like: "Wow, yeah." So, I bought her some champagne and flowers, and said: "*You're the champ.*"'

By rewarding her care work, Adam heightens its status. Care has often been unrecognized as work, perhaps because it is culturally constructed as feminine and because of its emotional nature. When fathers define it as hard work, this may be interpreted as masculine reframing, as men's status is associated with work. However, when this is also attributed to mothers, it does not mean their practice dominates over the feminine. It may thus indicate a slight 'undoing' of the gendered character of caring. Adam talked about how he had learned from being home alone: "I was a bit back to the old ways too. Thinking 'Okay, Siri has to take a bit more than me.' Changing the nappies and stuff, but now.... Before I probably would have argued about changing the nappy, now I just do it. So, it was a really good experience." He accepted that this was a responsibility that they shared, and did not bother to negotiate with his wife about whose turn it was to change the nappy. Thus, his previous understanding of care work as the mother's responsibility had been challenged, and he changed his practices towards more equal parenting.

We notice the same experience with many of the other fathers who compared care work to having physically demanding jobs, and who became much more tired from being home than at work. This also made them think about the mother and the work she did when staying at home. Through experiencing both types of work, they were able to recognize the heavy workload that mothers have, as well as commenting on how unfair this division of work between parents has been. Steinar is a 33-year-old graduate engineer with two daughters, one who was two-and-a-half and the other four months when we interviewed him. He stayed home alone with the oldest daughter when he had his father's quota of 12 weeks. Because the family moved to a new flat shortly after he started on his leave period, he had two different experiences while staying at home. He began by thinking that he would have ample time for himself, that care work would mean pleasant times, and that he might even be a bit bored. Nevertheless, he was warned by his more experienced friends that he would have little spare time. During his period at home, he experienced two phases. He followed his friends' advice in the first phase and focused on only being there for the child, which he called his "good father's quota" period: "And it was ... it was just as I had envisioned. Bliss, really. It was so nice, and peace and lots of cosy times with the baby." He talked about his experiences in the following way:

> 'Sure, you think you'll have oceans of time with a pleasant ... and almost boredom. And that's where you go wrong. The funny thing is that I was told by I don't know how many friends who'd been there, done that, that "Don't plan. Don't think you'll be able to do redecorating and ridiculous ideas like that, you won't be able to do squat, Steinar. You can't plan loads of projects. Just ... buy a book, you'll have time for that when she's sleeping".'

His description has a lot in common with the fathers in our previous study when the leave period was much shorter. They experienced 'slow time', meaning that they concentrated on the child and did not try to combine this with other tasks. The second phase of Steinar's leave was very different because the new flat needed to be renovated. In this period, he tried to combine doing care work with renovation tasks, and described this period as "awful" because of the stress of trying to combine both:

> '… you're chasing breaks from the kid to get things done, and every time you're like doing something and just need to get finished, then you hear her quack and start crying, and then you're working with a totally different sense of stress. You're not only working with the stress of having to hurry to mind the baby, but you're also full of guilt because you aren't there already. And then you can't let go of whatever you're doing, because then water will leak or whatever you were busy with. It really sucks, in other words.'

He felt caught between doing the renovation jobs and taking care of the child. Caring for his toddler required total commitment, and he experienced guilt when the child woke up and he was not able to be with her immediately because he was plumbing or in the middle of some other maintenance task. He saw very clearly that this was an impossible combination and had only negative remarks about this period, which contrasted greatly with his first period at home when he experienced unconditional joy from being together with and looking after his baby daughter.

Integrating caring, cleaning and cooking

As reported in our previous studies (see Chapters 5 and 6), housework was not part of what fathers expected to be doing when on leave. When fathers in the current study discovered that being home on leave with a young child was very work-intensive, housework was included in their stories about the workload they had to deal with. In other words, the 'three Cs' – caring, cleaning and cooking – were all part of their total workload. This might be attributed to the length of the leave period, as they were not just popping in for a short period to be with the child. Being home alone on a longer leave meant more obligations. Steinar's opinion was that doing housework was expected from men today: "It's been two generations since men couldn't manage to do the laundry on their own." He explained that young men have had to learn to do it when they were students and/or living alone before starting a family. However, "… this can't compare to what you have to do when you have a partner and children. That's how it is … a whole world of difference! And, you can't understand this before you have children yourself."

Emil, who took all the parental leave, including the father's quota, while the mother returned to her studies, confirmed that he did most of the housework during the leave: "She wasn't always satisfied, though, ha, ha, because she's very strict about the cleaning." It seems his wife had a higher standard of cleanliness than he had. Having been home on leave with their children, the fathers told us how exhausting it could be, but also that they gradually got better at multitasking. After the first months of trial and error, when the daily routines were better established, things were running more smoothly, and it became less tiring. Adam, who was home alone with his daughter for 15 weeks, starting when she was six months old, described his daughter as a very active child who slept much less than he had anticipated she would: "Kids that age usually sleep for three hours maybe … she never slept that long. Maybe one-and-a-half hours, and then I had to [entertain her].… I would start with something [in the house], and then I'd just give that up." What he managed to do was "basically cleaning and vacuuming and stuff like that. And making the dinner when she was sleeping." His description of a typical day during his leave showed how care work and housework were intertwined:

'A typical day would be … all the family would get up at the same time because my kids are up at six o'clock. So we'd get up, and me and my daughter would set the breakfast table because I knew I didn't have to rush, so I'd make breakfast for everyone. Thelma would sit and eat her breakfast. Afterwards we'd tidy up together. It would be sunny, so we'd go out on the back balcony and then we would have all the toys out. And she'd play and we'd play, and we would go around the garden. Then it would maybe be time for her to sleep. So then she'd sleep, and then I would clean up the breakfast and vacuum and do the washing. Just like my sister said: "you'll be the housewife".'

This shows how he involved his daughter in setting the table and making breakfast. Some of the housework became a common task for both father and child. Adam put value on doing the housework, as it gave him something to do while the child slept, "It's like what I'm used to doing at work", he said. As fathers learned to do housework, this work became visible to them.

Ian described a typical day as follows: "He [the son] slept twice a day, normally an hour each time, perhaps a little more.... In the mornings, I did tasks around the house, like tidying, remembering to take bread out of the freezer and making lunch. And then an activity and a trip in the afternoon." While some of the fathers anticipated taking trips to town and visiting cafes to have coffee with friends, Max had envisioned that he and his daughter "would go for trips in the woods, sleep in a tent, do some climbing and enjoy ourselves." In neither case did this turn out as expected. "I had to be home to make dinner every day", Max explained. Steinar's more experienced friends had warned him that he would have little spare time: "You need to do the laundry and you must ... really, take over the housekeeping." Even though he listened to his friends, he was disappointed that he couldn't get more done, for example, reorganizing his computer files: "I had to rename the 'father's-quota-to-do list' to the 'when-I-have-retired list'." Generally speaking, the fathers described periods of little sleep, exhaustion and loneliness, but at the same time they praised the leave period as having been very positive. Steinar expressed this dichotomy: "You really get completely worn out, and then it's worth it. And nobody will understand this before they have their own kid." Norwegian sociologist Helene Aarseth (2013) has studied the meaning of everyday work in the home as expressed by fathers. She maintains that there is no contrast between delight and responsibility since everyday life practicalities and delight are embedded within each other.

The other side of childcare: embodiment and delight

Fathers usually take their father's quota after the mother has returned to work and the child is approaching one year, which often means that the children are awake many more hours than when they were new-borns. This led to fathers doing many activities with their children, and these were experienced as emotionally rewarding. Steinar recalled when his daughter went on the swings:

> 'It was great fun. She still thinks it's great fun. But it's one of the first times I remember where I really know she had one of those special moments. Sitting safely on a swing and gaining speed, swinging back and forth, and it was all wonderful laughter. Because that's the true original definition of joy,

complete joy, no conditions. That's very good. So this is one of those moments I always recall.'

Fathers talked about this period with enthusiasm: "It's the greatest feeling in the world. It's a beautiful thing, I think." Talking about what he did together with his child, Adam said: "And after she woke up, we would sing and read. Old English songs and stuff, and she'd enjoy that. Some days were different; we'd try to make new things." Because he was from another country, he wanted to teach his daughter his native language, so he read and sung for her. He took great pride in being able to teach her, and he loved being with her:

> 'It was just being with.... Seeing her grow, and her understanding of English. And, everything was just coming, and she just changed so much. I witnessed her saying her first words and teaching her how to eat and everything. It was great! She just makes you laugh as well; Thelma, she's a great character.'

When he said, "I witnessed her saying her first words", he implied that this was a combination of interpreting her words and her body language in a special context. Because he had spent a long time with her, they had connected, and he understood what she was trying to express. He was also able to describe his emotions in a detailed language. His relationship with his daughter had benefited from the period when he stayed at home with her, and he compared their communication with his son who was older and with whom he had not stayed at home: "Yeah, I think we have got a lot closer.... I don't know... we seem like a little team. She understands when I talk to her, she just understands like this, whereas I really miss that I didn't do that with John." When his son was born he had only been in Norway for six months, and did not have the right to parental leave. He compared the two situations, stating: "It seems that it worked out a lot better when I had the time." He learned how to interpret the unspoken words of his daughter: "But she's really clever. I understood. She actually would come up and grip the chair, and I knew after a while that it meant she was hungry." Because he spent a lot of time with her, they developed a way of communicating between them. In fact, in the end the baby understood English better than Norwegian, and therefore understood the mother less well. He said:

> 'After a while, I think.... I saw that Thelma didn't understand Norwegian after the 15 weeks [of father's quota]. Siri would

talk to her after she came home from work, and Thelma would be like: "Huh, what are you saying?" And then I would talk to Thelma and she understood. Later, she went to daycare so she understands both languages now, so it's just amazing that they can adapt like that.'

This might exemplify a father who developed a close relationship with his child because he was alone with her at home while on leave for a long period. He was the parent who spent the time at home when his daughter started to talk, so she learned his language. Again, he made the comparison to his son: "I know ... we have a little bond. I have that with John as well, but it just seems a little different." When he is asked if that might be because he had time off and stayed at home alone, he answers: "Because of the father's quota, yeah." His best memory from when he was home with his daughter also illustrates their close relationship:

'I had a hammock sitting out on the lawn, and on sunny days she would lay on top of me and I would read my book, and she would just play with the trees and stuff. It was awesome. And I bought a trampoline, and that is what we did in the morning. We would go on the trampoline and roll some balls, and I would just lie in the middle and she would just roll around on top of me and it was a great time.'

They would be together both in the hammock and on the trampoline, and they would be close while he was reading or while they were playing. This is a story about how he experienced the days on leave as 'slow time', in which he could fully concentrate on the child and be emotionally absorbed with her. Their play was an embodied way of being together.

Max focused on how being home alone had impacted his relationship with his daughter. When we asked if it would have been the same if he had not been home alone, he talked about how nice it was to feel that she was dependent on him and to show her that he was a care person for her. An illustration of this bonding was that his daughter no longer automatically reached out for her mother when she was crying and needed comforting: "Yes, like suddenly it was ... she wasn't interested in her mother when she came home from work, and her mother was almost in tears. So then it was like ... it's so nice." These stories illustrate that the fathers staying home alone for a long period of time developed 'need-oriented care' (Bungum, 2013). Having had the main responsibility for their children, the fathers had learned how to read and understand their children's feelings. The fact that the toddlers had not yet developed a spoken language when the fathers stayed at home meant that they developed a different repertoire for understanding their children. They were doing fathering and taking part in the process of developing dual caring in these families.

Above, Adam described feeling tense and not being able to relax for eight weeks because he had sole responsibility for his little daughter. His story might be understood as an example of bodily alertness, with his lying in the hammock with the baby on top of him also being an example of embodied care. Another example was helping out when it was time to breastfeed the baby. Steinar's wife was working as a pre-school teacher in a daycare centre and had time off to breastfeed while he was at home with the baby. He told us how he would go to his wife's workplace every day with the baby so that she could be breastfed:

> 'Then I would put on my cross-country skis every morning and ski with Anna strapped to my body, and I would ski to her mother's workplace in the morning. And when I arrived, there would be a break for breastfeeding, and I would sit and read part of a book for Andrea while she was breastfeeding. Fantastic to have an hour or one-and-a-half hours off in the middle of the busy working day, where we just sat and read a book and enjoyed being with the baby. And then ... skiing back home. Really nice!'

Breastfeeding is usually seen to trump all other care work (Ranson, 2015: 60). Steinar's story showed how he actually took an active part in the breastfeeding by strapping the baby to his own body and skiing to the mother's workplace. While his wife was feeding the baby, he read for both of them. In this way they could both be together with the baby during the feeding session, and the baby could also hear her father's voice while she was being fed. By constructing an embodied place for himself in the breastfeeding, he deconstructed it as a strictly motherly or feminine practice. Despite this, he reflected on the biological difference, which represented limitations for what he could do while home on leave: "Because it's of course a drawback, that I'm not as free during my father's leave as she is in her mother's leave, because of the breastfeeding. And that's a little bit hard. I wouldn't mind having breasts. That would have been truly smart." Instead, he had to remember to bring "packed lunches' with him when he took his daughter outdoors.

Mons was home alone with his 11-month-old son during 20 weeks of father's quota four days a week. He described how this experience had an emotional impact on him, and he felt that being home alone with his son had affected their relationship: "I notice that now he's just as pleased whether it's me or the mother who comes in the door, but earlier it wasn't so important whether I came home or not. See? He probably feels more confident." His son displayed the same type of feelings whether his mother or his father was home – he accepted both parents as his caregivers:

> 'That's really wonderful. You really go all soft and are touched and proud. Many strange emotions come to the surface in this context. But there aren't so many of these "finally I have managed to procreate" emotions. It's a bit more infinite, sounds a bit tacky, but infinite love. And I get even more emotional over these feel-good stories than before. I get a feel for things more in situations others may have experienced. I'm probably getting more empathetic, if that's what it's called? Sympathetic? To the situations of others. And then it's how you understand that he's more important than you are. There is no half-way, plain and simple. It's difficult to explain.'

He focused on the emotional impact from having a child and getting to know him well, and felt that he had changed, although not dramatically, but felt that he had become less categorical. In addition to having an effect on the relationship between his son and himself, he explained how his caring qualifications had increased by becoming what he labelled as more "empathetic".

Conclusions

Concentrating on solo leave takers, we have been interested in the possible impact of the father's quota on fathers' experiences of childcare. During the years it has existed, the quota has been extended and become a normalized practice among Norwegian fathers. Our previous study (Chapter 6) underscored the importance of distinguishing between parental leave patterns where fathers on solo leave displayed a different involvement than fathers on joint leave. In this chapter, we have explored similarities and differences among solo leave users in the two studies conducted 15 years apart.

Two aspects of their experience as solo caregivers have been in focus: the extent to which their involvement includes sharing the housework, and whether they experience joy and delight in caring for their child, which was salient in the first study. While the fathers in our first study concentrated on taking care of their children when they stayed at home, and housework was an area of conflict in the family, the current fathers integrate cleaning and cooking with caring. This may reflect the general pattern of a gendered change in society, in which fathers' take-up of housework works together with having a longer period of leave, and manifests itself in them taking on more responsibility for the household. It also confirms Coltrane's (1997) finding that involved fathers often begin with childcare and only over time become involved in housework. The interviewed fathers experience how staying at home on leave with the baby means taking on many tasks, and they learn to multitask. They do not see themselves as assistant carers, but as fully-fledged carers and home-makers.

While the fathers in the first study primarily tended to talk about the positive aspects of staying home alone looking after their toddler, the current fathers described care work as hard work. This change is probably a result of fathers taking on housework and being home longer with their child due to the extension of the quota. By staying home alone for a longer period, the fathers experience the total commitment that caring for a small child requires, as they are not only 'visitors' staying for a short period. This is an 'eye-opening' experience for them, which challenges their previous understandings of care work and leads to a greater respect for the care work that mothers have previously done.

The fathers in both studies expressed great enthusiasm with having the opportunity to stay at home. Because the second generation of home-alone fathers were home for a longer period and had the primary responsibility for their children's wellbeing, they seemed to develop parenting skills and a possible intensification of their emotional bonds to the child. When the child only understands the father's language, when they turn to him for comfort just as often as to the mother, it gives the fathers a confirmation of these emotional ties to their children. Consequently, having the opportunity to spend time alone with the child for a longer period seems to promote the development of embodied emotions and relational competence.

Research on what fathers do when they are home on leave has been in demand by researchers. Our findings show the day-to-day realities of men's caregiving practices and the ways in which their time alone with the baby may be transformative. The greater their involvement, the more likely it seems to be that they regard themselves as equal caregivers and incorporate care into their gender identity.

8

Immigrant Fathers
Framing Parental Leave
Use and Caregiving

Introduction

The other chapters in this section have provided an insight into how Norwegian-born fathers have used parental leave to develop their fathering practices. These chapters, that span several decades, demonstrate that fathers, from being anxious to maintain their sense of masculinity, have incorporated masculinity into their caring practices and used parental leave as an opportunity to develop and grow as competent caregivers. Fathers' time with their children includes the routine tasks of childcare but also nurturing and emotional bonding. We have seen how staying home alone on leave influences fathering practices differently than if the mother is also at home, and that today fathers incorporate housework into their practices when on leave.

In this chapter we explore how immigrant men frame themselves as fathers in the context of parental leave taking. As seen in Chapter 3, migrants are new to the Norwegian welfare state, but they take parental leave and value it positively despite the gender normative expectations embedded in it. We ask to what extent integration makes them practise caregiving in line with current political and social discourses of fathering – what is culturally understood as 'proper' ways to be fathers in Norway where men's involvement with their children comes in addition to their role as financial provider.

Transnational theories emphasize the multiplicity of migrants' belongings, and transnational ties have often been assumed to represent obstacles to successful integration (Erdal and Oeppen, 2013; Bell, 2016). However, integration and transnational ties need not be at odds with each other, but rather represent 'a balancing act of migrants who can access opportunities – but who may also have responsibilities – in two or more countries' (Erdal and Oeppen, 2013: 868). There are many positions in the literature about the relationship between transnationalism and integration, and the 'pragmatic approach' seems to be the most dominant. This approach understands relations between integration and transnationalism as social processes with migrants as actors with agency (Erdal and Oeppen, 2013: 877). An illustration of this approach may be Hoel's (2013) study of middle-class fathers from predominantly Muslim countries. Exploring their fathering practices, including the use of the father's quota, she finds that they act in accordance with the ideals of 'involved fatherhood'. They frame the father's quota as an opportunity to be with their children and think that it is important that they do so. At the same time, they believe that the mother is more important and ought to have the main responsibility. Complying with both complementarity and equality in gender relations, Hoel suggests that they represent a modern version of the nuclear, complementary family. Their practices are formed in an interplay between cultural, local and individual circumstances. This leads to the second question to be explored in this chapter, namely the extent to which their transnational ties inform their caregiving.

The analysis below is based on interviews with 20 immigrant fathers from 12 different countries who are all employed and have permanent residence in Norway. All the interviewed fathers in the study have chosen to take the father's quota in one way or another. In so doing, they depart from traditions in their countries of origin and act in compliance with common practices in their new country (see Chapter 3).

Framing as an analytical perspective

This chapter focuses on the cultural dimension of fatherhood, in which the frames or discourses that inform fatherhood are central. Fathering practices are embedded in cultural narratives – in this case, from two countries – and women and men use framing devices actively when they work out their positions, speaking and acting within the boundaries that are available to them. Goffman's (1974) concept 'frame' was developed in order to analyse how people identify and make sense out of practices and events. Practices are constituted and given meaning by particular frames, and when the frame changes, so, too, may the practices of the actors. Different frames or discourses and practices are complexly intertwined with each other, and one practice may be traced back to several frames (Alasuutari, 1996: 111).

Fatherhood thus acquires its many meanings through framing processes. Frames develop and vary across cultures, times and places. Fathering practices are not only justified by one frame or another, but may also travel between and be transformed in relation to different frames. Because they include normative assumptions, frames may constitute conflicting meanings.

The notion of frame in this chapter helps us understand how fathering is produced on the individual level in everyday practices. The fathers will use different frames in order to justify their fathering practice in the contexts in which they live. Cultural frames both reflect and shape the fathering practices and play a key role in defining 'the boundaries of the plausible, the possible, and the acceptable' (Wall and Arnold, 2007: 509).

In the literature on fatherhood, studies have shown how fathers lean on particular frames to legitimate their practices. For instance, Yarwood's (2011) study from England finds that fathers construct themselves as 'good fathers' in line with the current political and social discourses of parenting. They shape their practices in relation to what can and cannot culturally be thought of as 'proper' ways to be men and fathers. This is further illustrated in Brandth's (2019) study of two generations of farmers who justify their fathering practices in very different ways. The oldest generation use farm-related, local accounts of complementary gender roles, 'good farming' principles, apprenticeship and farm succession, to justify their practices, while the current generation refer to the broader accounts of contemporary society such as involved and intensive fathering. The study shows how cultural understandings of fatherhood change from decade to decade as social and political conditions change. Furthermore, in Eerola and Huttunen's (2011) study of Finnish fathers, most of the men framed their fatherhood using storylines such as shared parenting, nurture and caregiving, and no features of pre-modern, traditional frames were found. Since fathers talk to make sense of their everyday experiences, research needs to consider the ways fatherhood is enmeshed within societal norms and practices of working and caring.

There has been an academic debate within the literature on fatherhood concerning culture versus conduct; that is, some studies have identified a contradiction between words and deeds (LaRossa, 1988; Wall and Arnold, 2007; Dermott, 2008). So, although cultural understandings of fatherhood suggest a new model of increasing involvement, more nurturing and commitment to spending time with children, it is argued that the actual practices of fathers indicate much less change towards equal sharing. The cultural understandings of motherhood and fatherhood are part of the explanation as to why fathers undertake only a fraction of what mothers do in terms of childcare, but may also explain the increasing participation of fathers in the day-to-day care of their children. This chapter intends to study both the conduct and culture of immigrant fathers in exploring how the cultural frames can be identified in their reported practices.

The term 'involved fatherhood' denotes the main cultural framing of fatherhood in Norway (Farstad and Stefansen, 2015), and it is associated with dual caring as well as dual earning. The meaning of 'father involvement' has varied over the years and between countries, making it hard to define involvement as an analytic concept and to make comparisons. Recognizing this difficulty, attempts have been made to identify components of involvement. Lamb (2000) distinguishes three components: *engagement* involves face-to-face interaction with the child such as feeding, washing, changing, reading and playing. Lamb's definition does not include child-related housework (Lamb, 2000: 31), but for small children much interaction happens during such activities (see Chapter 6). A second category is *accessibility*. This means a less intense degree of interaction than engagement as fathers may be available to the child even if they are not engaged in direct interaction with the child. They may, for instance, be cooking or reading the paper while the child plays nearby. The third type of involvement, *responsibility*, is the hardest to define, according to Lamb. It may nevertheless be the most important because it deals with the extent to which the father takes responsibility for the organization and scheduling of the child's wellbeing and care. It does not necessarily mean being in direct interaction with the child; rather, it involves thinking ahead, for instance, making sure that the child has clean and appropriate clothes to wear, planning the next day, upcoming social activities and babysitting arrangements. This component has been called 'the third shift' by family researchers as it comes in addition to the first shift (work) and the second shift (house and care work). Arlie Hochschild (1997) includes 'emotional work' in the third shift, which means responsibility for seeing and hearing the children in a hurried daily life.

Andrea Doucet (2017) has defined responsibility as a three-fold set of practices: emotional, community and moral responsibilities. Emotional responsibilities include attentiveness and responsiveness, being aware of a child's needs. This includes direct care when the child is upset and needs comforting. Community responsibility means an awareness that parenting not only takes place in the home; it is also community-based and includes others who are involved in children's lives such as schools and kindergartens. Moral responsibility brings attention to the social values and norms in the contexts where the parenting takes place. The responsibility component of involvement is found to be the most resistant to gender-equal sharing (Doucet, 2017; Smeby, 2017).

Despite the theoretical development of responsibility, Lamb's three dimensions may seem too narrow. In addition, therefore, the quality of the father–child relationship, the love and emotional bonding, has increasingly come into focus in recent research on father involvement (Hanlon, 2012; Elliott, 2015; Brandth and Kvande, 2018). Moreover, fathers are found to measure self-worth in terms of building care competence rather than as status in working life, and this may have an impact on their personal identities, changing into less self-centred and more emotionally oriented men (see Chapter 9). The other chapters in this section of the book also show fathers' emotional attachment and experiences of unconditional love towards their children, which we expect may also be a part of immigrants' experiences.

Data

The analysis is based on data from our most recent study where about half of the sample of 40 fathers consisted of immigrant fathers. Their countries of origin are South, East and West European (16), North and South American (2) and African (2). The interviews with the 11 well-educated European fathers in Chapter 3 are included in this sample. The educational and employment backgrounds of the nine additional fathers are more varied. Most of the 20 fathers came to Norway to study or work, and nine are married to Norwegian women. They have transnational family ties in the sense that parents, siblings and often in-laws live in another country. They also have friends in their country of origin. They are thus quite distinctly in-between cultural assumptions and influences from two cultures.

Most of the interviews were conducted from late 2012 to early 2014, when the youngest child was about two years old. Two of the interviews were done more recently. We located the fathers in various ways, some primarily through contact with a university and other work organizations, others by means of snowballing. Interviews lasted from 90 minutes to two hours, were conducted face-to-face, recorded and transcribed. The fathers have been given fictitious names, and their background information is limited to help secure anonymity.

As demonstrated in Chapter 3, the immigrant fathers used the father's quota and this is how they have related to the 'master frame' of changing fatherhood and masculinity in Norway (Korsvik and Warat, 2016). In subsequent sections we will tease out how the various components of involvement are visible in their stories, and how their transnational position impacts on how they frame themselves as fathers.

The involved father frame

The importance of involvement becomes visible when comparing their fathering practices to the way they themselves were fathered as children. Fabio said: "I remember very little about my father from my childhood. I felt that was sad, and maybe that's why I feel it's so important with leave – to bond with your own child at an early stage." He distanced the absent mode of fatherhood to emphasize why he was aiming at another model. Others, like Juan (Argentina), referred to their father's participation and presence in the home when speaking about their ideal model of fatherhood. Both cases show the value they put on involvement.

As noted, the involved father frame is articulated in various ways, and the components are woven together in the fathers' accounts. Accessibility, for instance, is illustrated by Adam when he spoke about the importance of 'being there' for the children: "[You must] make time for them, and other things are not important. The children … if you decide to have children that should be the most important thing, the time for your kids. Use the time the best way you can; as much as you can!" Daniel seemed to agree, and said: "The most important thing is to be with him [the son] … to be there and give love. Kiss him a lot and cuddle him. Follow his development, talk to him and teach him."

Daniel mentioned several aspects of what he felt fathering entails. It is, however, using the father's quota that makes fathers available for their children. Ismael, who came from an African country, framed having to take leave as an opportunity: "It is an opportunity for fathers to be with their small children. To get some time off from work. I looked forward to it. In any case, it is good to be with my children." The father's quota is a premise for presence. As we will see below, accessibility is also important for the other components of involvement.

Engagement: interacting with children and managing childcare

Relating to how friends and family in the homeland understood the leave, Simon, a father of two daughters, explained that they tended to frame the quota as a privilege or holiday and did not understand what it implied in terms of work and effort:

'They all thought it [staying at home] would be easy, that it is easy to take care of a child. When I talked to some of my friends, they couldn't understand what made me so busy.... It was right before Christmas and there was a lot to do.... I told them about all the work in taking care of the children, and ... "Why are you so busy?" they asked. So, they couldn't see what it implied, and that was mostly because they didn't have children themselves.'

That taking leave meant managing a lot of work was also something Ismael, a warehouse worker and father of two, had to explain to his family. His home country had few, if any, benefits for families, and Ismael did not have any knowledge of the Norwegian leave system, or what he was expected to do during his leave. Making a comparison to his homeland, he said: "Where I come from, men are not used to taking care of babies. They may cuddle them from time to time, but not change diapers and go for walks with them. I am not used to ... this was new to me." In a transnational perspective his masculinity was at stake. His brother living in his home country had children about the same age. "He has two kids and a very good job, and he only took one week's leave.... He was really shocked. He said 'What? What kind of country do you live in? A paradise?'" But when the brother heard what Ismael did during his leave, his tone changed as he had not envisioned all that was involved for Ismael, who told him: "I changed clothes, cooked, changed nappies. Then he wondered if I had become a woman because I change nappies. In my country, people would have pointed at you if you went for a walk with your children." Ismael is very clear that his care practices deviate from what is socially accepted of a man and a father where he comes from, but as a father in Norway, he has to be involved in the nurturing of his children.

Reactions from Fabio's family and friends in Italy were mixed, with friends feeling it was somewhat absurd that he was taking leave. Childcare was associated with a feminine practice, and he was subjected to slight bullying by his Italian friends and family. In particular, the older generation of relatives found it to be very odd while others were more positive and said there should be more of that in Italy, too.

Staying home to do childcare was not described as positive in every case. Jean, who came from France, worked as a researcher and had two children. Like many others, he experienced caregiving as extremely demanding, but his description distinguished itself from all the others in primarily stressing the negative aspects:

'I have always felt that babies, that's very … it's very demanding work, … it differs a bit, really, but it was 90 per cent sweat, toil and trouble, challenges and poo and preparing food and all, and only very little hugging and nice experiences … that's really how it was.'

Jean took his father's quota as part time, agreeing to shorter working hours for a period. He justified his choice because of his time-consuming research projects, but also by his lack of taking delight in childcare. In framing caregiving as secondary to work, his choice did little to challenge the breadwinner model of fathering. This model, based on an unequal gender division of roles, is a contrasting model to the master frame of father involvement in Norway. Although he didn't like having to take parental leave, Jean nevertheless did help with the children and the couple was a dual-earner couple. He thus may illustrate what Hoel (2013) found in her study, that the immigrant fathers represented a modern version of the complementary family, where the ideals of participation are combined with the idea that the mother must do most of the care work.

Framing fathering as strenuous work says something about the engagement required. Like Norwegian-born fathers in the study, engaging in childcare during the father's quota period provided a new insight into care work and the effort involved.

Framing themselves as competent carers

Through being accessible and engaged with their children, the fathers develop as involved caregivers. Their engagement during the leave clearly shows that childcare is a type of competence that must be learned (see also Chapter 6). In the beginning of the leave the fathers were quite apprehensive about managing care for such a small child. This apprehension may be tied to how fatherhood is framed in their homelands, which is demonstrated by the fact that friends and family in their homelands shared this worry. Daniel's mother, for instance, often called from Spain when he was home on his leave: "My mother called me every day to ask 'How are you doing? Has he eaten his porridge? Is he sleeping?' and stuff like that. I don't think it really was to check … but rather because it was nice to hear how things were going." Knowing well what childcare implies, it seems that his mother was anxious about him being able to handle it.

Fabio had a similar response from his mother, and had to convince her of his competence:

'My mother, I see that she's thinking about this as positive, but she still finds it a bit strange. So, the idea that I stayed home on leave with Maria [daughter] was good, but when I visited in Italy it was like "I can wash, I can do... I can change ..." I had to tell her it's not necessary, I can do it!'

Here Fabio described what being engaged in childcare represented in terms of tasks for him to do. By taking leave and carrying out the concrete menial work tasks necessary for the baby, such as doing the laundry and changing nappies, he differed from the traditional division of tasks in Italian families, and needed to negotiate with his mother to be allowed to do this for his daughter when he visited in Italy during his leave. He experienced little faith in his care competence: "... for instance, when I was changing diapers. It was almost 'Oh, ha, as if you can do that.'"

Similarly, neither Adam's friends nor family thought that he would manage to stay at home with two children. "They said I would pull my hair out and it would be a disaster! But I managed it pretty well", he said. Maxime's family in Belgium, however, was more concerned about his employment than about him being able to cope with the care work: "They were quite positive; their main concern is 'Oh, what is your employer going to say if you leave for so much time?' That was also my concern, but everything is fine, so...." In expressing this worry, they referred to a fatherhood frame in which economic provision is primary.

The lack of confidence in fathers' caregiving from family and friends in their homelands seems to have made some fathers even more determined to manage! "I'll show them", Johannes said, keen not to make his transnational ties an obstacle to his fathering practice. "Theoretically, there is a possibility in Austria, and in Italy there is something that the man can also take a part of. But nobody takes it, and the reason is that it isn't socially accepted." He was very proud that he, against expectations from home, had managed childcare so well. He wished to break with the dominant framings in his homeland to show that it was possible for the father to take leave and become an engaged father like he felt it was expected of him in his new country.

The expectations importantly voiced by the employed mothers contribute to the shift in this framing. Many of the fathers in our sample were married to Norwegian women, which may influence their fathering model. Ismael's story is a prime example that fathering cannot be defined in isolation from mothering and mothers' expectations. Ismael was home on leave with their youngest child for 12 weeks, starting when his wife, a lawyer, returned to work. With no initial confidence at all in his own ability to manage caregiving for two small children alone, he talked about how he had become a competent father:

> 'I was scared in the beginning, before the leave started. What shall I do? Will I manage? When she left for work at 7–7.30, I stood there with two children, and had to make lunch bags and take care of them. Dress them. Drive to the kindergarten. I worried about this. I asked if she could work less the first weeks and then come home to help me. "No, it's your turn now!" she said. She said I would manage.'

His wife was not worried about Ismael caring for the children alone while she went to work, and in giving him this responsibility and showing confidence in him, she played an important role in his development into a caregiver. Although she sometimes called to hear how they were doing at home, the fact that she returned to full-time work and left the responsibility to him pushed him into a learning situation. He said: "Sometimes I call and ask her to come home. But she doesn't come. Says I have to cope by myself." Although he was very reluctant at first, Ismael continued to tell his story about the start of the leave in the following way:

> 'The first weeks were very heavy. Stress! Particularly in the mornings before I delivered the oldest in kindergarten. And, what was there to do afterwards? We went for walks, one-and-a-half hour walks. Went home, played, slept, ate.... There is not so much you can do. But it became better and better! I developed a routine. After a while I knew what to do.'

In addition to hands-on caring, he gradually learned to differentiate between various types of the baby's crying: "For instance, when she drops her comforter and cries. I rush to check what is the matter. Tell her it will be okay. Other times she has a bellyache." He could hear from her crying that she was in pain. Likewise, Simon said: "I can read what my daughter needs and give a lot of love." Steve, a father of two, originally from Germany, told how he by caring for them had developed sensitivity and started to understand the child's non-verbal language during the leave. Fathers thus develop a capacity for emotional responsiveness, an ability connected to 'good' fathering (Ranson, 2015) and 'emotional responsibility' (Doucet, 2006) – addressed below. The development of 'need-oriented' care practice is also described in Chapter 7.

It is a common story among the fathers that their initial worries disappear, and things improve after a while. Daniel said:

'I experienced that I became better and better and better. I learned that it was important to have routines. Now he must eat; now sleep. We must go for a walk. I became calmer, and so did the child. It was important to have a plan. It was very important!'

In sum, we have seen the interplay between different models or frames of fatherhood expressed both as lack of confidence (with little support from family in their homeland) and confidence in their ability to be good fathers (from their wives). It is a balancing act where frames from two or more countries inform their fathering. As they learn the skills necessary to become able caregivers, their stories underscore an intention to be significantly involved in their small children's lives. In the process they changed their framing, and in their stories we recognize what Korsvik and Warat (2016) identified as a Norwegian master frame.

Responsibility

A third component of involvement in Lamb's (2000) theory is *responsibility*, a concept with many definitions. While some of the fathers spoke of responsibility in terms of becoming a more serious and mature person, caring for someone else, others, like Andreas, defined 'good' fatherhood as a sense of responsibility for sharing tasks more equally. Andreas illustrated responsibility the following way:

'In my opinion, a father must manage everything! He must not think that it is the mother's duty – that it is the mother who has the child. It is both of them! In Norway, many fathers do everything possible for children.... It is super-important that also fathers learn the everyday tasks. Both have 50/50 responsibility.'

The word 'help' is often used in relation to fathers' involvement, thus implying that mothers hold primary responsibility. Here, however, Andreas discards the father-as-a-supporting-player frame and stresses an equal position where responsibility for home and children is shared. This way of understanding responsibility reflects Lamb's (2000) definition as it indicates the extent to which the father takes ultimate responsibility for the child's daily needs.

Responsibility, however, also concerns the management of children's lives, as we see in Daniel's story of planning ahead. He says:

'When she [wife] is home, she always takes care of the many small details that a father doesn't think about, such as: what is he to wear tomorrow? Does he have enough porridge and baby food and stuff? Do I need to shop? Get everything ready to go out. I needed a plan in order not to forget something.'

Although Daniel reported that he also had responsibility for specific tasks and activities with his child, this quote is interesting regarding the question of whether men are able to plan, schedule, organize, remember and take action in relation their children (Doucet, 2006). One of the fathers from Poland, who had three children, experienced some of the same development as Daniel: "It [taking leave] was a great challenge for me. When I worked, my wife remembered most of the things in the morning. Suddenly it's *me* who is responsible!"

Taking primary responsibility for organizing and managing the family is noted to be women's responsibility (Hochschild, 1997), even in couples who define themselves as gender-equal. However, fathers who have taken the father's quota seem to be also more responsible for planning (Smeby and Brandth, 2013), and as Doucet (2017) highlights, taking leave alone is very important in this respect. Thus, the father's quota seems to make it feasible that the fathers manage the 'third shift' – at least during the leave period (Smeby, 2017). As demonstrated in previous research, responsibility for caregiving is constructed differently among fathers (Miller, 2011), and tends to have a moral undertone (Dermott, 2008).

Emotional gains

In the literature, there is an increased awareness that getting involved in the everyday care of children concerns additional aspects to availability, engagement and taking responsibility. A further aspect deals with men's emotions and their own gains from loving and caring.

Talking about the kind of father they would like to be often resulted in comparisons with their own childhood. Daniel explained an effect of his own father's involvement: "You understand how much your parents loved you ... and understand a lot from when you were little." Daniel spoke for many of the fathers when he framed fatherhood as giving time and love. He expands: "It is incredible how much you can love a person, right, and become so engaged with him [the child]. It changes you; suddenly you are a new person – a father!... It's not just about you anymore, but about you as responsible for a new, little being." Experiencing fatherly love as almost overwhelming at times is existential, and giving love is held as an objective by fathers, regardless of what country they live in.

Tomasz, an academic from Poland with two children, described a transformation that for him was about a new orientation in life. Being a first-time father, the leave experience was new to him, and he resisted it at first, but he said:

> 'One must learn to find delight in different things. It [the leave] was frustrating; it felt like I was losing control over my life.... I wanted to read, talk or call someone, but had to prioritize something different, namely the child. But after a while, things fall into place, one changes one's approach and thinks "children are fabulous!" The leave was nice. I woke up [after a nap], birds were singing, the sun was shining and beside me was this little boy. Life had changed its meaning!'

Tomasz missed the sociability and structure of his regular job, which gave him status and respectability, and it took some time for him to accept the new reality of staying away from work and to be a 100 per cent caregiver for some months. When he did, he found a new delight. In adapting to the Norwegian parental leave legislation, they describe experiencing an individual transition as very similar to stories told by Norwegian-born men (see Chapters 6 and 9).

Many of the interviewees stressed the importance of 'getting connected' with their baby: "I wanted to bond with my daughter, so I did, and it was a very nice experience" (Adam). They applauded the quota for the possibility it gave to develop close bonds with their children, and expressed a commitment to be a loving and involved presence in their children's lives.

Father involvement as gender equality?

According to Hanlon (2012), processes of change in masculinity are at work when men no longer suppress nurturing to the advantage of participation in the labour market. Although the fathers in the study use the leave in various ways, many seem intent to undergo a change in the direction of what leave policies for fathers are aiming at, namely a more gender-equal involvement in childcare. Comparing his situation to his friends and family in Germany, Steve described mothers' and fathers' roles as more complementary in Germany than in Norway: "In Germany, I still see that the father is an 'activity person' and mother is the one to go to if you have a problem and need a hug." Steve, however, defined emotional involvement as an obvious component of equal fathering practices when he wanted to be the parent to whom the children came for comfort.

However, even if the fathers in our sample spoke about being engaged and available fathers sharing caregiving, it was not necessarily in a gender-equal way. Mothers seem to take the bulk of responsibility and fathers help out: "Concerning practical tasks, I thought that it was okay with mostly mama the first part of the first year. I experienced it like this because we did it like that", Simon said.

Nevertheless, in taking leave they get a better understanding of a mother's effort during her leave. "It [taking leave] really opened my eyes", Adam said. He suddenly understood what the leave had been like for the baby's mother (see Chapter 7). Like most fathers in the study, engaging in childcare and giving children time during the father's quota gave a new insight into care work and the effort involved. Men upgrading care work, traditionally performed by women, unpaid, time-consuming, demanding, invisible, and historically placing women in an inferior position, refers to gender equality in the sense of equal worth.

In some of the accounts, mothers' jobs were a justification for the fathers' involvement. Simon understood this to be the main objective of the parental leave policies, and agreed that it was important. Daniel also used the increased opportunity for the mother to focus on her work as a justification for his leave use, but at the same time it was his own opportunity to be together with his child, to establish a bond and take responsibility, that he stressed as most important. Other fathers didn't think a few weeks of leave could do much for gender equality and the mother's work situation, but "it is first and foremost in relation to the child.... To set aside dedicated time for the child is priceless." Their involved father frame tends to prioritize care at the expense of housework. In comparison to the Norwegian-born fathers in the study who, as described in Chapter 7, combined housework with childcare, this might mean that the inclusion of housework is a later stage of involved fathering.

Only a few fathers understood gender equality as an objective of parental leave use, and it did not seem to motivate their involvement. This resembles how Norwegian men framed the father's quota when it was first introduced, namely as an opportunity to be with their child and to take care of the child (Brandth and Kvande, 2003a), but not as a gender-equality effort. This, again, underscores that gender egalitarianism and involved fatherhood are not synonymous concepts, and that the links between them may be complex. However, when men become involved, attached and responsible fathers, it may lead to a change in the direction of caring masculinity (Brandth and Kvande, 2018), and such a change is an aspect of gender equality.

Conclusions

The analysis has explored how our sample of immigrant fathers speak and act within their normative frameworks that are influenced by the processes of transnationalism as well as place of settlement. We have seen how the two contexts are continuously referred to in their framing work, something that emphasizes their concurrent dual belongings – albeit on different levels of engagement.

The analysis has been concerned with the extent to which their framings are in accordance with or depart from the 'involved father frame' and the Norwegian 'dual earner/dual carer' model. Generally, the 'involved father frame' seems to work well for the fathers' understandings. It fits with Norwegian culture and has had an international breakthrough, judging from the fatherhood literature (Lamb, 2000). Involved fathering has come to ideologically signify the culture of 'new fathers'. Being a broad concept, without a unified definition, involved fathering comes in different forms, as ideology but also practice (Wall and Arnold, 2007).

We can conclude that various aspects of involvement, with sub-frames such as the importance of engagement, 'being there'/spending time, responsibility and practical, hands-on care and emotional bonding are applied as fatherhood frames, although entangled with each other. Gender equality is more rarely used explicitly as a frame, but we notice it sometimes in terms of equal worth and equal sharing of care work in addition to privileging women's employment in line with the dual carer/dual earner norms.

All the first-time fathers and first-time leave users start the leave period with no prior experience of caring for a baby, but as shown, changing men's capacities to provide emotional and practical care for their children need not be a slow process. During the leave, they become competent to do so, and in most cases, they find it fulfilling. The content of the leave, describing what they do in terms of caregiving, brings them down to the everyday situation of care work. In a transnational perspective, doing care work sometimes tends to frame them as 'women'. This is not a frame they are part of; rather, they fight it, since it will not work where they live in their new country. As they learn to master caregiving they often speak of its enjoyable sides, the love and intimacy that they experienced.

We have been interested in the ways in which immigrant fathers create cultural distinctions or similarities when framing parental leave and their fathering practices. Other studies have shown that fathers' practices in various home countries are different from the settling country because the new model of involved fathering faces fewer barriers at the social and structural levels in Norway (Żadkowska et al, nd). Immigration creates a geographical distance to family networks and friends in their homelands and therefore greater freedom to do family and childcare differently. However, the main finding to come out of this analysis concerns the similarity with Norwegian-born fathers analysed in the other chapters. The immigrants may have faced more barriers to cross, but they use and support parental leave and thus Norwegian welfare and gender equality policies. In so doing, the way they frame fatherhood is not very different from native fathers. This may mean that we are on the scent of what involved fathering in the current societal context is about, universally speaking.

PART III

Reconciling Work and Care

9

Changing Fathers
and Work–Life
Boundary Setting

Introduction

This chapter deals with how fathers manage their work life in conjunction
with their home life. When Norway debated the father's quota prior to
its introduction, there were three main arguments for such a reform. The
first was a gender equality argument: if fathers became more involved
in the provision of care for their children, this would lead to a more
democratic sharing between men and women of the obligations and
rights in family and working life. The second argument was that the
relationship between father and child would be strengthened by fathers'
greater presence and participation in day-to-day care tasks. Third, it was
argued that involvement in childcare would benefit fathers themselves and
give men the opportunity to work on and develop new aspects of their
emotional repertoire (Mannifest, 1989). Making fathers out of men was
thus deemed favourable for mothers, children *and* the fathers themselves.
The benefits of the leave for fathers themselves is one point of departure
for this chapter, which aims to explore what emotional and personal
changes the fathers have experienced.

   In the aftermath of the introduction of the father's quota, research has
been concerned to see the effects of this reform. As noted, the father's
quota has made a large majority of fathers use this leave fully or in part
when they have a child. Thus, it has had a significant effect on the way
fathers spend their time during their baby's first year. Fathers with small

children are now temporarily away from work much more frequently than was previously the case (Kitterød and Kjeldstad, 2006). However, as Lammi-Taskula (2006: 95) observes, welfare state attempts to encourage (or promote) parental leave use for fathers are effective only up to a point. The major part of the total parental leave time is still taken by mothers, and the fact that fathers have taken leave and become more involved in childcare has not had much effect with respect to reducing their working hours after their leave is over (Brandth and Kvande, 2003a; Kjelstad, 2006; Kitterød, 2007). We are interested in exploring if becoming a father, having taken leave and cared for a child have any consequences for their time investment in working life.

Emotional involvement and work–family boundaries

Since the politicizing of fatherhood has proved to be slow in contributing to gender-equal time use, some scholars have looked towards the father–child relationship and men's self-development for explanations of father involvement. It has, for instance, been suggested that men's orientation towards childcare can be understood in terms of a new child-oriented masculinity (Bekkengen, 2002; Brandth and Kvande, 2003a, 2011; Aarseth, 2008). This new discourse of masculinity connects to the increasing status of childhood and the growth of child-centredness in late modern society. Consistent with this, Beck and Beck-Gernsheim (1995) argue that families are being pulled apart in contemporary society, meaning that love and intimacy between men and women in the family have become frail and threatened, resulting in greater propensity for divorce. As a consequence, relations between parents and children remain the only life-long relationships (Beck and Beck-Gernsheim, 1995), something that has important consequences particularly for fathers who are not secured access to their children in a cultural or naturalized way like mothers (Aarseth, 2008). When fathers are no longer guaranteed access to their children through the marriage relationship, they must earn connectedness to the child through developing good fathering practices. And, especially since women are still the 'ground crew of the family', men can do so without disturbing their stakes in working life (Aarseth, 2008: 9). This leads to new questions when it comes to researching men's fathering practices in relation to working life and how they reconcile the two spheres. How do fathers, for example, conform to the new cultural norms of spending time with their children without reducing their working hours?

Relatively new approaches to the study of the relationship between family and working life have emphasized cultural elements and the emotional resources of family members (Smart, 2007; Lewis et al, 2009; Ba', 2010). This emphasis is in answer to a criticism that the sociology of family and intimate lives has paid 'insufficient attention to the ways in which such relationships are saturated with emotions, feelings and affect' (Smart, 2007: 53). The 'emotional turn' is a consequence of the insight that emotions play a great role in how people choose to act (Wettergren et al, 2008). Thus, the emotional attachment that fathers develop for family or working life is central to the analysis undertaken in this chapter, which explores what is meaningful work and family time and what kind of boundaries fathers manage to negotiate between the two.

Working time and boundary setting

On average, long working days are less common among Norwegian fathers than previously, but fathers with small children work predominantly full time (Kitterød, 2007). Statistically speaking, there is very little change in the length of fathers' working days after the parental leave, with contracted hours remaining the same and actual hours being only slightly reduced (Dommermuth and Kitterød, 2009). Despite national differences in the levels of part-time work among women and men (O'Reilly and Fagan, 1998), part-time work is universally gendered feminine and not a way fathers are known to combine caregiving and work to any great extent (Delsen, 1998; Sheridan, 2004). Nor do 'family-friendly' hours that are offered by some companies get much positive response by fathers (Hochschild, 1997).

In Norway in 2005, only 6 per cent of employed fathers with children aged 0–15 had contracted part-time hours (Kitterød, 2007), most of them being students or men approaching retirement. In contrast, close to 50 per cent of employed mothers with children aged 0–15 worked part time, making eight out of ten part-time workers in Norway to be women. Thus, the common adaption in Norwegian families seems to be that work and home is reconciled by women adjusting their working hours to the care needs of the family (Ellingsæter, 2003). This has been termed a 'neo-traditional' division of work between men and women (Kjelstad, 2006) or a 'one-and-a-half-earner-family' (Lewis, 2001). Changes in women's participation in working life and their working hours have received much research attention, with less attention focused on the (small) changes in men's hours. Indeed, most sociological analyses of part-time work include women only.

Men's working hours are much less varied than women's (Kjelstad, 2006). They are sparsely researched, and we know little about the relationship between men's family situation and their working hours (Dommermuth and Kitterød, 2009). That men infrequently work part time may be seen in connection with the salience and symbolic meaning of work for men and what it represents as a source of identity (Brandth and Kvande, 2003a; Morgan, 1996). Furthermore, what we know about changes in parental time use is for the most part based on an analysis of quantitative data. Such data cannot capture meanings and help us understand how fathers' choices and practices may be motivated by symbolic and emotional factors (Ba', 2010). In this chapter the aim is to investigate fathers' time strategies after parental leave by means of qualitative interview data.

Home and work are commonly regarded as separate spheres with their different activities and logics – the workplace being associated with competitive individualism, rationality and profit, and the home with relational and nurturing concerns (Nippert-Eng, 1996; Hochschild, 1997). In his book *Family connections* David Morgan (1996) points out that the boundaries between work and family are vital for parents' everyday life, and that an important question is how mothers and fathers draw the boundaries in terms of strategies in the every day. Clark (2000: 748), who introduces border theory in order to address integrations and segmentation of family and work, describes parents as border-crossers who make daily transitions between work and home. Strong identification with a sphere increases people's motivation to manage borders, and if the parents are central participants in one or both spheres, they are more likely to be able to exercise control over the borders. Moreover, it is noted that shaping and handling borders are intersubjective activities with several actors involved (for example, bosses, colleagues and partners) (Clark, 2000). It has been assumed not only that work and personal life are separate, but also that work receives priority for men. A demanding work situation has contributed to a strengthening of the conflict perspective between work and home for time and attention, making boundary construction important as a tool for handling both spheres (Chesley, 2005; Golden and Geisler, 2007).

However, research has increasingly come to contest the existence of separate spheres and the significance of fixed boundaries. Lash (1990) describes current society as a de-differentiated society in which the separate areas of social life break down. Modern organizational practices have tended to move towards encouraging workers to blur the boundary between the two domains (Dumas and Sanchez-Burke, 2015), and integrate practices and thoughts associated with work and home. In particular, the rapid changes in communication and computer technologies have accelerated this development, as work can be carried out in various settings and at various times. It facilitates working anytime and anywhere; technology can be used 'to bring home to work as well as work to home' (Chesley, 2005: 1237), which promotes permeable boundaries. Nonetheless, there is disagreement about the consequences of permeable boundaries. Some argue that blurred boundaries are bad because they promote overwork, whereas others argue that blurred boundaries have the potential to reduce conflicts between work and family (Valcour and Hunter, 2005).

Both employees and employers attend to boundary work – employees because it may affect their experience of work–life balance, their relationship with colleagues or career outcomes, and employers through specific policies or practices that can shape employee wellbeing and productivity (Dumas and Sanchez-Burke, 2015: 804). The research literature on boundary work has not been particularly concerned with how state regulations such as parental leave may play a part in the management of boundaries.

The focus of this chapter is on the connection between fathers' emotional and existential changes and the way they manage the boundary between work and home. The chapter is organized into two sections. First, it explores how men experience becoming fathers and reflects on how fathering affects their lives. Second, it asks how their fathering practices influence the boundaries between home and work and their negotiation of these boundaries.

Sample

This chapter is based on our second study (1997) which includes a series of in-depth, semi-structured interviews with 30 couples (60 individuals) living in and around one of the largest cities in Norway. Dual-earner couples eligible for parental leave were chosen. Thus, both parents were employed either full or part time. The sample over-represents middle-class couples who constituted two-thirds of the participants; the remaining third was working class. Their occupations represent a wide variety. The interviews were undertaken when the leave period (which, broadly speaking, lasts for one year) was over, and the children were between two and three years old. Some of the couples also had older children. At the time of the interviews the father's quota was four weeks. The duration of the interviews was 2–3 hours each.

Becoming a father: emotions and new meanings in life

In their accounts of what it meant to have become a father, the importance of intimacy and emotional belonging was considerable. Each father we interviewed described the positive aspects of happiness, love and emotional involvement. In addition, they mediated a new moral obligation to be present and available for the child.

Becoming a father was reported as representing a transition to a new phase of life, something that was evident when they described what becoming a father meant by way of change. By taking responsibility for another person, the baby appeared as a symbol of the transition to 'adult life'. "Starting from this point in time", said Emil, "I developed along another path than I would have otherwise." Steinar, a transport worker with three daughters, told the following about what the new life phase represented for him:

> 'It's something about assuming responsibility. Perhaps it's easier to horse around and play the "lad" when you're an unattached bachelor – when you don't have kids. You need to be more of a man when you have kids, then you need to get your act together. You can't just diddle around. You really become more adult when you have kids.'

His is a narrative of maturing and growing and reaching a new level of responsibility in life. The fathers expressed how adult life with a small child had given them a new sense of purpose in life. Rolf said: "There's nothing that has meant so much to me, there simply isn't. I think about everything differently than I used to do." The child and the new life phase represented changes in many different ways. For instance, fathers gained experience in tolerating trivialities and chaos. When describing his own development, Magnar, a warehouse worker, said: "There were qualities in me that I didn't know I had, you could say. Something surfaced in me." We also heard how he was almost surprised to find these new aspects of himself rising to the surface.

Fathering also seemed to make these men more open to emotions and there were many descriptions of their new emotional qualities. They reported having grown calmer, more harmonious, more patient, more humble and less selfish: "I've become more caring. I think a bit more about others. I think I perhaps was more selfish before", one of them said. Most fathers had the main responsibility for childcare while they stayed at home on leave, and this made them "a little bit more tolerant and flexible, more willing to compromise", in the words of one of them. Jacob, a mailman who also had two children of school age in addition to his one-year old, confirmed this: "I have become better at thinking about others." He had learned to listen better, to adapt, and to take seriously what others felt.

Fathers also said that their emotional register had expanded and that they had acquired new values: "You get other perspectives on things; the little things become more important." Those who stayed home alone while the mother returned to her job full time were particularly likely to have learned to let the child's needs take over. They had been forced to accept the 'slow time' where it was not necessary to have so many big projects on the agenda, but where care for the children and 'simple things' needed to be given priority. It is precisely the aspects of being more open to others and having more empathy that made many fathers feel that they were developing as people and gaining another focus. For example, Jacob said: "I think I react more strongly when I read about accidents and stuff involving kids." Such incidents seemed to touch them in a way that was different than before they had had children. Another element of this emotional change was that it brought anxiety: "You're perhaps more worried than you used to be. You're more afraid of dying or getting ill, or you're afraid they'll be injured, get sick or something." These emotional dimensions of fatherhood, with hopes, enjoyment and anxieties, arose from an awareness of the child's dependence and their importance in the fathers' lives.

In other words, what they had experienced through fathering made men reflexive about themselves, for better or worse. Some of them felt that caring for the child demanded more patience than they had. When asked what participating in childcare had given him, Jacob had the following to say:

> 'I learn about myself, really, how I am. The older they [the children] get, the more feedback you receive as to how you really behave. Then you start thinking a bit about how you react to things, what you say and how you do things.'

The children functioned as a clear and unmistakable corrective with respect to their father's ways of acting. In communication with the child they interpreted themselves and developed a form of competence in intimacy and emotional intelligence. This is parallel to what Daly, Ashbourne and Brown (2009) found in their study of how children influence fathers. The fathers became more mindful of their own behaviour and values, and believed it was important to manage anger and set a good example for the children.

Dynamics of the work and home interface

As seen from their accounts, fathers' involvement with their children meant opportunities for personal development. Childcare constituted a relationship that required them to empathize with others and to expose their own emotions. In this section we explore what influence this emotional competence has in the area of work life.

The fact that fathers had learned needs-oriented communication and 'care rationality' (Wærness, 1984) appeared to make personal interactions easier with people other than their children. Paul, an economist with a senior administrative position in a private company, took several months of leave in addition to the mandatory father's quota when his son was born. He was keenly aware that his fathering experience was also useful in his work situation. He said the following about the consequences it had for him personally to take an active part in childcare:

> 'I really think I've become nicer. And ... I'm probably quite firm and head-strong and a pretty determined person. And quite dependent on ... like I work with administration and management and manage many employees and depend on building up a structure and making things work and all that. So suddenly, having a child and dealing with somebody who does anything but stick to the stipulated system, this really has forced me to think in many other ways, and I also deal with people differently now. Not that I deal with them as if they were children, but there are always those who do things differently than you had planned, and it may even be a good thing that they do. What I mean is that it may be necessary to have people who do things differently because they put systems to the test and this kind of thing, and fathering has taught me much in this way.'

Work and family are commonly seen as different cultures building on completely different values and logics (Clark, 2000). A child represents the counterpoint of the rationality, efficiency and discipline that characterizes working life. Paul spoke about how the experiences he gained during his period of parental leave, when he had the care of his son, had helped him develop a greater understanding of other ways of seeing and doing things in a work-related context. Fathering had thus influenced his managerial style in a more inclusive and softer direction. He described himself as 'firm' and 'head-strong' to start with, and the change had gone in the direction of his listening more to others and interacting and cooperating. In short, by becoming a father he had also become a better manager.

This is a narrative about maturing and greater self-insight, which was also experienced by other fathers who reported greater understanding, conscientious monitoring, empathy and flexibility – qualities that are linked to good fathering (Marsiglio, 1995). That fathers develop skills during their parental leave period that are useful in working life is also pointed out in a study of Canadian and Belgian fathers (Doucet and Merla, 2007). In this study, the childcare activities helped fathers become more skilled in the area of emotions, and they developed their managerial skills and gained better organizational understanding because they learned to master a greater diversity of tasks and solve conflicts. In the new economy, emotional and communicative competence has become an important form of capital (Illouz, 2007).

The new reflexivity created through intimate relations with the child seemed to be appreciated by workplaces. Axel, a computer engineer who took six months of leave when his daughter was less than a year old, reported that staying home and caring for his baby did not put brakes on his career, as is often believed. He said:

> 'Men really benefit from staying home and seeing a slightly different world ... and, perhaps even become a better person and thinking more of others. In my type of career job I think it might be an advantage to have stayed at home, too. I actually found a new job while I was at home, and I was of the understanding they found it positive that I had stayed at home with my child.'

Here, fathering and what it implies was defined as a qualification, becoming a new type of capital that the fathers brought to working life. This affected the boundaries between life in the family and at work, where one sphere was made relevant for the other in a new way. These narratives show that taking an active part in childcare may provide experiences that lend themselves well for transfer to working life.

To be unencumbered by obligations or relations beyond work has traditionally been considered the optimal state in working life. It is interesting if men with care obligations are valued as an asset in working life; that they are not regarded as problems, but rather the opposite. If workplaces appreciate the varied experiences one can gain from prioritizing childcare responsibilities, perhaps the idea of the 'universal worker' (Acker, 1990) will be redefined? This says something about how fathers may be part of an important political change project when it comes to the understanding and definition of men as employees.

Managing the boundaries between home and work

Since men do not reduce their hours to part time after parental leave (Kjelstad, 2006), in this section we explore their strategies for combining work and childcare. Can we, by means of qualitative data, see changes in their time practices? The focus is on time use after the leave. Once the period of parental leave is over, the day-to-day time problems emerge as great challenges.

That fathers do make several changes concerning work is something that became evident in a conflict Emil, a construction engineer with three children, had with his boss about adapting his working hours so that he would be able to pick up and take his children to daycare. He recounted:

> 'We had two of these conflicts. We had one in connection with daycare for our youngest. I said that once a week I would start work at nine, and once a week I'll quit at three so I could pick up and take my kid to the daycare centre. The rest my wife would take care of. But he [the boss] found this unacceptable.... Working hours were from eight to four! If I started at nine, that was one hour late, and if I quit at three, I quit one hour early.... The conflict went all the way up to the managing director level, where I simply gave an ultimatum to the main office that this would have to stop. And it did. He [the boss] accepted it. That is to say he pretty well had to when given directives from above.'

This was a job in the private construction industry, often involving many hours of commuting to the construction site and long working days. Some time later, when Emil wanted to adapt his working hours even more to his children's needs by reducing them down to 45–50 hours per week, there was new conflict. Finding the situation untenable, he finally quit this job. His new workplace, which was in the public sector, had greater acceptance of fathers who wanted time for their children: "[In this sector] there are more people than I who have taken father's leave with great success", he said.

As demonstrated by this example, we see that fathers are redefining their boundaries to achieve what they feel is a more ideal balance between work and family. When they found that "the child becomes the principal person in your life", as one of them put it, they wanted to make changes in accordance with this new identity. They no longer just saw themselves as an employee; rather, in the words of one of the other fathers: "You become very involved with your children. Not only emotionally, but also your practical life changes. You change much of the content of your life when it comes to what you actually spend your time on." What he meant was that his use of time in relation to work had changed.

Emil's story illustrates several strategies used to establish boundaries between work and home. One is flexi-time. There were also other similar stories, including Magnar's, a warehouse worker who negotiated to have his working hours start at six in the morning rather than seven so he could end earlier and have longer afternoons with his children.

A second strategy is to reduce overtime and additional working hours. This is not about shifting to part-time work, but a reduction in work hours to approach normal working hours. In the fathers' narratives, the child was an important life interest in addition to work. Life had gained more dimensions than work, and these aspects led them to reprioritize. Håkon stated:

> 'It's really true, I remember before we had children it was so much easier to spend more time at work, and perhaps continue into the late afternoon and work, and stuff like that, doing things you felt were good to have finished. You don't do this anymore now, really. I'm in a situation where I can do this. And I also notice that when I come home the job is a little more distant because you're thinking of something else. I used to spend much energy when I was off work thinking about my job. Thinking about work and solutions. I really notice this. But I don't think people do a worse job because of that. Rather I'm more focused when I'm at work.'

Håkon's strategy was to spend less time thinking about work when he was at home, making work seem more remote. He felt that this did not negatively impact his work effort and performance, as it was compensated for by higher efficiency and concentration when he was at work. In effect, he re-established clearer boundaries between work and home. Hans, an engineer who also taught, said much the same:

> 'During my first years at this workplace I had no family, and then I worked a lot, much more perhaps without getting so much more done. So I have thought about this later that I have become much more efficient because of this.'

What they were saying was that their new life interests and obligations that came from having children contributed to making them more efficient at their job. The job did not necessarily suffer even if new time boundaries were set. A third strategy was thus to become more efficient at work to prevent the necessity of bringing work home. Fathers were not necessarily less dedicated at work, but they were less willing to sacrifice family time for work and career. The need for fathers to maximize the use of time and to put effort into becoming more efficient is also described by Daly et al (2009), who studied children's influence on fathers' identity and development.

A fourth strategy that may be inferred from the interviews concerns choosing a job that can be combined with more time for children. We saw this strategy used in Emil's story of the conflict with his boss over the boundaries between work and home – a conflict that resulted in him finding a new job. Håkon describes the strategy of choosing a job that contributes to an acceptable balance between job and home:

> 'I don't want to make a career at the expense of my children. I want to make a career, if you can call it that, doing the best possible job in what are approximately normal working hours. I don't want to spend much more time working at the expense of my children and family, my wife. This gives me reduced choices and job opportunities. You can't work in private business then. If you are a graduate engineer and work for a private company, you must assume that you need to work around 60 hours a week. If you are to work at a university and do research, you must also assume a working week of 60 hours. I need to find a job that pays me reasonably and gives me adequately stimulating work where I won't have a managerial position.'

The strategies mentioned were all examples with consequences for time boundaries between home and work. The relation between family and work was not necessarily seen as a conflict, but when something special came up, problems began: "If there is something special going on or you are working overtime then you might have a poor conscience at times", said Ivar, an electrician:

> '... like when it's approaching the end of a project. Then you might perhaps like to chuck your job out the door and rather stay home with your family, really. It happens I do so at times, too, that I say "No, no more tonight!" And fortunately, this is possible where I work.'

Becoming fathers made it more important for these men to reassess their time use and rethink how they would now like to combine the two spheres. However, their strategies did not lead to an 'either or situation', as in home *or* work, but rather a 'both situation'. Hans, who stayed home for a year with his two children, said that "there's never enough time at work, and never enough at home, so the thing is to just shoe-horn it in." And in the words of one of the other fathers: "We juggled the time between us, but it does not show up in the statistics." The aim was to find a balance, or an adaptation that did not trigger a conflict.

These strategies may be seen as examples of how fathering made these men look differently at their work and/or appreciate it differently, as one of them said: "My job has become less important because my children have become more important." These are signs that the meaning of the two spheres is being redefined. Fathers who made no specific attempts at changing the boundaries also confirmed this. Anders, an academic in a managerial position with three children, stated: "I have continued in the same manner, really, this is a *problem* with work." The change for this man who was devoted to his career consisted of defining his all-consuming working hours and his efforts in an exciting job as a problem. Anders' solution was to 'wear several hats' at the same time. His story thus did not exclude time and emotional involvement in his children and family responsibilities, as is often described by men trying to climb the career ladder. Rather, this account provides the contours of a fifth strategy, which is redefining the importance of work, a redefinition that can exist alongside a definition of themselves as good fathers. This is a more phenomenological understanding of the time relation between home and work. The emphasis is not on the number of hours here or there, but on the content of what is going on and its importance. Thompson and Bunderson (2001) have pointed out that such a perspective is not in conflict with a time bind or balance perspective that focuses on the division of time between work and childcare. It is, rather, a supplemental perspective that is also important when it comes to achieving a multidimensional life and meaningful integration of work and childcare.

As we have seen in this section, becoming a father and providing childcare impacted the relation between fathers and their work. The emotional attachment that fathers developed for the child was important for their management of the boundaries between the two spheres. Strategies chosen by fathers did not lead to major reductions in their working hours (part time), but they did try to give their child a larger share of themselves.

Conclusions

This chapter aimed to connect men's self-development into fathers with changes in their relation to work and family. In line with the research focus on emotions in family sociology (Smart, 2007), we have seen how they described their emotional gamut as being widened after having become fathers. They described how they had developed in a softer, more emotional and less selfish direction. The child represented a new life phase in that they felt more adult and more responsible. Children and the family had become more important in their lives, and they assessed changing their priorities.

The second question for the analysis was how this change had affected the boundaries between work and home. According to border theory (Clark, 2000), we expected that their strengthened identification with the home sphere would make management of the borders more relevant. We have seen that the boundaries are influenced in several ways by their new interest in life and by their experience in childcare during their parental leave period. Fathering had, for instance, raised competencies of value to working life, something that is a sign of overlapping spheres, rather than conflicting and contrasting ones. Work and family may be different spheres, but they connect and give each other importance. Analyses show that fathers use 'inclusive strategies', where a good father and a good employee are compatible identities. Even though they are more involved in their children, they believe this does not hurt their effort at work or their male identities as employees. Managing boundaries between two spheres, which might appear incompatible, are not, in fact, incompatible when working life and childcare both become arenas for optimizing opportunities and life quality.

The last section of the chapter has illuminated strategies that fathers use to manage the border between work and home. As expected from the literature review, reduced hours are not an option for these fathers, but the analysis has shown their effort in establishing better boundaries. Boundaries are primarily built to benefit the family sphere. Reduction of unregistered working time and overtime represents the drawing of such boundaries for their professional work. Their new temporal awareness and the fact that they do not typically reduce working to part-time hours may, however, also be understood as drawing a boundary for their childcare activities. Thus, they choose strategies that imply drawing boundaries for both their caregiving and their professional work. We may conclude that fathers are good at boundary drawing, and that this may be part of the reason why the two spheres of work and home are not presented as terribly conflicting in their accounts.

A qualitative understanding of time helps put emphasis on the content and meaning of the time spent on childcare and at work. Fathers' boundary work is related to the meaning they ascribe to the spheres, and this meaning has importance for how they perceive the relation between them. One could ask, however, whether this is a shift of mentality more than of practice. As seen in these accounts, fathers do not initiate drastic changes when it comes to the use of time, but they define themselves as active fathers – something that gives both spheres new meanings.

10

Negotiating Parental Leave
and Working Life[1]

Introduction

Internationally, studies have identified a contradiction between words and deeds and a lack of commitment among men to their rhetoric of more involvement in childcare (LaRossa, 1988). Scholars have referred to the puzzle that although fathers express great willingness to take a greater part in childcare, little is reported in terms of actual change (Hobson and Fahlén, 2009). In order to explain this agency gap, attention has turned towards workplaces and how lack of support for fathers taking leave might be embedded in the structure and culture of work organizations. As we saw in Chapters 6 and 9, when the father's quota was in its infancy, the interviewed men in our study expressed not only enthusiasm about having become fathers; they also had serious intentions to take an active part in childcare and to deal with hindrances at work. This chapter shows how fathers deal with the father's quota in the context of their work organizations.

The gendered character of organizations is a constraint that has received much attention in feminist research. In her classic article, Acker (1990) develops an understanding of gendered structures and processes in organizations, and discusses how working life's apparently gender-neutral ideas and routines build on unwritten implicit ideas about gender. This

---

[1] The empirical analysis in this chapter is previously published as B. Brandth and E. Kvande (2002) 'Reflexive fathers: Negotiating parental leave and working life', *Gender, Work and Organization*, 9(2): 186–203. Reprinted by permission from John Wiley & Sons and the Copyright Clearance Center.

means that policies and practices are embedded in gendered workplace norms and expectations (Höygaard, 1997; Brandth and Kvande, 2009b). Organizations seek employees without particular gender or ethnic backgrounds, that is, 'abstract' or 'ideal workers'. Terms such as 'worker', 'leader' or 'manager' are abstract constructions until filled with people. These abstract workers are without commitments and obligations that might disrupt their concentration on work. Accordingly, fathers' problems with work–family balance measures are regarded as rooted in the traditional structures of gendered work organizations where practices and norms are based on the assumption that there is 'someone else' to take care of necessary reproduction work, expecting men to prioritize work over family.

With this in mind, we explore how father-specific parental leave policies and actively engaged fatherhood reconcile with gendered norms and structures in the workplace. From fathers' perspectives, the chapter focuses on how the work setting facilitates or hinders fathers' aspirations and obligation to take the father's quota. We expect the work demands and the gender norms at the workplace to influence how leave is used, as work is where leave is taken from, and we are interested to learn about individual efforts, supportive influences as well as barriers. There are differences between fathers when it comes to actual working conditions and how they cope with or negotiate on these conditions. (Father/mother negotiations are important in understanding the construction of fathers' practices. They are, however, not included in this chapter.) We explore how fathers construct different practices through negotiations with the leave schemes and their working conditions.

Choice and capabilities

The relationship between fathering and employment is dynamic. In *The transformation of intimacy* Giddens (1992) discusses the variety and ambivalence characteristic of modern society. Developments are not, he claims, unambiguously positive or negative; the individual has many choices, but in reality, many of them are inaccessible. The father's quota is meant to make family time accessible to fathers. It is, however, often understood to represent limited choice (see Chapter 1) because of the obligation built into it, even though it empowers men to obtain involvement in childcare without having to risk their labour market status. The father's quota, in other words, is a policy intended to increase men's opportunity to care for their children – which is often men's own preferred choice. The existence of the father's quota, however, may not be a guarantee for more father involvement. Notwithstanding, we need more knowledge of what fathers are up against in working life attempting to exercise their parental leave rights.

In this analysis, we focus on the different approaches employed fathers have to becoming more involved with their children. Obtaining a desired outcome is dependent on several factors on many levels. These levels are *individual*, for instance, resources, qualifications and class, etc. A second level is *institutional* such as parental leave policy and work organization. As noted, work organizations have been regarded as change-resistant gendered institutions that can undermine active fathering (Lewis and Stumbitz, 2017: 227). Lastly, there is the *cultural* level of norms and discourses where gender norms may have a large impact when fathers want to change their work–family practices (von Alemann et al, 2017). For men, this means that more dimensions other than those connected to employment and job careers will have a place in their everyday lives.

Our aim is to examine how fathers actively shape their fathering practices through various negotiation processes in working life. Institutions do not exist unless practised by actual people, and a considerable amount of individual agency enters into the negotiation of parental leave in working life. The concepts of 'negotiation' and 'reflexivity' can be considered close relatives. The difference might be that it is easier to link *negotiation* to the individual and interactional levels. 'Negotiation' as a concept has been successfully applied in women's studies (Haavind, 1992) and in the sociology of organization (Strauss, 1978). It is commonly linked to interaction between family or organization members. In our context, we will use it to show that fathers are negotiating with the institutions (working life and leave schemes provided by the state). Thus, a focus on negotiations enables us to consider the many situations of choice that fathers enter into when constructing their everyday lives with tensions between work and family demands.

The chapter discusses two types of institutional demands faced by Norwegian fathers: first, the father's quota with its mandatory pressure towards active engagement in family and childcare, and second, work organizations with their request for availability and loyalty. We ask what the strategies are to reconcile caring for children with work. Are fathers faced with (in)compatible demands?

Data and methods

The analysis is based on both quantitative and qualitative material. A questionnaire was sent to all men who became fathers in the period

May 1994 to April 1995 in the municipalities of Trondheim and Orkdal in central Norway. As the father's quota was introduced in 1993, it had not long existed when the interviewees became fathers. A total of 2,194 questionnaires were mailed and the response rate was 62 per cent. From the same sample, in 1997 we interviewed 30 couples who used the parental leave system in various ways.

The questionnaire data provides an overview of the various factors linked to fathers' working conditions and the impact they have on their use of leave. The dependent variable is the length of leave taken based on fathers' reports on the number of weeks taken. We distinguish between those who (1) did not stay at home or were home for less than one week; (2) used the 'daddy days' (paternity leave) and/or the father's quota; and (3) shared the parental leave with the mother (that is, took more than the quota of four weeks).

In order to show how fathers' practice is constructed differently and emerges as the result of different negotiations, we also carried out qualitative analysis. In this chapter, we present four different types of practices to show the variation in the outcome of the negotiating process between fathers, their work and the state (parental leave schemes). To pinpoint these types, we start the analysis with the quantitative material where we find variations in the use of leave according to the work situation. The quantitative findings suggest some guidelines, but the construction of types is based on the fathers' narratives. First, we read all the interviews with the aim of finding variations in the negotiations, before we started working *abductively* switching between induction and deduction (Alvesson and Schöldberg, 1994). Using such an analytic process, we have been able to establish that there is an ongoing active and reflexive process of choice. We show the individual choice and what happens when general legislation must be adapted to a complex and shifting reality.

The four cases we present are exemplified by specific people who illustrate some main patterns, that is, typical cases of variation in the use of leave. The cases are not exhaustive, as there may be other practices constructed by the interviewed fathers that we have not presented in this analysis. An advantage with a small number of cases is that they present context-dependent knowledge. A story can be followed and presented in more detail than if the presentation cut across many cases (Flyvbjerg, 2006). Each case represents a unique story, but it may also represent processes that exist more widely. Speaking generally, in qualitative research the generalizations that can be made are about the nature of a process and not about a group or a population (Gobo, 2006).

The importance of working conditions for fathers' use of leave

Table 10.1 presents a total overview of the various working condition factors that influence how fathers use their leave. It shows that a greater proportion of fathers working in the public sector use the 'daddy days' and father's quota and the shared parental leave. Twice as many fathers with lower education compared to those with higher education do not use the leave rights. Those with low education are the ones who are most content with only using the 'daddy days' and the father's quota. As to the importance of occupational level, we see that most workers stay home for one to six weeks, that is, they use the 'daddy days' and/

Table 10.1: Use of leave according to various working-life variables

Variable	Categories	% 'daddy days' and users of the father's quota	% users of leave beyond 'daddy days' and father's quota
Sector	Private	61.9 (375)*	10.1 (60)*
	Public	79.9 (259)	19.3 (61)
Education	Primary school	56.3 (40)*	2.9 (2)*
	Upper secondary school	59.9 (217)	8.3 (29)
	College/university	75.9 (347)	18.7 (84)
Profession	Blue-collar	62.8 (150)*	6.0 (14)*
	White-collar, lower	57.9 (33)	3.7 (2)
	White-collar, higher	72.5 (411)	17.6 (98)
	Self-employed	30.4 (7)	13.6 (3)
	Other	75.6 (34)	7.0 (3)
Overtime use	Many times per week	58.7 (178)*	9.5 (28)
	Every second week	71.4 (142)	15.3 (30)
	At least once a month	73.7 (137)	17.7 (32)
	Less frequently	73.9 (150)	13.0 (26)
	Never	74.3 (26)	11.8 (4)
Position level	Non-managerial	70.9 (373)*	15.1 (78)
	Supervisory	65.1 (114)	12.4 (21)
	Middle management	72.2 (114)	9.6 (15)
	Senior management	47.0 (31)	11.1 (7)

Notes: Correlation testing by means of chi square.

This table includes only fathers with the right to leave, given as percentage points and number in parenthesis.

*$p \geq 0.01$.

or the father's quota. Few blue-collar workers and lower white-collar workers share leave with the mother beyond this, which is also true of those who are self-employed. The higher-level functionaries have the decidedly largest portion of fathers who use the opportunity to share the leave with the mother.

Fewer managers than non-managers take leave beyond the father's quota and 'daddy days'. Management duties thus appear to restrict the sharing of leave. However, this only applies to leave beyond the six weeks. Having management tasks does not appear to prevent fathers from taking the father-specific leave. This applies to the middle management level only; among senior managers, a smaller proportion uses the father-specific leave ('daddy days' and the father's quota).

Table 10.1 indicates that a high expectation of overtime reduces the use of leave. Fathers in such workplaces most frequently neglect to stay home on leave, and rarely share the parental leave. On the other hand, it appears to be easier to use one's rights as a father when there is little expectation for overtime.

After this brief overview of how leave rights and working conditions are distributed in relation to leave use, we now analyse how fathers actively construct various father practices through 'negotiations' with the leave policies (the state) and working conditions (the market). These choices result in four different fathering practices. The concepts we apply to designate these practices refer to the way the leave rights are used in relation to work demands, that is, not only the length of the leave, but also its content and construction. Thus, we are not concerned with the personal qualities of the fathers but rather with their practices as fathers. The concepts primarily indicate how they cope with demands and opportunities in their work situation.

Limit-setting practice

Fathers in this category take the father's quota and 'daddy days'. Moreover, they share parental leave with the mother. These fathers are strongly motivated to stay at home. Their motives for doing so vary, but they have a common wish to have as much time as possible with their child. They see the leave as a necessary part of becoming thoroughly acquainted with their child. Their strong motivation can also be seen by the way these fathers share parental leave with the mother even if this causes them financial losses.

A typical representative of those setting limits to their work is Lars. He is 30 years old, a computer engineer and a cohabitant with Lise, who is also an engineer. They have a daughter who is two. When she was born,

Lars was home on paternity leave for two weeks in addition to the Easter holidays. They shared parental leave so that they had a total of six months of leave each, including the father's quota. While Lars was at home, his wife returned to her full-time job.

This couple reflect on how their work situation would influence their time with their child. They decided that cutting out work completely for six months would be best. Lars' reasons were that it would be difficult to set limits in relation to the job if they were to choose, for example, a time account scheme and return to work part time, and he states, "… from experience you know that you'll get full-time tasks anyway." What we see is that leave considerations take prominence, and work is adapted. This means that he had to challenge the structures of working life. He kept pressing and negotiated a leave arrangement that satisfied his wishes. He said:

> 'When a woman gets pregnant, it's completely natural that she should stay home for a year, and everybody seems to accept that. But if a man says that he wants to stay home for six months, reactions are like "Oh, yeah", "Why should you?", and this is the basis for negotiations. You have to ask your employer whether you may, while the ladies aren't even questioned.'

His employer was not exactly happy when he chose to take his leave, and Lars was forced to give his employer good reasons for his choice. However, his employer's attitude made him even more certain that he wanted his leave. At the time, he was employed in a small computer business with 10 employees and was in charge of developing software products. He was the manager of a small project organization, responsible for customer contacts and developing a product that the company placed much faith in. The company no doubt felt that they would lose an important cog in the wheel if he stayed away for too long:

> 'They proposed various other solutions, including paying for daycare and asking whether…. I could spend some time at work, not every day, only some days, or perhaps half days or such . really, I understand them, you know. However, I never felt their thinking was "Sure, Lars, we really think you should do this, this'll be good for you!" I got no support from my boss. I had support from colleagues, but not from the boss. One female colleague said, "Don't give in, Lars. I really think you should go for it!"'

This demonstrates that even if fathers had been granted rights, they encountered resistance in their company. Lars was working in a small knowledge-based company where his skills were in demand, and this company would easily become a 'greedy organization' (Coser, 1974) in which his skills were a resource that must be exploited continuously. It is also worth noting how Lars not only negotiated with his employer who offered resistance, but also with his colleagues who supported him.

The leave period had other consequences for Lars, as he discovered when he wanted to switch jobs: "I was a step removed from work, and I had time to think of other things." He wanted a job that was less demanding, something that would not be so mentally draining, but that allowed him to be in the shape he wanted and to spend time with his child. This illustrates how room to think was created within which fathers could then reflect and act.

Unrestrained practice

Fathers who fit this category of practice used both the 'daddy days' and father's quota but never shared the parental leave with the mother. They had earned rights to all types of leave and received full wage compensation. Nevertheless, they had not used the leave according to the policy intentions, that is, as a chance to have main responsibility for the child over an extended period of time in order to strengthen the father–child relation. There were two main varieties of unrestrained father's practice. The first was when the leave or father's quota was adapted to the father's job, and the other was when the father's quota was taken when the mother was at home or as part of a joint holiday.

Anders was an example of constructing an unrestrained practice. A graduate engineer with a PhD, 36 years old, he had made what he himself called "a comet career". He was now the manager of a research organization. He was married to Anne, a social worker, and they had two girls, one three years old and the other 18 months. When we interviewed them, child number three was on the way. When they had their first child, he was formally on leave, but due to him having to give a lecture abroad immediately after the birth, he only stayed home with Anne for a few days. This pattern was repeated when he was to use the father's quota. He stated:

> 'Both of us agreed that I would use the quota, but in actual practice I found it hard, even if my intentions were clear. It was difficult because of my job, my obligations – lectures I

had to give and preparing for them. It was tough because they couldn't be delegated to somebody else. Nobody else can do it for you when you have a job where you are the one to set the priorities. It was difficult to use one hundred per cent of the leave. I took some days off, and then some days I just couldn't take off. This, in fact, happened with both my children.'

Fathers in this group were not opposed to taking leave in principle, but they were subjected to what they themselves felt were conflicting interests. They had found opportunities to develop in jobs which demanded much from them, and which they also wished to pursue. Thus, they felt it was difficult to set limits in relation to the demands they felt in their working conditions. Anders recalled:

'I start eight thirty and work until five thirty, and then I often go back in the evening, like eight thirty, and then I keep working, often, perhaps not so rarely either, into the night, like one or one thirty or two. And then I work weekends. I often work all night too, when there are lectures I have not been able to prepare for I often work all night, really. On many occasions I have worked until six or six thirty, then I've gone home and taken the kids to the kindergarten before going back to work and received customers. You keep thinking this phase will pass.... I worked hard as a researcher and senior researcher, but I found it more rewarding then. I have great ambitions, far too big. I think this has snowballed. More and more people are working very hard, and this department has operated at a profit for many years and should continue doing so. So, we keep pushing each other.'

He was very aware that there were *choices* between various ways of coping with leave, and that he had chosen his job, as he put it:

'But really, it's the job and my job ambitions and my career I give priority to. I think that with a management position like I have ... I feel that the way I live now, ... it may be hard [to be away on leave]. Anyway, a person doesn't relish the idea of trying. This might be it just as much. I had expectations that I would have time off, I would have time to do lots of things with my kids, much more than actually happened in practice. I had these ideas, right up to the time it actually started going wrong. At work this and that had to be finished, and you're going here and then there. Lots of things were happening at work just then. When we had the first child there was this conference, and when the second.... It may have been slightly better then, I don't know.'

He realized he could not win in both arenas. He had tried, but eventually gave in and let his job have first priority, although this was not so simple:

'There's something about becoming too conscientious regarding your job. Too anxious it will have consequences if you don't do what you should. Too hard to see things in perspective, like. The father's quota is only four weeks out of fifteen, twenty years in the job, but in the midst of things it's sort of hard to see. Of course, if you manage to take four straight weeks, then you'll manage to forget your job, I think. Instead of trying to cope with both.'

This illustrates what is 'reflexive' about leave choices and working life adaptations. No absolute conditions or structures are at work; rather, there seems to be active negotiations or choices that influence the construction of fathering. Anders was also under pressure from his work, which is a characteristic of what we call 'greedy' or 'unrestrained' working life. Competition is rife for projects in the research area where he was working. The employees had to keep selling projects, and moreover, new deadlines kept popping up. Thus, they had to put in long hours in a work culture where they were expected to keep going, always doing their best and giving their utmost. Hence as we saw in the general overview, it appears that being a manager and having high overtime expectations negatively affected the use of leave.

Rights-using practice

This category comprises those fathers who take the father's quota according to what it was intended for – they stay at home with the child while the mother goes back to work. The mothers work either full time or part time. The majority would not have taken any leave beyond the two weeks of 'daddy days' if the new scheme had not offered it. Thus, many of them accept the offer given to them by the state while expressing some surprise or perhaps even some resistance. Nevertheless, the father's quota has been given them as a right, virtually equivalent to a reduction in working hours, and accordingly, they must use it. Like the limit-setting practice, this is an example of how leave schemes set guidelines for the work situation, and there was little individual bargaining in relation to the workplace.

Magnar may serve as a good example of this. He is 36 years old, a warehouse worker who had been working since he was around 16 years old. He is married to Siri, an industrial worker. They have two boys, one three years old and one eight months old. He had been home on the father's quota with the first child and was planning to do so with the second one. First, the mother stayed at home with both children and then she went back to work. They had, however, made a special arrangement where the father's quota was stretched to two months as both were working part time and the grandmother looked after the children. They were planning for Siri to have one year off without pay when his leave had been completed, because as she said, "Really, there's not much money left when you have two kids and you use a childminder or daycare, like, as I only have a regular income, you know." Here we see how working conditions influence the adaptations parents make. The father's income was considerably higher, so he could not even consider taking unpaid leave.

This is also why we have chosen to call this practice 'rights-using'. This couple exhibits the common pattern where the father's pay is higher than the mother's, and if the father's quota did not exist, the mother would have had the entire leave, even if the father was entitled to full wage compensation if he took leave. However, as this type of sharing may be rather difficult to envisage for these couples, the father's quota functions as the extra incentive or inspiration needed for them to choose that route. Magnar told how they opted to stretch the father's quota out in time to ease their boy's transition:

'I thought it was fine that we worked half so we could stretch it. For his [the child's] sake. Like he would be with me some and with his mother some. You know, when kids are so small they want to be with the ones who they have most contact with, that's the way it is. If he is with his mother, he wants to be with his mother, and if he is most with me, he wants to be with me. So that's why we did it that way.'

Magnar also indicated that he might be interested in using more of the leave: "There was nothing at my workplace which made that difficult – if they are notified in advance, it's very easy to get leave. I thought perhaps it would be stickier to get my leave than it turned out. They were very accommodating, you know." He stated that the period with a father's quota had given him "a taste for it", and that he therefore wanted more of the leave the second time round. This illustrates how the experiences he had made influenced the choices he made in the next instance, becoming expressions of his reflexive father's practice.

Magnar did not encounter the same type of demand from his work as the other two fathers. He was at a workplace where having leave rights was considered an obvious employee's right that the company would ensure they got.

Tradition-bound practice

Men who choose this practice have given less priority to fatherhood as they have not used the leave rights they are entitled to. Some of them have taken a few days off in connection with the birth, the 'daddy days', but they have not used the father's quota. As shown earlier, a relatively large proportion of self-employed fathers are among those who do not use the leave. We also find working-class men in this group who either suffer financial losses if they take leave because their wives are in part-time work, or they do not see the point in taking leave because they are at home so much anyway, due to shift or rota work.

Steinar is representative of this group. He is 32 years old, married to Solveig, and they have three children. He previously operated a small business but closed the shop some years ago and is now working for a small private transport business. Solveig works half time for a cleaning company. Steinar had little information about leave rights. He had not studied them and was thus unaware of the differences between 'daddy days', the father's quota and parental leave. Steinar thought he used his 'daddy days' for all three births. When we asked him what type of leave he had in connection with his youngest child of three years, he stated: "Well, it was a week then too, I think. I have taken one week, like, every time. No, I only had 2–3 days the last time. Then I brought the oldest girls to work with me."

His company did not have any wage agreement on paid welfare leave ('daddy days') when men have children. The days he took off were thus earned overtime. He said, "When you're working for a private company, you have to negotiate to have leave, so I just took my overtime as days off. I didn't take any leave." Steinar and Solveig could not afford to take unpaid leave. After his shop folded, he had struggled with old debts.

Steinar did not use any of the father's quota: "It was never really possible…. I can't remember that I was thinking about it in particular then." He explained his choice was based on financial and work considerations. His employer kept pressing, and there was always too much to do at work. He said: "At my job the working hours keep changing … there's so much overtime. Getting some pay extra each month is important, because our finances always come into the picture ... the tax man is after me all the time." When asked whether he would have taken any leave if his finances had been better, he was not quite sure that he would.

In addition to the financial importance he ascribed to his work, social expectations at work obviously also influenced his decisions. He described the working environment as follows:

> 'I work in a terminal, with the rough parts of transport. The majority there are men, and, you know ... it's a rough environment. Talk is pretty brutal, and.... We know each other, we party together and do things together after work. We talk bad about each other, and when that's done, we're friends anyway afterwards, really.... It's a private company ... lots of businesses are working in transport, and this is one of the toughest markets to be in. You depend on things working right. If one link in the chain lets go, then you've had it.... No company is stronger than the weakest link.'

If somebody was off work for a period, the others had to do the same amount of work even if they were short of one person. Once before, a father took leave from the company for a period of time, and then the others had to work extra to cope with the workload. "We really burned the midnight oil then, like", he said. "Taking leave signals what you as a *man* are interested in", he said. "... That you are interested in such things, like." Perhaps it is not very 'macho' to stay at home caring for a baby when you are part of a hard, male environment working by the quayside?

Here we have a type of workplace without wage agreements, which does not make it normal practice to use 'daddy days'. Moreover, the work situation is characterized by irregular working hours and great demands as to flexibility and availability. Opportunities for working overtime are great. As his finances were tight, Steinar wanted to work some overtime, so this was his rationale for not using the father's quota. He also worked in a type of working-class environment where taking leave from work to care for children was not among 'the things a man should do'. This set important limitations on the freedom to act that Steinar felt he had.

Conclusions

In this study, we focused on how Norwegian fathers construct a variety of practices when they negotiate the new parental leave scheme in combination with work demands and opportunities. Our intention was to demonstrate that the fathers' choices may be understood as part of the increased reflexivity and negotiations that characterize modern society. Fathers choose differently, thus they also construct different father practices.

Within the *limit-setting practice*, the first consideration is how the father can get as much time with his child as possible. He is able to set limits on the demands of working life, having the resources that come from being attractive to his employer and from having been given statutory leave rights. This practice may have grown during the last few decades as setting boundaries for work during the leave is also shown in other chapters. It is, for instance, common practice for fathers in a similar occupational group in Chapter 13. The opposite is the case in *unrestrained practice*, where work comes first, and leave is adapted to it. The father exemplifying this practice sets no limits to work, although he may have the freedom to do so.

A third practice, *the rights-using practice*, is based on the state 'allowing' and demanding the fathers take leave, since it is a right they have been given that cannot be transferred to the mother. The workplace facilitates leave-taking, and fathers may take it without having to go through lengthy negotiations with the employer. Many of the fathers in this group would not have used the leave had it not been reserved for them. Over time, the individual, non-transferable characteristics of the father's quota have changed it into a norm for what men do when they become fathers. The fourth practice examined, the *tradition-bound practice*, shows that little priority is given to any of the available leave rights. While boundless work is the basis for not prioritizing leave in the unrestrained practice, the restraining factor for the tradition-bound practice is the norms of masculinity in a rough male environment with the accompanying demand for flexibility.

All four fathers, whom we have used to illustrate the different cases, work in male-dominated workplaces in which gendered norms influence their combination of work and family. Steinar, who work on the quayside where the gendered expectations on fathers' work are overt, is the only one to pass up the opportunity to take the father's quota. In the other organizations, gender is more a subtext that can be negotiated in the process of enabling fathers' leave-taking.

Another interesting finding is that Anders, with the unrestrained practice, and Steinar, who represents the tradition-bound practice, belong to two different social classes. Anders is a computer engineer with a PhD degree and a management position, while Steinar is a transport worker. In both cases, their fathering practice gives priority to work. The difference between these two is nevertheless that Anders reflects more on the choices he makes. He belongs in an environment where expectations as to gender equality are greater, and feels that he is on the horns of a dilemma. In Steinar's environment, childcare is not one of the things men normally do, so he finds no dilemma attached to his choice. This is an example of how gender and class work together, albeit with a similar outcome concerning priority put on leave use.

One concern of this chapter is whether the father's quota provides enough individual choice in relation to prioritizing childcare before work. The results of the questionnaire show that 80 per cent of the sample used the quota. This might indicate strong state pressure on fathers to choose similar work–family solutions. Through analysis of how fathers use the quota, we have, however, shown that there is great variation in their leave practices. Thus, the standard, non-transferable part of the leave scheme, which is represented by the quota, is used in different ways depending on how the institutional setting enables or constrains fathers' leave-taking. We can conclude that the quota connects individual choice and the opportunity structure in work organizations.

When the fathers in this study used the quota, it had only existed for a few years, and it was relatively short (four weeks). Our findings show variation in how seriously the fathers and the work organizations took up the new policy, and how they adapted to it at that time. The bargaining processes indicate that some fathers and organizations were opposed to it, as the father's quota had not yet become incorporated as normal practice. Something was, however, set in motion, as their right to leave was transformed into take-up.

11

Workplace Support of Fathers' Parental Leave Use[1]

Introduction

How employed fathers experience their workplaces' reactions to parental leave is the topic of this chapter. The aim is to understand how the Norwegian policy regime contributes to workplace practices and cultures that can promote active fathering. In Norway, the father's quota has become a mature institution. Internationally, fathers are increasingly becoming the target for government incentives to encourage their involvement in the family, father-specific leave from work being one such measure.

Work organizations contribute to construct fathering practices, and because they are increasingly confronted with the demands of social policy regulations, they are an interesting context for studying change in fathering practices (Liebig and Oechsle, 2017: 9). Research on greater father involvement has often been concerned with barriers represented by work organizations, and many work–family studies have shown how gendered assumptions at the workplace have made them change-resistant towards fathering. Lewis and Stumbitz (2017) raise the question of how research can progress beyond describing barriers and instead identify conditions of change and shifts in workplaces to contribute to involved fatherhood.

[1] Adapted from B. Brandth and E. Kvande (2019) 'Workplace support of fathers' parental leave use in Norway', *Community, Work & Family*, 22(1): 43–57, doi:10.1080/ 13668803.2018.1472067. Republished by permission from Taylor & Francis.

A concern of this chapter is to explore how national parental leave policies with a father's quota affect the workplace. Parental leave is now available to fathers in many countries, but its usage is often low (see Koslowski et al, 2019). This is different in the Nordic countries, something that directs our attention to the importance of institutional context, which not only includes welfare state regulations of parental leave rights, but also their implementation in working life.

How the leave is implemented in working life has received little attention by parental leave researchers, and compromises between fathers and organizations have hardly been addressed (Liebig and Oechsle, 2017). Scarce attention has also been directed towards the wider institutional contexts of which the parental leave regulations are part. According to Lewis and Stumbitz (2017), work–family studies in general have neglected context-sensitive research, particularly when it comes to understanding how the various contextual levels interact. Contextual awareness is important to catch the impact of different and changing institutions. Contexts include working life and social policies that vary over time as well as between countries, and include a country's family and gender norms. Responding to Lewis and Stumbitz's (2017) call for contextual awareness, this chapter focuses on two contextual levels: the welfare state in terms of parental leave regulations and working life culture.

The book, *Work–family dynamics* (Brandth et al, 2017), illustrates the importance of context. It demonstrates how parental practices can be understood as a competition between different institutions and their cultural logics in various countries. The institutions of the welfare state, labour market and family with their respective logics of regulation, economy and morals confront each other differently according to time and place. The logics of parental leave regulation and good fathering are, for instance, challenged by the economic logic of working life in various ways. Even if fathers on parental leave are legally granted job security, leave may still have negative effects on their careers, particularly in professions where the career logic is strong. Among business lawyers, for instance, the cultural logic of the career game is found to overrule formal regulations, resulting in low, if any, take-up of the father's quota (Halrynjo, 2017).

Although many organizations are changing their views to support fathers' leave-taking in response to national policies, change may be uneven. Differences in national contexts are, for instance, illustrated in a study of a Norwegian company trying to introduce the Norwegian parental leave system to their branch office in New York. This led to tensions between two national work cultures, but at the same time forged the introduction of new local practices (Heggem and Kvande, 2017). Such pockets of change are promising for men's family involvement. Most often studies report how the economic logics of work privilege men who have uninterrupted career trajectories, few care responsibilities and long working hours (Miller, 2017). In Rudman and Mecher's article from the US (2013), men who request family leave are penalized and given the stigma of being 'poor workers'. In a study of reasons for non-use of paternal leave (Additional Paternity Leave, APL) in the UK, Kaufman (2017) finds perceived workplace resistance to be one of four central barriers, and Romero-Balsas et al (2013) show that men who do not use parental leave in Spain justify their choice as a result of workplace culture and their own feeling of being indispensable at work. Fathers who do not take leave tend to argue that they cannot be away from work. Comparing the UK and Sweden, Kaufman and Almqvist (2017) found Swedish employers to be more accepting of men's use of long parental leave than UK employers.

In the Nordic countries, several studies show that workplaces may not represent particularly serious hindrances to fathers taking parental leave. Haas and Hwang (2009) hold that corporate support for fathers taking parental leave has increased in Swedish companies, and attribute this to the larger supportive cultural environment and institutions in which the companies are embedded. Men in Sweden are met with positive attitudes when taking parental leave – sometimes to an even greater extent than women; this can be connected with the strong support for gender equality in the Nordic countries (Bekkengen, 2002). A Finnish study also shows that attitudes toward men's paternity leave are predominantly positive, as very few fathers who take leave get negative reactions from colleagues and supervisors (Lammi-Taskula, 2007). This is confirmed in a later study that finds negative attitudes at Finnish workplaces to be rare obstacles to taking leave (Närvi and Salmi, 2019). Furthermore, studies from Norway find the workplace level to have little negative effect on parental leave (Halrynjo and Kitterød, 2016), emphasizing that in all kinds of work organizations it has become acceptable that fathers take their father's quota (Naz, 2010). This is also the result of an interview study among Norwegian employers who wished to accommodate their employees and accept the costs that followed leave use (Hagen, 2017). For fathers, the work situation is found to be important for when and how they take parental leave (Østbakken et al, 2018).

In order to understand why fathers in the Nordic countries encounter different reactions than those found in the larger literature, this chapter will explore how contextual factors and the policy regime in which workers operate shape the use of leave among fathers. Thus, the research question concerns how working life and the welfare state interact in a Norwegian context to promote take-up of leave among fathers.

This research draws on an interview study involving 40 cohabiting or married heterosexual fathers who had been home on leave with the father's quota, their total leave ranging from 2 to 10 months. The fathers selected for interviews had become fathers after the father's quota was extended from 6 to 10 weeks in 2009, thus assuring their experiences with a fairly long leave. The interviewed fathers were recruited by contact with various work organizations, in addition to snowballing individual fathers. Extra effort was put into finding interviewees with lower educational backgrounds. This was only a partial success as a little over two-thirds of the sample have a college or university education. The occupational composition of the sample was, however, varied, comprising craftsmen, teachers, consultants, researchers, health, administrative and service staff. They worked in many different forms of organizations. A majority of the sample was employed in private companies of various sizes, and 10 per cent were self-employed. Most of the interviews took place in 2012 and 2013. The fathers and mothers had all been employed before the birth of the child. Most fathers were employed full time, and only a couple of students held temporary work. A majority of the fathers were in their thirties, the age range being between 27 and 43 years.

The analysis in this chapter is based on a subsample of 20 fathers who used the leave on a full-time basis and not flexibly. Two questions are explored in the subsequent empirical sections: (1) In what practical ways do workplaces support father's leave-taking? (2) How do fathers themselves manage their leave in relation to work?

The Norwegian model of working life

There is a long research tradition focusing on the Nordic model of working life, which is important to take into account in order to understand how laws and regulations work in Nordic countries (Kangas and Palme, 2005; Bungum et al, 2015). Although there are great similarities between the Nordic countries, there are also significant differences. Here we focus on the Norwegian working life model that has been labelled a 'conflict partnership' and is based on an understanding that there is both a conflict of interest and a common interest between employer and employees. At the societal level this is characterized by cooperation between the social partners and state authorities, called 'three-party cooperation' (Dølvik et al, 2014). This is considered a competitive advantage and is successful in increasing productivity in working life (Levin et al, 2012). Based on this collaboration, laws and regulations have been developed and institutionalized in work life.

At the workplace level, the model includes various ways of involving employees in decisions within the companies, through formal and informal participation. Formal participation is connected to the professional organizations of the employees and cooperation between employee representatives and employer, for instance, by appointing employees as members of the board of directors. The Work Environment Act §12 also grants employees the right to informal participation in decision-making concerning the daily work situation. This has been called the Norwegian 'micro model' (Hernes, 2006) or 'micro democracy' whereby employees have the opportunity to influence how the company is organized and managed. The emphasis on cooperation and representation has also been characterized as employees being 'citizens of the companies' in order to underline the democratic aspect. An important feature of the model is the mutual recognition of rights and obligations. Employees' individual rights anchored in laws, agreements and unions influence institutional conditions that limit managers' autonomy (Gooderham et al, 1999). Managers are expected to encourage employees' participation and empowerment and in return they can expect employees to be devoted to work and increased productivity (Levin et al, 2012).

In a study of the Norwegian model, Ravn (2015) finds that the management function is often exercised in collaboration between managers and employees. This implies that the Norwegian model also includes a management model that embraces values and norms of equality, solidarity and democracy (Grenness, 2003). These values are reflected in the fact that work organizations often have few hierarchical levels and are characterized by a small distance between managers and workers (Gallie, 2003).

The Norwegian model also includes collaboration between employers, employees and the state in developing social and economic policies. There is a long tradition of strong trade unions combined with regulated working conditions that has been thought to both protect employees and enhance productivity. A consequence that is often emphasized is the high degree of *trust* between managers, union representatives and employees. Trust means that the parties can negotiate wages and collaborate on productivity. Thus, all social partners in Norway support the father's quota. Some even argue for its extension in order for an equal distribution of leave between mothers and fathers. The father's quota is understood to have the potential to promote the dual earner/dual carer model, which is seen as having a positive effect on productivity.

This Norwegian micro model empowers employees and focuses on the development of democratic work relations, helping employees to accept, trust and feel responsible for working life laws and regulations. This model provides the important institutional context for our analysis of the usage of parental leave by fathers in Norway.

Realization of the regulations

The fathers are aware that the design of the leave is important for their use of it, and that it has a special effect on their relation to the workplace. There are strong moral obligations for fathers to take the father's quota and for employers to accept it, produced in part by its design. This section explores how workplaces support usage of the father's quota in practice.

None of the fathers in the study reported that they had experienced any serious problems with their employers when planning to take their leave. That men take the father's quota when they become fathers seems to be expected at workplaces, which can be understood by the acceptance of regulations in Norwegian working life. When talking about reactions at work, Charles, a schoolteacher who took his 12 weeks' father's quota, said, "It was all right, and it [the leave] was expected! It had been more of an issue if I hadn't taken it. Public work places have to play by the rules." This observation is also more general. Fathers seem to take it for granted that working life adapts to the regulations of the welfare state. Christian, a senior advisor in the county administration, argued that even though the father's quota might sometimes represent challenges at workplaces, organizations do adapt to parental leave legislation. He said:

> 'We have five weeks of vacation every year. Workplaces manage to adapt to that, and when employees turn 60 they get one additional week. So, we manage that, and we have managed to adapt work to the fact that mothers are home for one year [on parental leave]. Why shouldn't we manage to adapt to fathers taking their quota of 12 weeks? It is a question of planning and organizing.'

Fathers report that as leave-takers they do not stand out as special or as tokens in any way. Arne, a communication adviser in a transport company, told us that at his workplace, "many of my male colleagues had a child at about the same time as me, which was great! We were about three or four who had kids within a 2–3 months span. In addition, there are many employees with small children working here." The norms that are produced by these practices make it easy for fathers to take the leave and for organizations to accept it. Dahl et al (2014), who studied the peer effect of father's quota usage in social security data, found that Norwegian fathers were even more likely to take the quota if their colleagues and peers did, described as 'a snowball effect'. The effect was greatest if the peer was a manager at a higher level in the organization.

The general pattern is that fathers inform their employers of their plans, and the employers approve it. The plan also includes how their work would be handled in their absence. Arne had a long leave of nine months, consisting of the father's quota plus six months of sharable parental leave. This could have caused negative reactions, because at the time when he wanted to start his leave, he was new at his job and things were busy. When he told his boss that he was going to become a father and wanted to take a long leave, he received only positive reactions: "The boss messed with me and said he would authorize everything that had to do with the leave as long as I promised to give him a high score in the next appraisal meeting. But that depends since I had to find my own substitute, ha, ha. So we'll have to see." That he had to plan for the coverage himself can be interpreted as an obstacle to leave-taking, but Arne mentioned it as evidence of the trust his boss showed him and the freedom he was given.

Burt, who worked in a bank, said that his employer supported whatever would function best for Burt himself: "So, I had to do the planning myself. The boss signed what had to be signed, and I didn't discuss much with him. I just said what I wanted, and he said okay." Martin, who worked as an architect, explained how he experienced applying for parental leave for 16 weeks at his workplace:

'I just asked, how do we do this in practice? Should I send in the paperwork or should you do it? I didn't feel that I had to negotiate about this. I knew that it was a right I had, and I just informed them [employer] quite early about when I planned to take leave. Because we are so few people working in this office, we need a bit of organizing when one of us is on leave a few months, so I let them know as soon as I could. That was that! There were no negative reactions.'

Like Burt, Martin's story illustrates a lack of negative reactions. They just informed their employers about their plan, and their employers approved it. There were not many people working in Martin's firm, which might have presented a problem with an employee going on leave because of having fewer people available to replace fathers on leave. Yet, this wasn't a problem.

The parental leave rules are complicated and may be quite difficult to understand in all their detail. Harold, a schoolteacher, explained that the principal at the elementary school where he worked did not know the parental leave rules very well and gladly accepted Harold's own plan: "I think he [the boss] had a very pragmatic attitude to it and thought: 'Okay then, let us find a substitute!' The administration didn't get actively involved in the paperwork, but they seemed to think: 'This is how it is; so we just have to adjust as best we can.'"

Ismael, a warehouse worker with two children, told yet another story of supportive employers. He took his father's quota after the mother returned to work. During his leave he learned that their daughter had been granted a place in kindergarten and was due to start two weeks *after* his leave had ended. His manager, who had been positive to his leave-taking all along, suggested that Ismael extend his leave by moving two weeks of his summer holidays towards the end of the father's quota period in order to close this care gap. This solution made him able to stay at home for a total of 12 weeks to care for his daughter until she could be cared for by the kindergarten. This shows that supportive employers are not only found among organizations that employ highly educated workers in the knowledge industry.

We get a further impression of employers' support of fathers' leave use when fathers compare their employer with NAV, the institution that validates the application for leave and pays out parental benefits. Fathers found their employers to be more understanding and easy to deal with than NAV. For instance, Arne, who took nine months leave because his wife wanted to return to her studies, had many meetings and phone calls to negotiate with NAV: "They could not fit my case into their forms – that I, by the way, discovered were outdated." His employer, however, helped him straighten things out. "I received a lot of backing from them", he said. Also Dave, who was a student and held four part-time jobs in addition to his studies, and thus gained leave eligibility, talked of how all of his employers assisted him more than he had expected in his rather difficult negotiations with NAV. Research has documented that one of the main reasons why some Norwegian fathers do not take the quota (or less than the full quota) is problems in relation to NAV (Kitterød et al, 2017).

According to the master narrative of workplace hindrances, it is often expected that employers not only resist men's leave-taking, but that fathers also stall their careers or interpret their family involvement as an indication that they are not dedicated employees. Niels pointed to the opposite, and said that *not* taking leave would have been understood to mean that he was not concerned about his children. When asked whether his leave was taken as a sign that he was not enough interested in his work, Arne said:

> 'No. I think most employers today live in the modern world
> and understand that they must live up to that. This is how it is.

They need employees who are happy with their job and have a good family life. Now, we see that both managers and middle managers in companies, 35–40 years old, also experience the same tensions concerning career, childcare, parental leaves and work hours. I have a mate who is manager of marketing, only a few years older than me in a top job; he had four months' daddy leave, so that says a lot.'

Arne pointed out that a person's overall effort and performance at work are what counts as a signal of work devotion, not whether they take temporary leave from work. What particularly surprised fathers who were migrants to Norway was that taking leave did not have any negative consequences for them in terms of job or wage loss. One of them said: "I knew we were not supposed to have problems at work, but I was a little concerned whether that was actually true because sometimes things look good on paper, but it may be that you get some problems. But I had no problems, and I felt really privileged I could have leave."

None of the fathers in the sample had experienced any problems with their employers when taking their leave. Tore, who worked as a doctor at a large hospital, illustrated this when we asked about how his leave-taking was received by his director, a 65-year-old chief physician: "He is updated on the father's quota ... he has got young children himself.... And I am not the first father to be in this situation." The fact that many fathers before him had used the quota and paved the way made it easy for him. The hospital where he worked had adapted to the fact that like mothers, fathers have the right to parental leave. He continued:

'With us [at his job] this is no big problem.... I believe that employers understand that this is part of life, society has decided that this is the way to organize; therefore, I believe that employers just adjust. It might be that they experience a lot of organizing. People stay at home without anyone grumbling. It's part of life.'

By calling fathers' leave-taking a 'part of life', he illustrated the change that has taken place in Norwegian society concerning fathers' caretaking. It has become the 'normal' thing to do for fathers. Daniel, who worked as a research scientist in a private company, confirmed this, saying: "In my job everybody has full understanding – I felt that my colleagues supported it.... I feel that there is total acceptance for taking leave and staying at home with children...." He also included his colleagues when he talked about the support he had received at his workplace. In order to illustrate the generally positive attitude, he told the story about when he sent an email to his manager on a Sunday and got the following response: "Dani, it's Sunday, and you must take time off." This illustrates that there might be a greater degree of consciousness at workplaces about respecting that employees have a life outside of work.

Because the father's quota has existed for 23 years in Norway, it seems to be well known, and as stated in the introduction to this chapter, the great majority of Norwegian fathers use it. It has been a widely used practice for Norwegian fathers from the early days of the father's quota, and may have led to what can be called a 'normalization process' or institutionalized practices at most workplaces.

Reconciliation processes: give and take

Employers who are supportive of fathers' leave-taking may obtain more loyal and committed employees in return. This may be attributed to the trust and cooperative practices between employers and employees that are inherent in the Norwegian model. In this section, we look into how fathers manage their leave-taking in order to be at home for several consecutive weeks.

According to Hagen's (2017) interview study of Norwegian employers, it is considered to be up to the fathers themselves to be available or not during the leave period. The fathers in our study did not suddenly abandon their jobs when the leave date came, but were prepared to be considerate to the needs of the workplace. Martin, who took full-time leave for 16 weeks, was willing to help out a bit if it had been necessary, saying, "I would have been there for them an hour or so and explained matters to them." Small businesses may be particularly vulnerable when it comes to fathers taking leave from work. Fredrik was the only one holding technological competence in the small architectural firm where he worked. He stated that he took his leave in one continuous period, as this was easiest to handle for his firm: "My way of organizing the leave was for the most part in consideration for the job. It is simplest for the job. When I am away, I am away!" Fredrik preferred to keep work and home separate. However, even if he tried to maintain a strong boundary between work and home during his leave of 26 weeks, he was still available, to a limited extent:

'I own the data skills in this firm, so they called and asked for assistance sometimes. We agreed on that. It is okay, but I told them to limit it as much as possible, and they are very good at it, I think. They called mostly in the beginning of my leave as there were matters they had forgotten to ask me about before I started leave, but lately they have been good at refraining from calling. And, it's important to me, because I don't want to think too much about my job when I'm home on leave.'

Beyond "helping a bit over the phone when they worry about things", Fredrik did not work during his leave. He seemed to volley back and forth a bit between work and home at the start of his leave, but managed to keep the two separate as time passed. His employer could have been negative towards him for taking leave because his competence was essential to the firm, but the solution they agreed on was satisfactory to both of them. The employer respected the aim of the parental leave regulation. In return, Fredrik respected the needs of his workplace and adapted the start of his leave to it. Hence, it seems to be a win-win situation, as happy employees mean productive employees.

Many of the interviewed fathers appeared very confident when portraying the quota as being *their* leave. They conveyed a sense of entitlement and beliefs about what is right and fair. Peter, an engineer with one daughter, took 10 weeks' father's quota, although he was sometimes contacted by his workplace and asked to help out:

'I sometimes helped out when she slept, but I let them know that it had to be on my conditions, that I couldn't promise anything, I would only do it when I had the time, and I would register the hours I worked, generously. If I worked one hour, I would register two or three. It was okay as it only amounted to five or six times during my leave, and only 2–3 hours at a time.'

From this quote we observe that Peter felt empowered by his right to parental leave. Hobson and Morgan (2002: 14) hold that family-friendly policies provide men with discursive resources with which they can make claims on their employers. Peter communicated that it was *he* who controlled how much to work and when to work, and he was not afraid to insist on his time priorities.

Daniel, a research scientist who started leave with his first child before he had completed a project, told another story about how he managed leave in relation to work. What made it extra challenging was his position as head of an international research group in which people from other country contexts did not have the same respect for fathers' parental leave rights. "Working outside Norway makes it extra challenging. In Norwegian projects, people are more used to ... 'Okay, he has his daddy leave', so they handle it differently", he said. Consequently, he did some work at home after the children were put to bed: "I have to work a bit at home. It is like … you have to find out what functions for you, find your balance."

There were many different examples in the interviews of how work and leave were planned to fit each other, such as various internal redistributions of work tasks and assignments or work put on hold. For instance, Cristopher planned his leave to fit in with the seasonal variations in his work, and Martin, who started preparing for his leave far in advance, finished assignments and gave responsibility to his colleagues. John, a university teacher, planned to take his leave when the students worked on their term papers, and Inge, who worked in property development, was very concerned about timing his leave period in relation to work demands. He said: "I have been fortunate with my employer. I work in projects; I finished a project before the leave, and I won't start a new project before I come back. So, because of this I don't have a bad conscience for anything at work. It is very positive that I am not in conflict with my employer." Sometimes, the employer just had to accept that the leave took time away from work. Steinar said: "It's quite clear that the project we are involved in will have to be put on hold, and we'll lose customers because of that, but too bad!" This is a story in which the moral obligation of fatherhood overrules the logics of work.

It is interesting to see that so many fathers organized their leave with the needs of their workplaces in mind. It is also interesting that the leave often gained priority. The interviews show give-and-take concerning the leave. Employers are supportive, and fathers, who want to take the father's quota and be home with their children, are willing to have an easy transition period in order to reduce possible problems at work. It seems very important, however, that they are able to control the amount of work themselves so that work does not interfere too much with their caregiving.

Conclusions

While much work–life literature has documented how workplaces often work counter to fathers' involvement in family and childcare, Nordic research has shown different tendencies. The aim of this chapter has been to understand how Nordic policy regimes, using Norway as an example, contribute to workplace cultures that promote active fathering. The findings show that fathers do not encounter much opposition to their parental leave use, but rather enjoy considerable support at their workplaces. This is different from the fathers in Chapter 4 who chose to take flexible leave and tended to be available for work during their leave. They often organized their leave with the needs of their workplaces in mind. These findings stand in contrast to the picture painted in the existing literature, and are promising as they show that workplaces can be organized both structurally and culturally in ways that support fathering.

The study has identified the Norwegian working life model as one context for opening up opportunities for involved fathering. Work organizations in Norway are generally law-abiding with respect to government regulation, and accustomed to ensuring worker protection and employee rights. Since the father's quota is an employment-based right, it seems to be handled in the same way as other types of rights and regulations in working life. Employers leave it to the fathers to plan their leave; they assist in negotiations with NAV if necessary, and adjust work, prepared to find solutions. In short, workplaces take leave use into consideration and deal with it pragmatically. When the findings show how the use of the father's quota is subject to acceptance, trust and respect, we recognize elements of the Norwegian model of working life, based on democratic work relations (Dølvik et al, 2014), with a mutual recognition of rights and obligations, which also includes parental leave regulations. Our findings are in accordance with the findings from a study of employers' attitudes towards parental leave (Hagen, 2017), which showed that employers were positive and generous towards employees on parental leave. There were three main reasons for this: first, because they needed to attract and keep productive employees; second, because they wanted to demonstrate a give-and-take attitude towards their employees; and third, because of a normative commitment to parenthood among employees and employers alike.

This chapter answers the call for research on the wider institutional contexts of which parental leave regulations are part (Lewis and Stumbitz, 2017). It has shown how the Norwegian context with its working life model and social policy regulations may account for an optimistic picture concerning the implementation of parental leave rights for fathers in working life. This may be an inspiration for other countries and encourage them to look beyond organizational constraints when explaining low take-up. A positive attitude to the implementation of leave may make fathers' leave use a 'normal' decision in the workplace. To gain more knowledge, research with different samples and comparative studies on the linkages between various institutional contexts may be important contributions from future studies.

12

Managers: Irreplaceable in Caregiving and Replaceable at Work

Introduction

Although the use of the father's quota has become a majority practice among Norwegian fathers, there is variation between different groups of fathers. Highly educated fathers are more positive to the father's quota compared to other groups of fathers (Lappegård and Bringedal, 2013), and the actual use of leave by this group of fathers is also the highest. Fathers with very high incomes are, however, among those who use the father's quota the least (Grambo and Myklebø, 2009; Kitterød et al, 2017). In their research on career fathers with an elite education, Halrynjo and Lyng (2010, 2013) find that in the particular part of working life where the job is an investment in career development, fathers' use of leave may have indirect and long-term consequences that can reduce career opportunities. This may, in turn, explain the lower use of leave in this group. However, their research is founded on studies of career fathers who have generally not used the leave; what is lacking is research that explores what actually happens when male managers use leave. Moreover, their data material was collected between 2005 and 2007; in the decade since their study there has been more normalization of the fathers' use of parental leave in Norwegian society (Kitterød et al, 2017).

The point of departure for this chapter is the significant changes that have taken place in Norwegian society when it comes to the participation of fathers in caring for their children. Based on a qualitative interview study of male managers who are fathers and who have used the father's quota, this chapter explores the experiences these fathers have had, both in terms of caregiving for their children and their own career development. These issues have not been adequately researched as the focus has rather been on men in this group of fathers who do not use the father's quota. This chapter will therefore attempt to answer the following research questions: How are the caregiving activities of male managers influenced by their use of parental leave? What is the impact on the career development of male managers when they use the parental leave?

Implementation of the father's quota in working life

A study of what prevents men from taking parental leave in Canada (McKay and Doucet, 2010) points to four factors: the preferences of mothers, no earmarking of the leave that is too short and social norms at the workplace. Research in the US (Blair-Loy and Wharton, 2002) has found that the use of flexible and family-friendly initiatives that either entails a direct or indirect break with 'the rules of the game' can come at a cost for the employees using them. Working part time, job sharing and flexibility programmes were available in a large US firm, but awareness of the actual rules of the game meant that these programmes were hardly ever used (Hochschild, 1997). This was the case even though workers expressed stress and conflicts when trying to balance family life and working life.

Fathers' use of parental leave is generally context-dependent as it varies according to the country in question and its welfare system, which may have highly divergent family policies and working life regulations. This use may also vary from one work organization to the next. In the Nordic welfare states, where family policies are no longer based on the male provider model but are rather based on both parents being providers and caregivers, there may be greater acceptance and use of parental leave. Chapter 2 showed that fathers have a strong sense of entitlement relating to the use of the father's quota, but not when it comes to the parental leave that can be shared. Reactions in the workplace to fathers' use of the father's quota are respect and support from their employers. One important reason for this respectful attitude is that the father's quota is a legally stipulated and earmarked right for the father. This should also be seen in light of the institutional importance of the Norwegian model in working life, with its focus on collaboration between employer and employee (Bungum et al, 2015). As described in Chapter 11, the model is based on mutual recognition of rights and obligations, where the employees have the opportunity to influence their working conditions. Employee rights are anchored in legislation and policies that limit the influence of the employer. This has led to a high level of trust between the parties in working life (Hernes, 2006).

However, as pointed out, there are variations in the use of the father's quota, where fathers in career professions take less leave. An earlier study has examined whether the use of leave by fathers in career professions may have indirect and long-term detrimental effects on their careers (Halrynjo and Lyng, 2013). Based on a questionnaire study of lawyers, business economists and graduate engineers from 2007, their data shows that the father's quota has had a great impact on the fathers' use of leave in the elite professions in general. After the father's quota was introduced, 71 per cent of fathers in their study used the leave compared to 15 per cent before it was introduced. When it comes to the link between career development and use of leave in this group, the researchers find that the use of parental leave does not influence the probability of fathers being promoted to middle-management positions. Nevertheless, they find that the probability of reaching senior managerial positions decreases with the use of leave.

They explain this by stating that parents in career professions are facing a dilemma when using parental leave, which is based on what they call a facilitation logic for parents, meaning that the right to leave can clash with a career logic that demands continuous input and performance (Halrynjo and Lyng, 2013). Career jobs are often characterized by individual competition where visibility and performance can provide an important competitive edge. Therefore, family policy programmes introduced to improve the possibility of combining work and family for fathers may have a counterproductive effect on this group of fathers, according to Halrynjo and Lyng (2013). In the competition with other colleagues, they may risk being demoted from the A team, dropping down to the B team because they have less time available for work if they use the leave.

The challenges are thus connected to the risk of being 'replaceable' in a career path, demanding that one is 'irreplaceable' by being available, according to Halrynjo and Lyng (2013). Even the earmarked father's quota may be negotiable in such a context. This is because the effect of the earmarking is undermined in career jobs where choosing not to use one's legal rights becomes a symbolic marker of dedication to job and career (Lyng, 2010). Although parental leave is a one-time and time-limited absence, when many highly qualified and motivated colleagues are competing for the same opportunities, projects and promotions, even a short-term absence, such as the father's quota, may leave a male employee lagging behind. The concepts of replaceable and irreplaceable have mainly been used in research focusing on the career logic in work organizations. We will, however, be using these concepts when analysing these managers' experiences with care work as well as in handling their careers.

Halrynjo and Lyng's study is based on interviews with a group of career fathers where the majority had not used the parental leave. This means that there is a lack of knowledge about managers who used the father's quota and their experiences of being both a caregiver and a manager. The studies were conducted from 2005 to 2007. Over the last decade, the use of the father's quota has become an accepted norm among the majority of Norwegian fathers (Kitterød et al, 2017). This may have had an impact on both the understanding and use of the father's quota by male managers and the culture in companies where career logic is prominent. According to some researchers, the increase in the fathers' participation in childcare in Norway and in the other Nordic countries has led to the 'emotionally involved father' gaining a key place in their culture (Bungum, 2013). In her work on the new child-oriented fathers, Aarseth (2013) argues that fathers' focus on the importance of having an intimate relationship with their children has led them to assume greater responsibility for family work. It is through being involved in the day-to-day life of the child that they are able to experience the power of love that the relationship with the child can give (Aarseth, 2013: 249).

To analyse how the caregiving activities and career development of male managers have an effect on their choice of taking parental leave, two concept pairs are central: (1) replaceable and irreplaceable and (2) available and unavailable. As shown above, these concepts have been used in analyses of the career logic in working life (Halrynjo, 2009; Halrynjo and Lyng, 2013). We use them here to analyse the fathers' experiences of both caregiving activities and career development during the leave period.

Method and design

This study of managers' experiences of the father's quota used qualitative interviews with nine managers who are fathers conducted in the autumn of 2016 and winter of 2017 (Moen, 2017). These nine fathers were found through strategic selection according to three criteria. First, they were fathers who had a management position; second, they had used the parental leave; and third, they had children young enough for the fathers to be able to remember the toddler period and how the leave was experienced in relative detail. Another reason for choosing this criterion was that fathers with children between zero and six years of age belonged to the group of fathers who had gone through great changes in terms of the father's role (Kitterød, 2013). In some cases, the fathers had older children, and some also had younger children.

The fathers were recruited according to the snowball method, and all were very helpful in contacting additional potential interviewees. Pseudonyms were used to keep the identity of both fathers and companies anonymous. The interviews, lasting approximately one hour, were held in meeting rooms at their workplaces, except for four interviews that were conducted in their homes or by telephone. The interviews focused on the fathers' day-to-day life at home and at work. The main topics of the interviews concerned work duties, wellbeing at work, the leave itself, the combination of work and home, caregiving responsibilities at home and detailed descriptions of 'an ordinary day' at home and at work.

All the informants used 10 or 12 weeks of the father's quota, respectively. In this study, only one informant used leave beyond the father's quota, the so-called shared leave between the mother and the father. For this informant the first leave was six months and the second four-and-a-half months. The male managers for the most part belonged to the same professional group, as they were educated as engineers and graduate engineers. All the informants were middle managers in their companies, either heads of section or department heads. Their duties in these positions could include human resources (HR) management, project management and team leadership.

Being irreplaceable in caregiving

This section focuses on the experiences of male managers when staying at home to care for their child during parental leave. What happens when they choose to make themselves available for caregiving activities?

"It was me and her"

Harald was one of the informants who had used the father's quota weeks consecutively, and who never considered flexible use. He was a graduate engineer and head of department with many demanding duties. During his leave he knew that a managerial position was waiting for him, but he managed to make himself relatively inaccessible while he was on leave, and did not start thinking about his job until the final week of his leave was approaching. He therefore had the opportunity to focus on being a caregiver for his child, saying: "This obviously helped me to get to know my child very well, and I could not have done that in the evenings or on the weekends. It was me and her." The intention of strengthening this relationship through the father's quota had succeeded in Harald's case, which illustrates the importance of having a relatively long continuous period alone with the child. He could not have achieved the same relationship with his child if he had only had the evenings or weekends to get to know her, as the mother would also be present and the caring time would be shorter and more split between them.

The feeling of having 'grown together' with the child brought strong emotions to the surface for Harald when the leave period was drawing to a close: "Towards the end, perhaps the last week, I was obviously quite emotionally moved in realizing that now the leave would soon be over. I could even call it anxiety about going back to work." He had made strong bonds with his child and was worried about what could happen when he was about to 'leave' the child. He said: "… but it went very well. What it's most about is having this little child you are now leaving to daycare and what not." He thus experienced both how it is to feel irreplaceable in relation to the child and also to feel relief that others can replace him when it is time.

Becoming number one

Didrik was also an engineer and head of department in the company. For the most part, he was the only one responsible for his particular work area in the company. He also had many other duties and was willing to take on additional ones than those stated in his job description. Didrik was one of the fathers at home alone with caregiving responsibilities during his leave, meaning that the mother of the child was at work while he had leave. He believed that his relationship with the children would have been different if the mother had been home at the same time:

> 'I feel that I would not have had the same relationship, because then they would have chosen the solution they were used to. And the mother has always been the rock…. It would probably have been very nice if she had been home and we could have gone on trips and stuff like that, but for the relationship between me and my children I think it was very good.'

He summarized that the father's quota could provide the opportunity to have sole responsibility for his child, and thus he could learn the everyday needs of the child. By being available for his child, he also believed that during this period the child would learn to trust him, and that it would be healthy for the child to become thoroughly familiar with him. He pointed out that the father's quota was important for his relationship with both his children, and were it not for the father's quota, he would have continued to be 'number two' in relation to his children. This can be understood as the father's quota having contributed to increased equality between the mother and the father in the care work, through him being empowered as a carer. This also illustrates how the father experiences the impact that the love and affection from the child might have (Aarseth, 2013).

Emil, also an engineer and head of department, was one of two informants who had used both the continuous and flexible father's quota. It is interesting to note how Emil found that his daughter was just as dependent on him as she was on her mother during his use of the father's quota. He therefore believed that there was no great difference between the father's role and the mother's role, and that it simply came down to how much time one was willing to invest: "Because I guess that a father who has stayed home for a year could have experienced the same closeness and dependency as when the mother is home. So I had a feeling that the father's role can be at least just as important." His experiences suggest that if a father makes himself available and spends enough time with his child, he will have as close bonds with the child as the mother.

About going into the 'leave bubble'

While the father's quota contributed to strengthening the father's relationship with the child during the leave period, the fathers also found that they gained an important role in the home in general. Aron had two children and worked as a head of section in his organization. He talked about how he had gained some new experiences about the father's role during his leave, and these experiences also included chores around the house: "So I noticed that minding a child was actually a bit more work than I perhaps had believed, really. With everything that needs to be done in the house in addition, I think that made me reflect a little bit." He found out that it was quite a job to stay at home with everything that needed to be done. Thus, he developed awareness about things he had not reflected on very much before this experience. He admitted thinking before the leave that the mother could have done more at home during her leave. He had not wanted to make something out of it, but was a bit annoyed at times when his dinner was not ready or if the washing machine hadn't been started. This "came back to haunt him a little" when he was alone home on leave.

Aron is not the only one to experience this after ending his leave. Karl had four children and was a head of department. Because there was a large gap between the first and the last of Karl's children, we focused on the last leave period where he had what he calls "an epiphany":

> 'You really do experience some things with this … that is, I think you become more aware of the responsibility you have for more than just going to work … but that you become a much greater part of the upbringing and a part of the home in a way, you know, it contributed to that. You get a bit more responsibility for planning dinner and activities. When you're home that's in a way your duty, really.'

The time spent at home during the father's quota helped Karl to become more aware of household responsibilities and chores. Being alone home over a longer period meant more household obligations. Several of the informants said that they found caregiving to be hard work (see Chapter 8). This means that they experience the total obligation that follows from being alone at home over a longer period of time. Similar to Aron and Karl, Leo also acknowledged that he could be a bit exasperated when finding that nothing had been done at home when he returned after a long day at work. Staying at home during the father's quota left him keenly aware of two things: first, that the caregiver role can be quite demanding, and second, that he personally experienced everything that should have been done in the house but was left undone. In Leo's own words: "… you enter this bubble, you know, the leave bubble".

In this section, we have seen that male managers who made themselves available for caregiving activities by staying at home on leave found that they got closer to their child. When the father and child were alone together most of the day, a close tie developed between them, making the fathers feel that they were bonding with their child, and some felt virtually irreplaceable in relation to their children.

Being replaceable at work

"Business goes on anyway"

The interviews show how several of the fathers considered themselves irreplaceable in their jobs before taking leave, but this view often changed during the leave.

Markus, an engineer and project manager who had used the father's quota, had the following to say:

'You might think that you're "one of a kind", that you're indispensable or things won't function at work. And, you might have learnt that if you don't do anything at all chaos will ensue, so that there will be loads of backlog at work when you return. Ten weeks is a long time.'

However, he found that both he and the company coped well during his leave. With a surprised tone he said: "everything didn't come to a standstill, and that's good." Thus, it turned out that he was not quite 'one of a kind' at his workplace after all, but that the company was able to find solutions without him, and colleagues were able to fill his role. He experienced that he was replaceable, and even that the company was quite successful during the weeks that he was away.

Karl experienced the same when he used 12 weeks of the father's quota, and he reflected on feeling irreplaceable in the job context:

'So I think it's quite good, both for the fathers and for the families, and maybe even for working life, really, that you find out that you're not irreplaceable, I can be away and the business simply goes on anyway. When you only keep working and working, you make yourself indispensable, you deal with everything yourself. It in a way forces you to stay away for some time.'

By making himself unavailable for the job, he discovered that the company managed without him; Karl experienced that he was actually not indispensable at work. He pointed this out when he said: "business goes on anyway". This also points out that it is possible to influence whether one wants to be replaceable or irreplaceable at work. The more you work, the more irreplaceable you become. Making himself inaccessible during a long continuous father's quota helped Karl to see this in context. He sees it as his own choice to make himself unavailable and does not see it as a "risk" of being made replaceable.

Making oneself inaccessible

Aron is one of the informants who had used both a continuous and part-time father's quota. With his last child, he used a father's quota of 10 consecutive weeks, and also took two extra weeks. He stated that his choice was based on the fact that he wanted to make himself less available for the job:

'… So I probably felt that if I was to do it [use the part-time father's quota] I would not get much time off. Say that if I had leave two days a week, for example, then I think it would have been difficult for me to turn off completely…, so I think that on those two days there would have been a lot of focus on the job, as I would have been available.'

His grounds for using continuous leave were his concern that he otherwise would not have been 'off the job' enough. Making himself less accessible for the job was important to him if he was to succeed at being fully present in caregiving. This choice was also based on his experiences from his first father's quota leave, where he "hit the wall" when he took the part-time father's quota: "I learned the hard way the first time … when you made yourself accessible, both for colleagues and clients, the phone would ring and mails would come, and then there was too much focus on it. So the first leave was not very good…" To manage to set a boundary between the job and caregiving during his second leave he chose to make himself less available for his job and more available for his child.

Similar to Aron, Harald found that he was able to put aside his job during his leave: "I received the odd phone call which I answered, but there was nothing that was really a bother. I tried to be very aware of it, and I think I succeeded." His focus was on being a caregiver – even with a new managerial position waiting for him. Several of the fathers had a few phone calls from their workplaces during their leave, but they spoke about them as being "pleasant", or not important. Leo chose to make himself unavailable for his job. For him, the caregiving quickly turned into regular routines that he got used to, and he was thus quite detached from his job.

Unlike the other interviewed fathers, August used the shared leave in addition to the father's quota, so his leave amounted to a full six months. He had two young children, and during the interview, he was on leave with his youngest child. One of the reasons why he succeeded at being unavailable for his job during his leave was that the project he was involved in was reaching completion. Thus, it was not necessary to introduce a completely new person to what he called an "intensive and important role"; instead, a colleague already working on the project took care of it. He only received the odd phone call with questions he needed to deal with during his leave. It is also interesting that he said that he had adopted a "normal working life" situation, which suggests that it was common to take leave. In his company, it was up to each employee to choose whether they wanted to be among the "ambitious ones" or among those with a "normal working life". The latter was defined as working "nine-to-five". At the same time, this can be interpreted to mean that a 'normal working life' also includes taking leave. Thus he opted out of the career logic that requires continuous effort and achievement, and it is instead working hours that allows a combination of work and family.

The leave as a boundary-setter in relation to work

Emil used two different leave periods, one continuous and the other part time. The first time he was to use the father's quota, Emil told us that his company accepted that he use the leave, but there was no encouragement to use it. He also encountered comments such as "Doesn't the child have a mother?", and he talked about his workplace as having an "old boys" culture. For this reason, Emil did not embark on his leave with the most favourable of conditions from the company's point of view, and like Aron, he chose to make himself unavailable during the weeks he used his father's quota full time: "During the first [leave] I didn't work at all, I removed the mail app from my phone too, and then I didn't work at all.... I didn't want them to rob me of the joy of the leave." He deliberately made himself unavailable for his job due to negative incidents that had occurred prior to the start of his leave. In this way, Emil's period of leave turned into a protest against his workplace and the prevailing 'old boys culture'. He adopted what may be called an oppositional role by not just having the right and opportunity to take leave, but also by using this opportunity as a protest. This is an example of one of the four factors that McKay and Doucet (2010) highlight as an obstacle to taking parental leave: social norms in the workplace. Nevertheless, in this case, he chose to defy the social norms and violate the 'prevailing rules of the game', which Blair-Loy and Wharton (2002) write about.

Markus said that he was able to choose when he wanted to make himself available or inaccessible during the leave. The period of leave became a boundary-setter for him in the sense that he chose not to accept work duties there and then: "… it felt good to be able to simply say 'no, I'm on leave, so you better come back in a couple of months', you know." He deliberately used his leave to set a boundary so he could put work assignments aside. Markus also told us that the period of leave enabled him to "turn down the pressure a notch or two" and be present at home and in his caregiving.

Career development

Several of the fathers found that they were neither 'irreplaceable' nor 'indispensable' in their jobs while home on leave. However, when in competition with colleagues, using parental leave may mean being demoted from the A team to the B team in a career context. The interview material shows, however, that our informants did not experience this. The perception of being replaceable at work may be connected to how the fathers experienced that the period of leave did not detrimentally affect their career. Halrynjo and Lyng (2013) describe how career fathers may risk being dropped from the A team to the B team due to their absence from work during leave. Our data material shows, however, that the fathers compared returning to work to returning from a long holiday. It must be pointed out that the leave itself is not compared to a holiday; the comparison refers only to the feeling when returning to work. One of the implications of this is that there is extra work waiting for them when they return, as is the case when returning from an ordinary holiday.

When asked whether the leave had an impact on their career development, Leo responded: "No, not at all." He returned to the same work assignments and nothing had changed. This was also clearly expressed by Emil, who found that the leave had not influenced his career development, and this was particularly clear in Harald's case, when a new position was waiting for him when he came back to work after his leave. Therefore, he did not in any way feel that his leave had constrained his career opportunities, but rather, he could claim that: "… I was promoted while I was at home." He was given a managerial position with greater responsibility.

Only one of the fathers in this study reported that the leave caused his career to stall. This informant took a total of six months' leave. His feeling that his career was stagnating may have come from the fact that he was absent from work for a relatively long period of time compared to the other fathers in the study. It is important to point out that this father did not experience the stagnation as problematic because he had chosen 'normal working hours' and his career ambitions belonged to the past. This may also say something general about fathers who use leave, as they may have possibly reached a phase in life where their priorities have changed. Their career is in part put on the back burner while being a caregiver rises to the top of their agenda.

It is interesting to take a closer look at how managers with experience of being home on leave presented their points of view on the father's quota and fathers' leave to their employees. Emil kept his own experience in mind when assessing applications for leave from his employees. He stated: "There's one worker now who I'm the manager for together with [name of wife] and he's planning to take 26 weeks, that's half of the total leave time. Of course he should be able to do this, that's the culture I want to have, that much tolerance." Emil's view on what type of culture he wanted

MANAGERS: IRREPLACEABLE IN CAREGIVING

to have in terms of leave for fathers also showed how he, as a manager, helped to determine the norms in his workplace. He used his experiences from his first leave where he received negative feedback from the company and did not want his employees to experience the same. Creating this type of culture was something Aron also wanted in the company where he worked: "There is acceptance for taking a large portion of the leave with no questions asked. We have people who take the minimum and also people who have been away for seven or eight months. I think this is good, and I hope it's a stamp of quality for our workplace."

Thus, it was up to the fathers themselves to decide how much of the leave they wanted to take. Having this positive attitude to the father's quota and leave was something Aron called a *stamp of quality* for the company. This illustrates that taking the father's quota has become a norm in many companies. Edvin, who was a head of section with responsibility for many employees, shared this attitude. He told us that no questions were raised about taking the father's quota and leave, and stated that: "It's the most natural thing in the world that people use the leave." He and the rest of the company were also interested in making this the basic policy: "... the bottom line in the company is that this programme is positive, and all the managers take leave." Therefore, it was not a problem to use the leave, even for the heads of the company.

Irreplaceable as a caregiver and replaceable at work

The point of departure of this chapter has been the major change that has taken place in Norway when it comes to the participation of fathers in caregiving for young children. The father's quota, which reserves part of the parental leave for the father alone, has played an important role in this respect. Earlier research has shown that there has been less use of the leave among fathers in career jobs. This is because these fathers are in jobs where the career logic indicates the need to always be available and irreplaceable. The data used as the basis for this chapter are interviews with managers who have used the father's quota and been at home on leave with their children. We chose to use the concepts 'available' and 'irreplaceable' to analyse the fathers' experiences of both their caregiving and career development.

We find that the concept 'replaceable' can also be connected to what the fathers experience when being home on leave. By going into the 'leave bubble' and making themselves continuously available, they experience being the main person in the caregiving of their child. Being 'irreplaceable' is thus connected to being the child's caregiver. At the same time, these managers chose to reduce their accessibility for their job and experienced being replaceable at work when they used the father's quota. Prior to taking leave, many of these fathers considered themselves to be irreplaceable at work. However, they found that the workplace managed well without them for a period of time, and that other colleagues could take over their roles without this damaging their own career development. By using 'replaceability' as a concept to analyse the experiences of male leaders when it comes to the effect of the leave, both in the fathers' caregiving and professional lives, we therefore find that the content of the career logic is shifting and changing. These fathers do not see refusing to use the father's quota as a symbolic marker of dedication to their work and careers. Their experiences of being on leave and being irreplaceable in childcare have also led them to encourage their colleagues and employees to use the leave. In this group, we can therefore observe signs of changes in career logic in that caregiving for one's own children is compatible with having future career opportunities.

Our findings may in part be understood bearing in mind that the study was carried out in 2017. By then the father's quota had existed for 24 years, with more 'normalization' of the fathers' use of parental leave over the last decade, both through an increase in the length of the father's quota and increased consensus in public debate (NOU 2017: 7). Earlier research in this field was based on data collected in 2007. Our findings may thus indicate that the norms for the use of leave are changing within the leadership group of fathers. In other words, they are following the majority of Norwegian fathers in this field. However, this study has few informants and they all have the same educational background. Earlier studies were based on data from economists and lawyers in addition to engineers. This may mean that fathers with engineering backgrounds are in industry branches that are more positive to the use of the father's quota than others. Perhaps career fathers in other organizations and with other educational backgrounds than these engineers have other experiences. It is also worth noting that we did not include career fathers who had not used the leave. Future research could show whether we can observe a general 'normalization process' among a larger group of male managers when it comes to using the father's quota.

13

Conclusions: Change in Policies, Fathers' Caregiving and the Ideal Worker Norm

Many countries are currently working to improve their parental leave policies and make leave available to fathers in various ways. Comparative international research has found that fathers in countries that offer earmarked, non-transferable leave have a higher take-up than in countries where such a leave design does not exist. In this book, as we were interested in how leave policies work, we approached leave use phenomenologically by studying fathers' actual perceptions of and experiences with taking leave. From their perspectives, we aimed to gain knowledge about the connection between leave design, its use and possible impacts. In so doing, we looked at meanings, cultural frames, practices, motivations and consequences. We studied attitudes to fathers' leave use in working life, and considered the consequences of their various uses for their work and careers, caregiving and father–child relations. We also looked out for aspects that may possibly harm the desired change process.

The studies behind the chapters span approximately 30 years. During this period parental leave policies have changed radically from a very short parental leave, where fathers could share only a few weeks with the mothers, to a long total leave, including a shared as well as an individual, earmarked period for both parents. In this concluding chapter, we will discuss the changes that we have seen happen in fatherhood and fathering over the years that the father's quota has existed, and the development towards equal quotas for both parents.

Policy works

After the introduction of the father's quota in 1993, great changes happened in a few years concerning the readiness of fathers in Norway to use the earmarked, non-transferable leave granted to them. Staying at home on leave looking after a baby has traditionally been the role of mothers. To change this heavily gendered field, policy measures such as the father's quota have proven to be important. Focusing on the connection between policy design and leave use, we have endeavoured to understand the processes behind fathers' high take-up of the father's quota. The analyses in Part I show how the fathers have become aware of their individual rights, and they regard the father's quota as *their* entitlement. Over time, in granting fathers this right, the welfare state has contributed to turning leave-taking into a norm for modern fathering practices. A statutory, earmarked and non-transferable right means that it is 'pre-negotiated' by the state, and this diminishes the need for negotiations with the mother. Furthermore, these design characteristics represent an advantage in relation to workplaces where fathers' specific parental leave rights have become accepted and respected. Individual leave entitlement is also experienced as a motivating factor for most fathers to take care of their children, and without the 'push' represented by an earmarked, non-transferable leave, some fathers would not have taken it. Fathers with a foreign country background identify well the elements of the design that makes the father's quota work for them: namely that it is statutory, non-transferable and not the least, that it is generously paid. These fathers represent an 'outsider-within' perspective that confirms the importance of the leave design.

Comparing the father's quota with shared leave, its advantages become even more visible. Contrary to the intent of the law, which was to encourage parents to share parental leave, the fathers didn't generally see shared leave as something they were entitled to. Rather, it is discursively defined as mothers' entitlement, and fathers wanting to use it had to negotiate with mothers as well as employers. The shared leave has not become a matter of fact like the father's quota, and it seems that fathers taking it must be particularly motivated and/or circumstances such as mothers' lack of rights or a wish to return to work may be behind this choice. Mothers consenting to fathers using this leave may thus represent both a possibility and a hindrance. In the recent public debate over the extension of the father's quota at the expense of the shared leave, a tendency to controversy between motherhood and fatherhood has become visible. Breaking with maternalistic presumptions still rouses conflict. However, there has been a certain increase in fathers' use of the shared leave over the last years, as some use a longer leave period than their full quota. This increase may mean that fathers are starting to expand their sense of entitlement based on their achieved competences as caregivers.

Some design elements of the father's quota may increase fathers' use of leave but work contrary to the aim of making men into fathers by building care competences and strengthening the father–child relation. Attention therefore needs to be directed towards the content of the leave – what fathers do when on leave. One of these design characteristics is the option to use the quota flexibly in terms of part-time leave combined with part-time work or taking bits of leave now and then over the first three years. The intention of this option to use the rights in a flexible way is to accommodate a need for parents to tailor the leave to families' various situations. However, flexible use also seems to be fitted to fathers' desire to be present at work and/or satisfy both home and work. There is thus a risk that flexible use supports the traditional path dependency that defines fathers as workers and breadwinners at the expense of caregivers. As such, it does less to back the transformation of men into carers and promote the dual carer/dual earner model. Change may still happen, but at a slower pace.

Towards caring masculinities

There is no doubt that taking leave alone has a great potential for developing father involvement and gender equality in terms of time invested in childcare. Fathers being home alone on leave means taking total responsibility for the child, which helps facilitate a move from being the mother's supporting player to being an equal co-parent. Our first study of fathers using the father's quota showed the importance of distinguishing between two situations: solo leave and leave with the mother at home. Fathers who stayed home alone displayed a different involvement than fathers on leave with the mother present. Having main responsibility leads to fathers developing a need-oriented care practice because they learn to read the child and thus develop competence as carers. When the mother was home at the same time, this type of process did not take place. These fathers represented the first generation of fathers who used the earmarked leave, which was then four weeks. Therefore, designing the father's quota with an option to take their leave when the mother is also at home means making men into involved caregivers at a slower pace. Through pregnancy, confinement, breastfeeding and a long leave, the mother has come to know the baby well before the father comes home on leave. Understandably, if the mother continues to be home during his leave, the father's role is easily constituted as a helper, or perhaps just a 'visitor' in caring.

In our second study, the fathers who had been home alone 10 years later had experienced a much longer period of leave because of the extension of the father's quota to 12 weeks. Exploring similarities and differences among home-alone leave users in the two studies we find both changes and continuities in their experiences of leave use. One clear similarity is that the fathers in both studies expressed great enthusiasm with staying at home with their children. Because the last group of home-alone fathers were home for a longer period and had primary responsibility for their children's wellbeing, they developed parenting skills and experienced an intensification of their emotional bonds with their child. Spending time alone with the child for a longer period seems to promote the development of embodied emotions and relational competence. These findings show that men's caregiving practices and their time alone with the baby may be transformative. The greater their involvement, the more likely it seems to be that they regard themselves as equal caregivers and incorporate care into their masculine identity.

We find a notable change concerning housework. While the fathers in the early study concentrated on taking care of their children when they stayed at home, the latter group integrated cleaning and cooking with caring. This may reflect the general pattern of a gendered change in society, which together with having a longer period of leave, led them to take on more responsibility for all household tasks. Another change is that while the fathers in the first study mostly tended to talk about the positive aspects of staying home alone looking after their child, the second group of fathers described care work as hard work. These fathers experience the total commitment that caring for a small child requires when staying home alone for a longer period. This challenges their previous understandings of care work and leads to a greater respect for the care work that mothers have done previously. Our interviews with immigrant fathers show the same development of involvement.

Changing the 'ideal worker' norm

Throughout several chapters, the book has addressed the role of working life concerning the change in leave behaviour of employed men who have become fathers. From our analyses conducted when the father's quota was new, until our last study 15 years later, the conflict between fatherhood and the ideal of the unencumbered employee seems to have weakened in many types of organizations. Over time, workplace norms of acceptance have been generated, and taking leave has become standard practice. Many fathers in the years of our first study made career advancements, and consequently today's managers have used the father's quota themselves. The analysis in Chapter 12 describes them as fathers who can accept being replaceable at work and who are able to break the 'career logic' to be available for their children. Fathers in general experience a supportive working life, and immigrant fathers learn this with surprise and gratitude. If this means that the leave has strengthened employees as fathers to the extent that their fathering practices challenge the ideal worker norm, the father's quota has been demonstrated to possess a radical potential. Taking leave has not only constituted a challenge to masculinist workplace norms but also to the notion of men as ideal workers.

Our second study, conducted right after the introduction of the father's quota, helps illustrate this change. At that time, fathers and workplaces seemed to be insecure about the new policy and did not know quite how to handle it and what to expect. As things were less self-evident to begin with, many workplaces demonstrated some opposition towards fathers' leave-taking. This happened both when fathers wanted to start their leave and later, when work needed to be adapted to employees' responsibilities as involved fathers. Often, negotiations were needed, both with employers and managers, but also with their own sense of irreplaceability and performance as men and workers. In these negotiations, fathers' individual motivations and agency were important for the outcome. To our surprise, and contrary to most international research results, in our last study there are no stories of strong resistance from workplaces when fathers want to use the quota. Workplaces respect parental leave policies and find ways to handle challenges and possible problems produced by employees on leave. At a national level, both employers' associations and trade unions support the leave system, which shows the advantages of the Norwegian working life model based on cooperation between employers and employees (see Chapter 11). In return for the positive attitude of the workplaces, fathers who are about to take leave adapt their timing and try to avoid putting their workplace in a tight spot.

The father's quota has provided the opportunity to provide care, and learning how to care has changed fathers' thinking, about the importance of their working life, too. Throughout the chapters in this book there are many reports of a change in personal priorities, and this change has also affected work–life balance after the leave is over. Although the real struggle for balancing work and care starts when the leave is over, and although there are work contexts that cannot easily be changed, we detected several strategies that fathers employ in order to reduce time spent working to the advantage of time for their children (Chapter 9).

In this book, one backdrop has been the dual earner/dual carer model that is an expression of the gender equality aim in the Nordic countries. We delimited this theme to focus on fathers as dual carers, and believe the observed change of fathers into more motivated and competent caregivers is one of the most radical contributions to this model. The non-transferable father's quota has greatly contributed to this change. However, the father's quota alone cannot bring about a new gender equality model. It has existed in a period where many other changes towards gender equality in family and working life have happened. The interplay between these other trends and the father's quota have magnified the speed and scale of the changes.

References

Aarseth, H. (2008) 'Samstemt selvskaping: Nye fedre i ny økonomi' ['Unanimous self-creation: New fathers in the new economy'], *Tidsskrift for kjønnsforskning*, 32: 4–21.

Aarseth, H. (2013) 'De nye barneorienterte fedrene' ['The new child-oriented fathers'], in B. Brandth and E. Kvande (eds) *Fedrekvoten og den farsvennlige velferdsstaten*, Oslo: Universitetsforlaget, 238–50.

Acker, J. (1990) 'Hierarchies, jobs, bodies: A theory of gendered organizations', *Gender & Society*, 4(2): 139–58.

Acker, J. (1997) 'Foreword', in L. Rantalaiho and T. Heiskanen (eds) *Gendered practices in working life*, New York: St Martin's Press, ix–xi.

Ahrne, G. and Roman, C. (1997) *Hemmet, barnen och makten: Förhandlingar om arbete och pengar i familjen*, Stockholm: Arbetsmarknadsdepartementet (SOU 1997:139).

Alasuutari, P. (1996) *Researching culture: Qualitative method and cultural studies*, London: Sage.

Almqvist, A.-L. (2008) 'Why most Swedish fathers and few French fathers use paid parental leave: An exploratory qualitative study of parents', *Fathering*, 6(2): 192–200.

Almqvist, A.-L. and Dahlgren, L. (2013) 'Swedish fathers' motives for parental leave take-up in different scenarios', in E. Oinonen and K. Repo (eds) *Women, men and children in families: Private troubles and public issues*, Tampere: Tampere University Press, 91–112.

Almqvist, A.-L. and Duvander, A-Z. (2014) 'Changes in gender equality? Swedish fathers' parental leave, division of childcare and housework', *Journal of Family Studies*, 20(1): 19–27.

Alvesson, M. and Schöldberg, K. (1994) *Tolkning och reflektion* [*Interpretation and reflection*], Lund: Studentlitteratur.

Anttonen, A. and Sipilä, J. (1996) 'European social care services: Is it possible to identify models?', *Journal of European Social Policy*, 5(2): 131–49.

Ba', S. (2010) 'Meaning and structure in the work and family interface', *Sociological Research Online*, 15: 10.

Backett, K. (1987) 'The negotiation of fatherhood', in C. Lewis and M. O'Brien (eds) *Reassessing fatherhood*, London: Sage, 74–90.

Bagnoli, A. (2007) 'Between outcast and outsider: Constructing the identity of the foreigner', *European Societies*, 9(1): 23–44.

Bauman, Z. (1998) *Globalization: The human consequences*, Cambridge: Polity Press.

Beck, U. and Beck-Gernsheim, E. (1995) *The normal chaos of life*, Cambridge: Blackwell.

Bekkengen, L. (2002) *Män får välja – Om föräldraskap och föräldraledighet i arbetsliv och familjeliv* [*Men may choose – On parenthood and parental leave in working life and family life*], Malmö: Liber.

Bell, J. (2016) 'Migrants: Keeping a foot in both worlds or losing the ground beneath them? Transnationalism and integration as experienced in the everyday lives of Polish migrants in Belfast, Northern Ireland', *Social Identities*, 22(1): 80–94.

Bengtsson, M. and Frykman, J. (1987) *Om maskulinitet: Mannen som forskningsprosjekt*, Stockholm: JÄMFO.

Bergqvist, C. and Saxonberg, S. (2017) 'The state as a norm-builder? The take-up of parental leave in Norway and Sweden', *Social Policy & Administration*, 51(7): 1470–87.

Bettio, F. and Plantenga, J. (2004) 'Comparing care regimes in Europe', *Feminist Economics*, 10(1): 85–113.

Bjerrum Nielsen, H. and Rudberg, M. (1989) *Historien om jenter og gutter*, Oslo: Universitetsforlaget.

Bjørnholt, M. and Stefansen, K. (2019) 'Same but different: Polish and Norwegian parents' work–family adaptations in Norway', *Journal of European Social Policy*, 29(2): 292–304.

Blair-Loy, M. and Wharton, A. (2002) 'Employee's use of family-responsive policies and the workplace social context', *Social Forces*, 80: 813–45.

Blum, S., Koslowski, A. and Moss, P. (2017) *International Review of Leave Policies and Research 2017*, www.leavenetwork.org/lp_and_r_reports/

Blum, S., Koslowski, A., Macht, A. and Moss, P. (2018) *International Review of Leave Policies and Research 2018*, www.leavenetwork.org/lp_and_r_reports/

Boje, T. and Ejrnæs, A. (2013) *Ulige vægt: Arbejde og familie i Europa*, Fredriksberg: Nyt fra Samfundsvidenskaberne.

Bonoli, G. (1997) 'Classifying welfare states: A two dimension approach', *Journal of Social Policy*, 26(3): 351–72.

Boyer, D. (2017) 'Fathers on leave alone in France: Does part-time parental leave for men move towards an egalitarian model?', in K. Wall and M. O'Brien (eds) *Fathers on leave alone: Comparative perspectives on work-life balance and gender equality*, London: Springer, 183–204.

Brandth, B. (2019) 'Farmers framing fatherhood: Everyday life and rural change', *Agriculture and Human Values*, 36: 49–59.

Brandth, B. and Kvande, E. (1989) 'Like barn deler best', *Nytt om kvinneforskning*, 13(3): 8–17.

Brandth, B. and Kvande, E. (1991) 'Når likhet blir ulikhet: Foreldres forhandlinger om barneomsorg', in R. Haukaa (ed) *Nye kvinner: Nye menn*, Oslo: Ad Notam, 117–42.

Brandth, B. and Kvande, E. (1992) 'Fedres arbeidsvilkår og omsorgspermisjoner' ['Fathers' working conditions and care leave'], *Søkelys på arbeidsmarkedet*, 9(2): 158–68.

Brandth, B. and Kvande, E. (1998) 'Masculinity and child care: The reconstruction of fathering', *Sociological Review*, 26(2): 293–313.

Brandth, B. and Kvande, E. (2001) 'Flexible work and flexible fathers', *Work, Employment & Society*, 15(2): 251–67.

Brandth, B. and Kvande, E. (2003a) *Fleksible fedre* [*Flexible fathers*], Oslo: Universitetsforlaget [Norwegian University Press].

Brandth, B. and Kvande, E. (2003b) 'Father presence in child care', in A.-M. Jensen and L. McKee (eds) *Children and the changing family: Between transformation and negotiation*, London: RoutledgeFalmer, 61–75.

Brandth, B. and Kvande, E. (2009a) 'Norway: The making of the father's quota', in S. Kamerman and P. Moss (eds) *The politics of parental leave policies: Children, parenting, gender and the labour market*, Bristol: Policy Press, 191–206.

Brandth, B. and Kvande, E. (2009b) 'Gendered or gender neutral care policies for fathers?', *Annals of the American Academy of Political and Social Science*, 624(1): 177–89.

Brandth, B. and Kvande, E. (2011) 'Free choice or gentle force? How can parental leave change gender practices?', In A.T. Kjørholt and J. Qvortrup (eds) *The modern child and the flexible labour market*, Basingstoke: Palgrave, 56–70.

Brandth, B. and Kvande, E. (eds) (2013a) *Fedrekvoten og den farsvennlige velferdsstaten*, Oslo: Universitetsforlaget.

Brandth, B. and Kvande, E. (2013b) 'Fedrekvotens valgfrihet og fleksibilitet', in B. Brandth and E. Kvande (eds) *Fedrekvoten og den farsvennlige velferdsstaten*, Oslo: Universitetsforlaget, 134–49.

Brandth, B. and Kvande, E. (2016a) 'Parental leave and classed fathering practices in Norway', in G.B. Eydal and T. Rostgaard (eds) *Fatherhood in the Nordic welfare states: Comaring care policies and practice*, Bristol: Policy Press, 121–40.

Brandth, B. and Kvande, E. (2016b) 'Fathers and flexible parental leave', *Work, Employment & Society*, 30(2): 275–90.

Brandth, B. and Kvande, E. (2017) 'Fathers integrating work and childcare: Reconciling the logics?', in B. Brandth, S. Halrynjo and E. Kvande (eds) *Work–family dynamics: Competing logics of regulation, economy and morals*, London: Routledge, 70–85.

Brandth, B. and Kvande, E. (2018) 'Masculinity and fathering alone during parental leave', *Men and Masculinities*, 21(1): 72–90.

Brandth, B., Halrynjo, S. and Kvande, E. (eds) (2017) *Work–family dynamics: Competing logics of regulation, economy and morals*, London: Routledge.

Breidahl, K.N. and Larsen, C.A. (2016) 'The myth of unadaptable gender roles: Attitudes towards women's paid work among immigrants across 30 European countries', *Journal of European Social Policy*, 26(5): 387–401.

Brighthouse, H. and Wright, E.O. (2008) 'Strong gender egalitarianism', *Politics & Society*, 36(3): 360–72.

Brittan, A. (1989) *Masculinity and power*, Oxford: Basil Blackwell.

Brod, H. (ed) (1987) *The making of masculinities: The new men's studies*, London: Allen & Unwin.

Brod, H. and Kaufman, M. (1994) *Theorizing masculinities*, London: Sage.

Bungum, B. (2013) 'Barnas fedrekvote – tid sammen med far' ['Children's father's quota – time together with daddy'], in B. Brandth and E. Kvande (eds) *Fedrekvoten og den farsvennlige velferdsstaten*, Oslo: Universitetsforlaget, 60–73.

Bungum, B., Forseth, U. and Kvande, E. (eds) (2015) *Den norske modellen: Internasjonalisering som utfordring og vitalisering*, Bergen: Fagbokforlaget.

Bünning, M. (2015) 'What happens after the "daddy months?" Fathers' involvement in paid work, childcare, and housework after taking parental leave in Germany', *European Sociological Review*, 31(6): 738–48.

Bygren, M. and Duvander, A.-Z. (2006) 'Parents' workplace situation and fathers' parental leave use', *Journal of Marriage and Family*, 68: 363–72.

Cais, J. and Folguera, L. (2013) 'Redefining the dynamics of intergenerational family solidarity in Spain', *European Societies*, 15(14): 557–76.

Carrigan, T., Connell, R.W. and Lee, J. (1985) 'Towards a new sociology of masculinity', *Theory & Society*, 14: 551–603.

Castro-Garcia, C. and Pazos-Moran, M. (2016) 'Parental leave policy and gender equality in Europe', *Feminist Economics*, 22(3): 51–73.

Chesley, N. (2005) 'Blurring boundaries? Linking technology use, spillover, individual distress and family satisfaction', *Journal of Marriage and the Family*, 67: 1237–48.

Christian, H. (1994) *The making of anti-sexist men*, London: Routledge.

Clark, S.C. (2000) 'Work/family border theory: A new theory of work/family balance', *Human Relations*, 53: 747–70.

Cockburn, C. (1985) *Machinery of dominance*, London: Pluto Press.

Collins, P.H. (1986) 'Learning from the outsider within: The sociological significance of Black feminist thought', *Social Problems*, 33(6): 4–32.

Coltrane, S. (1997) *Family man: Fatherhood, housework, and gender equity*, New York: Oxford University Press.

Connell, R.W. (1985) 'Theorizing gender', *Sociology*, 19: 260–72.

Connell, R.W. (1987) *Gender and power*, London: Polity Press.

Connell, R.W. (1995) *Masculinities*, Oxford: Polity Press.

Connell, R.W. (2000) *The men and the boys*, Cambridge: Polity Press.

Corsaro, W.A. (1997) *The sociology of childhood*, Thousand Oaks, CA: Pine Forge Press.

Coser, L. (1974) *Greedy institutions: Patterns of undivided commitment*, New York: Free Press.

Craig, L. (2006) 'Does father care mean father's share? A comparison of how mothers and fathers in intact families spend time with their children', *Gender & Society*, 20: 259–81.

Dahl, G.B., Løken, K.V. and Mogstad, M. (2014) 'Peer effects in program participation', *American Economic Review*, 104(7): 2049–74.

Daly, K. (1993) 'Reshaping fatherhood: Finding the models', *Journal of Family Issues*, 14(4): 510–31.

Daly, K., Ashbourne, L. and Brown, J.L. (2009) 'Fathers' perception of children's influence: Implications for involvement', *Annals of the American Academy of Political and Social Science*, 624: 61–77.

Daly, M. (2011) 'What adult worker model? A critical look at recent social policy reform in Europe from a gender and family perspective', *Social Politics*, 18(19): 1–24.

Daly, M. and Rake, K. (2003) *Gender and the welfare state: Care, work and welfare in Europe and the USA*, Cambridge: Polity Press.

Dearing, H. (2016) 'Gender equality in the division of work: How to assess European leave policies regarding their compliance with an ideal leave model', *Journal of European Social Policy*, 26(3): 234–47.

Delsen, L. (1998) 'When do men work part-time?', in J. O'Reilly and C. Fagan (eds) *Part-time prospects: An international comparison of part-time work in Europe, North-America and the Pacific Rim*, London: Routledge, 57–76.

Dermott, E. (2008) *Intimate fatherhood: A sociological analysis*, London: Routledge.

Deutsch, F. (2007) 'Undoing gender', *Gender & Society*, 21: 106–27.

Dommermuth, L. and Kitterød, R.H. (2009) 'Fathers' employment in a father-friendly welfare state: Does fatherhood affect men's working hours?', *Community, Work & Family*, 12: 417–36.

Doucet, A. (2006) *Do men mother?*, Toronto, ON: University of Toronto Press.

Doucet, A. (2017) 'The ethics of care and the radical potential of fathers "home alone on leave": Care as practice, relational ontology, and social justice', in M. O'Brien and K. Wall (eds) *Comparative perspectives on work–life balance and gender equality: Fathers on leave alone*, London: Springer, 11–28.

Doucet, A. and Merla, L. (2007) 'Stay-at-home-fathering: A strategy for balancing work and home in Canadian and Belgian families', *Community, Work & Family*, 10: 455–73.

Dølvik, J.E., Fløtten, T., Hippe, J.M. and Jordfald, B. (2014) *Den nordiske modellen mot 2030: Et nytt kapittel?*, Report 2014:46, Oslo: Fafo.

Drakich, J. (1989) 'In search of the better parent: The social construction of ideologies of fatherhood', *Canadian Journal of Women and the Law*, 3(1): 64–87.

Dumas, T.L. and Sanchez-Burks, J. (2015) 'The professional, the personal, and the ideal worker: Pressures and objectives shaping the boundary between life domains', *The Academy of Management Annals*, 9(1): 803–43.

Duvander, A.-Z. (2013) 'Er den svenske permisjonsordningen for fleksibel?', in B. Brandth and E. Kvande (eds) *Fedrekvoten og den farsvennlige velferdsstaten*, Oslo: Universitetsforlaget, 165–79.

Duvander, A.-Z. and Lammi-Taskula, J. (2011) 'Parental leave', in I.V. Gíslason and G.B. Eydal (eds) *Parental leave, childcare and gender equality in the Nordic countries*, TemaNord 2011: 562, Copenhagen: Nordisk Ministerråd [Nordic Council of Ministers], 31–64.

Duvander, A.-Z., Eydal, G.B., Brandth, B., Gíslason, I.V., Lammi-Taskula, J. and Rostgaard, T. (2019) 'Gender equality: Parental leave design, men's participation and evaluating effects', in P. Moss, A.-Z. Duvander and A. Koslowski (eds) *Parental leave and beyond: Recent international developments, current issues and future directions*, Bristol: Policy Press, 187–204.

Eerola, J.P. and Huttunen, J. (2011) 'Metanarrative of the "new father" and narratives of young Finnish first-time fathers', *Fathering*, 9(3): 211–31.

Ellingsæter, A.L. (2003) 'Når familiepolitikk ikke virker... Om kontantstøttereformen og mødres lønnsarbeid' ['When family policy does not work... On the cash-for-care reform and the employment of mothers'], *Tidsskrift for Samfunnsforskning*, 44: 499–527.

Ellingsæter, A.L. (2012) 'Ideational struggles over symmetrical parenthood: The Norwegian daddy quota', *Journal of Social Policy*, 41(4): 695–714.

Ellingsæter, A.-L. (2016) 'Kampen om familiepolitikken: Farvel til hybridregimet?', *Tidsskrift for Samfunnsforskning*, 56(3): 227–56.

Ellingsæter, A.-L. (2018) 'Familiepoltikkens kjønnsforståelser – to spor og fire tiår', *Nytt Norsk Tidsskrift*, 34(3/4): 246–55.

Elliott, K. (2015) 'Caring masculinities: Theorizing an emerging concept', *Men and Masculinities*, 19(3): 240–59.

Erdal, M.B. and Oeppen, C. (2013) 'Migrant balancing acts: Understanding the interactions between integration and transnationalism', *Journal of Ethnic and Migration Studies*, 39(6): 867–84.

Esping-Andersen, G. (1990) *The three worlds of welfare capitalism*, Cambridge: Polity Press.

Esping-Andersen, G. (2002) 'A new gender contract', in G. Esping-Andersen, D. Gallie, A. Hemerijck and J. Myles (eds) *Why we need a new welfare state*, Oxford: Oxford University Press, 68–95.

Esping-Andersen, G. (2009) *The incomplete revolution: Adapting to women's new roles*, Cambridge: Polity Press.

Eydal, G.B. and Rostgaard, T. (eds) (2016) *Fatherhood in the Nordic welfare states*, Bristol: Policy Press.

Eydal, B.B., Gíslason, I.V., Rostgaard, T., Brandth, B., Duvander, A.-Z. and Lammi-Taskula, J. (2015) 'Trends in parental leave in the Nordic countries: Has the forward march of gender equality halted?', *Community, Work & Family*, 18(2): 167–81.

Farstad, G. and Stefansen, K. (2015) 'Involved fatherhood in the Nordic context: Dominant narratives, divergent approaches', *NORMA: International Journal for Masculinity Studies*, 10(1): 55–70.

Fassinger, P.A. (1993) 'Meanings of housework for single fathers and mothers: Insights into gender inequality', in J.C. Hood (ed) *Men, work, and family*, London: Sage, 195–216.

Ferrera, M. (1996) 'The southern model of welfare in social Europe', *Journal of European Social Policy*, 9(4): 285–300.

Flyvbjerg, B. (2006) 'Five misunderstandings about case-study research', *Qualitative Inquiry*, 12(2), 219–45.

Fougner, E. (2012) 'Fedre tar ut hele fedrekvoten – også etter at den ble utvidet til ti uker', *Arbeid og Velferd*, 2: 71–7.

Fraser, N. (1994) 'After the family wage: Gender equity and the welfare state', *Political Theory*, 22(4): 591–618.

Frønes, I. (1989) *Den norske barndommen* [*Norwegian childhood*], Oslo: Cappelen.

Gallie, D. (2003) 'The quality of working life: Is Scandinavia different?', *European Sociological Review*, 19(1): 61–79.

Gatrell, C. and Cooper, G. (2016) 'A sense of entitlement? Fathers, mothers and organizational support for family and career', *Community, Work & Family*, 19(2): 134–47.

Geisler, E. and Kreyenfeld, D. (2011) 'Against all odds: Fathers' use of parental leave in Germany', *Journal of European Social Policy*, 21(1): 88–99.

Giddens, A. (1992) *The transformation of intimacy*, Cambridge: Polity Press.

Gobo, G. (2006) 'Sampling, representativeness and generalizability', in C. Seale, G. Gobo, J.F. Gubrium and D. Silverman (eds) *Qualitative research practice*, London: Sage, 34–47.

Goffman, E. (1974) *Frame analysis: An essay on the organization of experience*, Cambridge, MA: Harvard University Press.

Golden, A.G. and Geisler, C. (2007) 'Work–life boundary management and the personal digital assistant', *Human Relations*, 60(3): 519–51.

Gooderham, P.N., Nordhaug, O. and Ringdal, K. (1999) 'Institutional and rational determinants of organizations' practices: Human resource management in European forms', *Administrative Science Quarterly*, 44(3): 507–31.

Gornick, J.C. (2015) 'Leave policies in challenging times: What have we learned? What lies ahead?', *Community, Work & Family*, 18(2): 236–43.

Gornick J.C. and Meyers, M.K. (2009a) 'Institutions that support gender equality in parenthood and employment', in J.C. Gornick and M.K. Meyers (eds) *Gender equality: Transforming family divisions of labor*, London: Verso, 3–64.

Gornick, J.C. and Meyers, M.K. (eds) (2009b) *Gender equality: Transforming family divisions of labor*, London: Verso.

Grambo, A.-C. and Myklebø, S. (2009) *Moderne familier – Tradisjonelle valg. En studie av mors og fars uttak av foreldrepermisjon* [*Modern families – Traditional choices. A study of the mother's and father's use of parental leave*], NAV report 2/2009, Oslo: Arbeids- og Velferdsdirektoratet [Norwegian Labour and Welfare Organization].

Gregory, A. and Milner, S. (2011) 'Fathers and work–life balance in France and the UK: Policy and practice', *International Journal of Sociology and Social Policy*, 31(1/2): 34–52.

Grenness, T. (2003) 'Scandinavian managers on Scandinavian management', *International Journal of Value-Based Management*, 16(1): 9–21.

Grødem, A.S. (2017) 'Family-oriented policies in Scandinavia and the challenge of immigration', *Journal of European Social Policy*, 27(1): 77–89.

Haas, L. and Hwang, C. P. (2008) 'The impact of taking parental leave on fathers' participation in childcare and relationships with children: Lessons from Sweden', *Community, Work & Family*, 11(1): 85–104.

Haas, L. and Hwang, P.H. (2009) 'Is fatherhood becoming more visible at work? Trends in corporate support for fathers taking parental leave in Sweden', *Fathering*, 7(3): 303–21.

Haas, L. and Hwang, C.P. (2019) 'Workplace support and European fathers' use of state policies promoting shared childcare', *Community, Work & Family*, 22(1): 1–22.

Haas, L. and Rostgaard, T. (2011) 'Fathers' right to paid parental leave in the Nordic countries: Consequences for the gendered division of care', *Community, Work & Family*, 14(2): 177–95.

Haavind, H. (1992) 'Kvinners utviklingsmuligheter i en verden i forandring', in *Kjønnsidentitet, utvikling og konstruksjon av kjønn*, Memo 1/92, Trondheim: Centre for Women's Studies.

Hagen, I.M. (2017) *Arbeidsgivers holdning til foreldrepermisjon*, Report 2017: 40, Oslo: Fafo.

Håland, K. (2001) 'Kontantstøtten – et veiskille i norsk familiepolitikk?', Master's thesis, Trondheim: NTNU.

Håland, K. (2005) 'Fra enighet til strid i familiepoltikken', in B. Brandth, B. Bungum and E. Kvande (eds) *Valgfrihetens tid*, Oslo: Gyldendal akademisk, 26–43.

Halrynjo, S. (2009) 'Men's work-life conflict: Career, care and self-realization: Patterns of privileges and dilemmas', *Gender, Work & Organization*, 16(1): 98–125.

Halrynjo, S. (2017) 'Exploring the career logic with the Nordic work – family model', in B. Brandth, S. Halrynjo and E. Kvande (eds) *Work–family dynamics: Competing logics of regulation, economy and morals*, London: Routledge, 198–208.

Halrynjo, S. and Kitterød, R.H. (2016) *Fedrekvoten – Norm for fedres permisjonsbruk i Norge og Norden. En litteraturstudie* [*The father's quota – The norm for father's leave use in Norway and the Nordic countries: A literature study*], ISF report 2016: 06, Oslo: Institute for Social Research (ISF).

Halrynjo, S. and Lyng, S.T. (2010) 'Fars forkjørsrett-mors vikeplikt? Karriere, kjønn og omsorgsansvar i eliteprofesjoner' ['Father's right of way – mother's obligation to yield? Career, gender and caregiving responsibility in elite professions'], *Tidsskrift for Samfunnsforskning*, 2: 249–80.

Halrynjo, S. and Lyng, S.T. (2013) 'Fedrepermisjon i karriereyrker' ['Fathers' leave in career professions'], in B. Brandth and E. Kvande (eds) *Fedrekvoten og den farsvennlige velferdsstaten*, Oslo: Universitetsforlaget, 222–37.

Hamre, K. (2017) 'Fedrekvoten – mer populær enn noen gang', *Samfunnsspeilet*, 1, Oslo: Statistics Norway, www.ssb.no/befolkning/artikler-og-publikasjoner/fedrekvoten-mer-populaer-enn-noen-gang--298200

Hanlon, N. (2012) *Masculinities, care and equality: Identity and nurture in men's lives*, Basingstoke: Palgrave Macmillan.

Hansen, S.M.H. and Bozett, F.W. (eds) (1985) *Dimensions of fatherhood*, London: Sage.

Hays, S. (1996) *The cultural contradictions of motherhood*, New Haven, CT: Yale University Press.

Hearn, J. and Collinson, D.J. (1994) 'Theorizing unities and differences between men and between masculinities', in H. Brod and M. Kaufman (eds) *Theorizing masculinities*, London: Sage, 97–118.

Heggem, G.F. and Kvande, E. (2017) 'Nordic work-family regulations exported to a liberal context', in B. Brandth, S. Halrynjo and E. Kvande (eds) *Work–family dynamics: Competing logics of regulation, economy and morals*, London: Routledge, 156–72.

Hernes, G. (2006) 'Den norske mikromodellen. Virksomhetsstyring, partssamarbeid og sosial kapital' ['The Norwegian micro model. Performance management, collaboration between the parties in working life and social capital'], Report 07:25, Oslo: Fafo.

Hobson, B. (2002) *Making men into fathers: Men, masculinities and the social politics of fatherhood*, New York: Cambridge University Press.

Hobson, B. and Fahlen S. (2009) 'Competing scenarios for European fathers: Applying Sen's capabilities and agency framework to work/family balance', *The ANNALS of the American Academy of Political and Social Science*, 624: 214–33.

Hobson, B. and Morgan, D.H.J. (2002) 'Introduction', in B. Hobson (ed) *Making men into fathers*, Cambridge: Cambridge University Press, 1–21.

Hochschild, A.R. (1989) *The second shift*, New York: Avon Books.

Hochschild, A.R. (1997) *The time bind: When work becomes home and home becomes work*, New York: Metropolitan Books.

Hoel, A. (2013) 'Fedrekvoten i et kulturelt komplekst Norge', in B. Brandth and E. Kvande (eds) *Fedrekvoten og den farsvennlige velferdsstaten*, Oslo: Universitetsforlaget, 106–20.

Holter, T. and Brandth, B. (2005) 'Tidskonto: Valgfrihet for elitemødre?', in B. Brandth, B. Bungum and E. Kvande (eds) *Valgfrihetens tid*, Oslo: Gyldendal Akademisk, 79–94.

Holter, Ø.G. and Aarseth, H. (1993) *Menns livssammenheng*, Oslo: Ad Notam.

Hood, J. (ed) (1993) *Men, work, and family*, London: Sage.

Höygaard, L. (1997) 'Working fathers: Caught in the web of the symbolic order of gender', *Acta Sociologica*, 40: 245–61.

Hylland Eriksen, T. (2001) *Øyeblikkets tyranni* [*The tyranny of the moment*], Oslo: Aschehoug.

Illouz, E. (2007) *Cold intimacies: The making of emotional capitalism*, Cambridge: Polity Press.

Kamerman, S.B. and Moss, P. (eds) (2009) *The politics of parental leave policies: Children, parenting, gender and the labour market*, Bristol: Policy Press.

Kammer, A., Niehues, J. and Pleichl, A. (2012) 'Welfare regimes and welfare state outcomes in Europe', *Journal of European Social Policy*, 22(5): 455–71.

Kangas, O. and Palme, J. (eds) (2005) *Social policy and economic development in the Nordic countries*, Basingstoke: Palgrave Macmillan.

Karu, M. and Tremblay, D.-G. (2018) 'Fathers on parental leave: An analysis of rights and take-up in 29 countries', *Community, Work & Family*, 21(3): 344–62.

Kaufman, F.-X. (2002) 'Politics and policies towards the family in Europe: A framework and an inquiry into their differences and convergences', in F.-X. Kaufman, A. Kuijsten, H.J. Schulze and K.P. Strohmeier (eds) *Family life and family policies in Europe, Vol 2: Problems and issues in comparative perspective*, Oxford: Oxford University Press, 419–90.

Kaufman, G. (2017) 'Barriers to equality: Why British fathers do not use parental leave', *Community, Work & Family*, 21(3): 310–25.

Kaufman, G. and Almqvist, A.-L. (2017) 'The role of partners and workplaces in British and Swedish men's parental leave decisions', *Men and Masculinities*, 20(5): 533–51.

Kaufman, M. (ed) (1987) *Beyond patriarchy: Essays by men on pleasure, power and change*, Toronto, ON: Oxford University Press.

Kimmel, M.S. (ed) (1987) *Changing men: New directions in research on men and masculinity*, London: Sage.

Kimmel, M. and Messner, M. (eds) (1992) *Men's lives*, New York: Macmillan.

Kitterød, R.H. (2003) *Tid til barna? [Time for children?]*, Report 2003/5, Oslo: Statistics Norway.

Kitterød, R.H. (2007) 'Fremdeles et tosporet foreldreskap?' ['Still a double-track parenthood?'], in E. Kvande and B. Rasmussen (eds) *Arbeidslivets klemmer: Paradokser i det nye arbeidslivet [Squeezes and paradoxes in the new working life]*, Bergen: Fagbokforlaget, 221–48.

Kitterød, R.H. (2013) 'Mer familiearbeid og mindre jobb blant småbarnsfedre' ['More family work and less work among families with small children'], in B. Brandth and E. Kvande (eds) *Fedrekvoten og den farsvennlige velferdsstaten*, Oslo: Universitetsforlaget, 42–59.

Kitterød, R.H. and Halrynjo, S. (2017) 'Mindre spesialisering med fedrekvote? Foreldrepermisjonens potensial for å endre arbeidsdelingen blant foreldre' ['Less specialization with father's quota? A discussion of the potential for parental leave to change gendered work-family patterns'], *Tidsskrift for Samfunnsforskning*, 58(3): 311–33.

Kitterød, R.H. and Kjeldstad, R. (2006) 'Kortere arbeidstid for fedre – men fremdeles et tosporet foreldreskap' ['Shorter working hours for fathers – but still a double-track parenthood'], *Søkelys på arbeidsmarkedet*, 23: 159–71.

Kitterød, R.H. and Lømo, A. (1996) 'Småbarnsforeldres tidsbruk 1970–90', in B. Brandth and K. Moxnes (eds) *Familie for tiden* [*Families at present*], Oslo: Tano.

Kitterød, R.H., Halrynjo, S. and Østbakken, K.M. (2017) *Pappaperm? Fedre som ikke tar fedrekvote – Hvor mange, hvem og hvorfor?* [*Fathers who do not use the father's quota – how many, who and why?*], Report 2017:2, Oslo: Institute for Social Research (ISF).

Kjelstad, R. (2006) 'Hvorfor deltid?' ['Why part time?'], *Tidsskrift for Samfunnsforskning*, 47: 513–44.

Klinth, R. and Johansson, T. (2010) *Nya svenska fäder*, Umeå: Borea Bokförlag.

Korsvik, T.R. and Warat, M. (2016) 'Framing leave for fathers in Norway and Poland: Just a matter of gender equality?', *NORA – Nordic Journal of Feminist and Gender Research*, 24(2): 110–25.

Koslowski, A., Blum, S., Dobrotić, I., Macht, A. and Moss, P. (2019) *International Review of Leave Policies and Research 2019*. Available at: www.leavenetwork.org/annual-review-reports/

Kvande, E. and Brandth, B. (2013) '"Haha, skal du ta maternita?" Fedre mellom to velferdsregimer', in B. Brandth and E. Kvande (eds) *Fedrekvoten og den farsvennlige velferdsstaten*, Oslo: Universitetsforlaget, 74–90.

Kvande, E. and Brandth, B. (2017) 'Individualized, non-transferable parental leave for European fathers: Migrant perspectives', *Community, Work & Family*, 20(1): 19–34.

Lamb, M.E. (1976) *The role of the father in child development*, New York: Wiley.

Lamb, M.E. (2000) 'The history of research on father involvement', *Marriage & Family Review*, 29(2–3): 23–42.

Lammi-Taskula, J. (2006) 'Nordic men on parental leave: Can the welfare state change gender relations?', in A.L. Ellingsæter and A. Leira (eds) *Politicising parenthood in Scandinavia: Gender relations in welfare states*, Bristol: Policy Press, 79–100.

Lammi-Taskula, J. (2007) *Parental leave for fathers?*, Helsinki: Stakes.

Lammi-Taskula, J. (2008) 'Doing fatherhood: Understanding the gendered use of parental leave in Finland', *Fathering*, 6(2): 133–48.

Lappegård, T. and Bringedal, T.H. (2013) 'Stor oppslutning om fedrekvoten' ['Great support for the father's quota'], in B. Brandth and E. Kvande (eds) *Fedrekvoten og den farsvennlige velferdsstaten*, Oslo: Universitetsforlaget, 29–41.

LaRossa, R. (1988) 'Fatherhood and social change', *Family Relations*, 37(4), 451–7.

LaRossa, R. (1992) 'Fatherhood and social change', in M. Kimmel and M. Messner (eds) *Men's lives*, New York: Macmillan, 521–34.

Lash, S. (1990) *Sociology of post-modernism*, London: Routledge.

Lawrence, T.B. and Suddaby, R. (2006) 'Institutions and institutional work', in S.R. Clegg, C. Hardy, T.B. Lawrence and W.R. Nord (eds) *The SAGE handbook of organization studies*, London: Sage, 215–54.

Leitner, S. (2003) 'Varieties of familialism: The caring function of the family in comparative perspective', *European Societies*, 5(4): 353–75.

Levin, M., Nilssen, T., Ravn, J. and Øyum, L. (2012) *Demokrati i arbeidslivet*, Bergen: Fagbokforlaget.

Lewis, C. and O'Brien, M. (eds) (1987) *Reassessing fatherhood*, London: Sage.

Lewis, J. (2001) 'The decline of the male breadwinner model: Implications for work and care', *Social Politics*, 2: 152–69.

Lewis, R.A. and Sussman, M.B. (eds) (1985/86) 'Men's changing roles in the family', *Marriage and Family Review*, 9(3–4).

Lewis, S. (1997) '"Family friendly" employment policies: A route to changing organizational culture or playing about at the margins?', *Gender, Work and Organization*, 4: 13–23.

Lewis, S. and Lewis, J. (1997) 'Work family conflict: Can the law help?', *Legal and Criminological Psychology*, 2: 155–67.

Lewis, S. and Smithson, J. (2001) 'Sense of entitlement to support for the reconciliation of employment and family life', *Human Relations*, 54(11): 1455–81.

Lewis, S. and Stumbitz, B. (2017) 'Research on work and family: Some issues and challenges', in B. Liebig and M. Oechsle (eds) *Fathers in work organizations: Inequalities and capabilities, rationalities and politics*, Berlin: Barbara Budrich Publishers, 227–44.

Lewis, S., Brannen, J. and Nilsen, A. (eds) (2009) *Work, families and organisations in transition: European perspectives*, London: Policy Press.

Liebig, B. and Oechsle, M. (2017) 'Introduction', in B. Liebig and M. Oechsle (eds) *Fathers in work organizations*, Berlin: Barbara Budrich Publishers, 1–17.

Lyng, S.T. (2010) 'Mothered and othered: (In) visibility of care responsibility and gender in processes of excluding woman from Norwegian law firms', in P. Lewis and R. Simpson (eds) *Revealing and concealing gender: Issues of visibility in organizations*, Basingstoke: Palgrave Macmillan, 76–99.

Major, B. (1993) 'Gender, entitlement, and the distribution of family labor', *Journal of Social Issues*, 49(3): 141–59.

Mannifest (1989) *Førebels statusrapport frå mannsrolleutvalget* [*Preliminary report from the Male Role Committee*], Oslo: Forbruker og administrasjonsdepartementet.

Marsiglio, W. (1993) 'Contemporary scholarship on fatherhood: Culture, identity, and conduct', *Journal of Family Issues*, 14(4): 484–510.

Marsiglio, W. (1995) *Fatherhood: Contemporary theory, research, and social policy*, London: Sage.

Matzke, M. and Ostner, I. (2010) 'Introduction: Change and continuity in recent family policies', *Journal of European Social Policy*, 20(5): 387–98.

McKay, L. and Doucet, A. (2010) '"Without taking her leave": A Canadian case study of couples' decisions on fathers' use of paid parental leave', *Fathering*, 8(3): 300–20.

Merton, R. (1929) 'Insiders as outsiders: A chapter in the sociology of knowledge', *American Journal of Sociology*, 78: 9–47.

Messner, M.A. (1993) '"Changing men" and feminist policies in the United States', *Theory & Society*, 22: 723–37.

Miller, T. (2011) *Making sense of fatherhood*, Cambridge: Cambridge University Press.

Miller, T. (2013) 'Shifting out of neutral on parental leave. Making fathers' involvement explicit', *Public Policy Research*, 19(4): 258–62.

Miller, T. (2017) 'Making sense of motherhood and fatherhood', in B. Brandth, S. Halrynjo and E. Kvande (eds), *Work–family dynamics: Competing logics of regulation, economy and morals*, London: Routledge, 105–20.

Moen, L.V. (2017) '"Hun ble en pappajente". Å gjøre seg uerstattelig i omsorgen og erstattelig på jobb', Master's thesis in Sociology, Trondheim: Department of Sociology and Political Science, NTNU.

Morgan, D. (1992) *Discovering men*, London: Routledge.

Morgan, D.H.J (1996) *Family connections: An introduction to family studies*, Cambridge: Polity Press.

Morgan, K.J. (2008) 'The political path to a dual earner/dual carer society: Pitfalls and possibilities', *Politics & Society*, 36(3): 403–20.

Moss, P. and Deven, F. (2006) 'Leave policies and research: A cross-national overview', *Marriage & Family Review*, 39(3–4): 255–85.

Moss, P. and Deven, F. (2015) 'Leave policies in challenging times: Reviewing the decade 2004–2014', *Community, Work & Family*, 18(2): 137–44.

Moss, P. and Kamerman, S. (2009) 'Introduction', in S. Kamerman and P. Moss (eds) *The politics of parental leave policies*, Bristol: Policy Press, 1–13.

Moss, P., Duvander, A.-Z. and Koslowski, A. (eds) (2019) *Parental leave and beyond: Recent developments, current issues, future directions*, Bristol: Policy Press.

Mussino, E. and Duvander, A.-Z. (2016) 'Use it or save it? Migration background and parental leave uptake in Sweden', *European Journal of Population*, 32(2): 189–210.

Mussino, E., Tervola, J. and Duvander, A.-Z. (2018) 'Decomposing the determinants of fathers' parental leave use: Evidence from migration between Finland and Sweden', *Journal of European Social Policy*, 1–16.

Närvi, J. and Salmi, M. (2019) 'Quite an encumbrance? Work-related obstacles to Finnish fathers' take-up of parental leave', *Community, Work & Family*, 22(1): 23–42.

Naz, G. (2010) 'Usage of parental leave by fathers in Norway', *International Journal of Sociology and Social Policy*, 30(5/6): 313–25.

Neuman, B. and Meuser, M. (2017) 'Changing fatherhood? The significance of parental leave for work organizations and couples', in B. Liebig and M. Oechsle (eds) *Fathers in work organizations*, Berlin: Barbara Budrich Publishers, 83–102.

Nippert-Eng, C.E. (1996) *Home and work: Negotiating boundaries through everyday life*, Chicago, IL: University of Chicago Press.

NOU (Official Norwegian Report) 1993: 12, *Tid for barna*, Oslo: Ministry of Children and Family.

NOU 2012: 15, *Politikk for likestilling*, Oslo: Ministry of Children, Equality and Inclusion.

NOU 2017: 6, *Offentlig støtte til barnefamiliene*, Oslo: Ministry of Children and Gender Equality.

O'Brien, M. (2009) 'Fathers, parental leave policies and infant quality of life: International perspectives and policy impact', *The Annals of the American Academy of Political and Social Science*, 624: 190–213.

O'Brien, M. (2013) 'Fitting fathers into work–family policies: International challenges in turbulent times', *International Journal of Sociology and Social Policy*, 33(9/10): 542–64.

O'Brien, M. and Wall, K. (eds) (2017) *Comparative perspectives on work–life balance and gender equality: Fathers on leave alone*, London: Springer.

Oechsle, M. and Beaufaÿs, S. (2017) 'Hidden rules and competing logics: Working fathers within organizations in Germany', in B. Brandth, S. Halrynjo and E. Kvande (eds) *Work–family dynamics: Competing logics of regulation, economy and morals*, London: Routledge, 121–37.

O'Reilly, J. and Fagan, C. (eds) (1998) *Part-time prospects: An international comparison of part-time work in Europe, North America and the Pacific Rim*, London: Routledge.

Ostner, I. (2004) 'Individualization – The origins of the concept and its impact on German social policies', *Social Policy & Society*, 3(1): 47–56.

Pascall, G. (2012) *Gender equality in the welfare state?*, Bristol: Policy Press.

Pedersen, F.A. (1985) 'Research and the father: Where do we go from here?' in S.M.H. Hansen and F.W. Bozett (eds) *Dimensions of fatherhood*, London; Sage, 435–50.

Pleck, J.H. (1987) 'American fathering in historical perspective', in M.S. Kimmel (ed) *Changing men: New directions in research on men and masculinity*, London: Sage, 83–97.

Pleck, J.H., Lamb, M.E. and Levine, J. (1985) 'Facilitating future change in men's family roles', *Marriage and Family Review*, 9(3–4): 11–16.

Pollock, S. and Sutton, J., (1985) 'Father's rights, women's losses', *Women's Studies International Forum*, 8(6): 593–99.

Prop 64L (2011-2012) *Endringer I folketrygdloven (tredeling av foreldrepengeperioden)*, Oslo: Ministry of Children, Equality and Inclusion.

Radin, N. and Russell, G. (1983) 'Increased paternal participation: The fathers' perspective', in M. Lamb and A. Sagi (eds) *Fatherhood and family policy*, London: Lawrence Erlbaum Associates, 136–9.

Ranson, G. (2015) *Fathering, masculinity and the embodiment of care*, Houndmills, Basingstoke: Palgrave Macmillan.

Ravn, J. (2015) 'Forhandling, forvaltning og forvandling – den norske samarbeidsmodellens muligheter i fremtidens arbeidsliv', in B. Bungum, U. Forseth and E. Kvande (eds) *Den norske modellen: Internasjonalisering som utfordring og vitalisering*, Bergen: Fagbokforlaget, 37–52.

Ray, R., Gornick, J.C. and Schmitt, J. (2010) 'Who cares? Assessing generosity and gender equality in parental leave policy designs in 21 countries', *Journal of European Social Policy*, 20(3): 196–216.

Rehel, E.R. (2014) 'When dad stays home too: Paternity leave, gender, and parenting', *Gender and Society*, 28(1): 110–32.

Risman, B.J. (1987) 'Intimate relationships from a microstructural perspective: Men who mother', *Gender & Society*, 1(1): 6–32.

Romero-Balsas, P., Muntanyola-Saura, D. and Rogero-García, J. (2013) 'Decision-making factors within paternity and parental leaves: Why Spanish fathers take time off from work', *Gender, Work & Organization*, 20(6): 678–91.

Roosalu, T., Pajumets, M. and Hansson, L. (2016) '"Experts" arguments for paternity leave: Social-democratic and post-socialist frames compared', in T. Roosalu and D. Hofäcker (eds) *Rethinking gender, work and care in a new Europe*, London: Palgrave Macmillan, 47–63.

Rudman, L.A. and Mecher, K. (2013) 'Penalizing men who request a family leave: Is flexibility stigma a femininity stigma?', *Journal of Social Issues*, 69(2): 322–40.

Sainsbury, D. (ed) (1994) *Gendering welfare states*, London: Sage Publications.

Sainsbury, D. (1999) 'Gender, policy regimes and politics', in D. Sainsbury (ed) *Gender and welfare state regimes*, New York: Oxford University Press, Chapter 8.

Saraceno, C. (2004) 'De-familization or re-familiarization? Trends in income-tested family benefits', in T. Knijn and A. Komter (eds) *Solidarity between the sexes and the generations: Transformations in Europe*, Cheltenham: Edward Elgar, 68–86.

Schmidt, E.M., Arieder, I., Zartler, U., Schandler, C. and Richter, R. (2015) 'Parental constructions of masculinity at the transition to parenthood: The division of parental leave among Austrian couples', *International Review of Sociology*, 25(3): 373–86.

Schou, L. (2017) 'Fedrekvoten – uttak og holdninger' ['The father's quota – take up and attitudes'], *Arbeid og Velferd*, 3: 81–95.

Schutz, A. (1944) 'The stranger: An essay in social psychology', *American Journal of Sociology*, 49: 499–507.

Schwartz, B. (2004) *The paradox of choice: Why more is less*, New York: Ecco/HarperCollins.

Seidler, V. (1988) 'Fathering, authority and masculinity', in R. Chapman and J. Rutherford (eds) *Male order: Unwrapping masculinity*, London: Lawrence & Wishart.

Segal, L. (1988) 'Look back in anger: Men in the 50s', in R. Chapman and J. Rutherford (eds) *Male order: Unwrapping masculinity*, London: Lawrence & Wishart, 68–97.

Segal, L. (1990) *Slow motion: Changing masculinities, changing men*, New Brunswick, NJ: Rutgers University.

Sheridan, A. (2004) 'Cronic presenteeism: The multiple dimensions to men's absence from part-time work', *Gender, Work & Organization*, 11: 207–25.

Sherrod, D. (1987) 'The bonds of men: Problems and possibilities in close male relationships', in H. Brod (ed) *The making of masculinities: The new men's studies*, London: Allen & Unwin, 213–40.

Simmel, G. (1921) 'The sociological significance of the stranger', in R.E. Park and E.W. Burgess (eds) *Introduction to the science of sociology*, Chicago, IL: University of Chicago Press, 322–7.

Smart, C. (2007) *Personal life*, Cambridge: Polity Press.

Smeby, K. (2013) 'Stykkevis og delt eller fullt og helt?', in B. Brandth and E. Kvande (eds) *Fedrekvoten og den farsvennlige velferdsstaten*, Oslo: Universitetsforlaget, 150–64.

Smeby, K.W. (2017) 'Likestilling i det tredje skiftet? Heltidsarbeidende småbarnsforeldres praktisering av familieansvar etter 10 uker med fedrekvote', PhD thesis, Trondheim: Norwegian University of Science and Technology.

Smeby, K.W. and Brandth, B. (2013) 'Mellom hjem og barnehage: Likestilling i det tredje skiftet', *Tidsskrift for kjønnsforskning*, 37(3/4): 329–47.

Smith, D. (2005) *Institutional ethnography: A sociology for people*, Lanham, MD: AltaMira.

SSB (Statistics Norway) (2014) 'Innvandrere etter innvandringsgrunn', 1 January, www.ssb.no/befolkning/statistikker/innvgrunn

Stortingsmelding [Report to Parliament] no 4 (1988-89). Langtidsprogrammet 1990–1993. Oslo: The Government.

Strauss, A. (1978) *Negotiations*, San Francisco, CA: Jossey-Bass.

Strohmeier, K.P. (2002) 'Family policy: How does it work?', in F.-X. Kaufman, A. Kuijsten, H.J. Schulze, and K.P. Strohmeier (eds) *Family life and family policies in Europe, Vol 2: Problems and issues in comparative perspective*, Oxford: Oxford University Press, 321–62.

Stryker, S. (1987) 'The vitalization of symbolic interactionism', *Social Psychology Quarterly*, 50(1): 83–94.

Sumer, S. (2009) *European gender regimes and policies: Comparative perspectives*, Farnham: Ashgate.

Suwada, K. (2017) '"It was necessary at the beginning to make this whole revolution": Men's attitudes to parental leave in Sweden and Poland', *Men and Masculinities*, 20(5): 570–87.

Tervola, J., Duvander, A.-Z. and Mussino, E. (2017) 'Promoting parental leave for immigrant fathers – What role does policy play?', *Social Politics*, 24(3): 269–97.

Thompson, J.A. and Bunderson, J.S. (2001) 'Work-nonwork conflict and the phenomenology of time', *Work and Occupations*, 28: 17–39.

Valarino, I. (2017) 'Fathers on leave alone in Switzerland: Agents of social change?', in K. Wall and M. O'Brien (eds) *Comparative perspectives on work–life balance and gender equality*, London: Springer, 205–30.

Valarino, I. and Gauthier, J.-A. (2016) 'Paternity leave implementation in Switzerland: A challenge to gendered representations and practices of fatherhood?', *Community, Work & Family*, 19(1): 1–19.

Valarino, I., Duvander, A.-Z. and Haas, L. (2018) 'Exploring leave policy preferences: A comparison of Austria, Sweden, Switzerland, and the United States', *Social Politics*, 25(1): 118–47.

Valcour, P.M. and Hunter, L.W. (2005) 'Technology, organizations, and work–life integrations', in E.E. Kossek and S.J. Lambert (eds) *Managing work–life integration in organizations: Future directions for research and practice*, Mahwah, NJ: Erlbaum, 61–84.

Vollset, G. (2011) *Familiepolitikkens historie 1970–2000*, Oslo: Nova.

von Alemann, A., Beaufaÿs, S. and Oechsle, M. (2017) 'Work organizations and fathers' lifestyles: Constraints and capabilities', in B. Liebig and M. Oechsle (eds) *Fathers in work organizations: Inequalities and capabilities, rationalities and politics*, Opladen: Barbara Budrich Verlag, 21–40.

Wajcman, J. (1991) *Feminism confronts technology*, Cambridge: Polity Press.

Wall, K. (2014) 'Fathers on leave alone: Does it make a difference to their lives?', *Fathering*, 12(2): 196–210.

Wall, G. and Arnold, S. (2007) 'How involved is involved fathering? An exploration of the contemporary culture of fatherhood', *Gender & Society*, 21(4): 508–27.

West, C. and Zimmerman, D.H. (1987) 'Doing gender', *Gender & Society*, 1: 125–51.

Wettergren, Å., Starrin, B. and Lindgren, G. (eds) (2008) *Det sociala livets emotionella grunder* [*The emotional basis of social life*], Malmö: Liber.

Wærness, K. (1984) 'The rationality of caring', *Economic and Industrial Bureaucracy*, 5(2): 185–211.

Yarwood, G.A. (2011) 'The pick and mix of fathering identities', *Fathering*, 9(2): 150–68.

Żadkowska, M., Kosakowska-Berezecka, N. and Ryndyk, O. (no date) 'Two worlds of fatherhood – Comparing the use of parental leave among Polish fathers in Poland and in Norway', Unpublished paper.

Østbakken, K.M., Halrynjo, S. and Kitterød, R.H. (2018) *Foreldrepengeordningens betydning for likestilling i arbeidslivet og hjemme*, ISF report 2018: 15, Oslo: Institute for Social Research.

Appendix: Data and Methods

The chapters are based on three research projects conducted in different decades. All of them contain extensive interviews with fathers about their use of and experiences with parental leave, particularly the father's quota.

The first study was conducted at the end of the 1980s when the parental leave rights were much less generous than today. The fathers had no leave period reserved for them as the study took place before the introduction of the father's quota. The rights allowed a total period of 20 weeks at 100 per cent pay, in addition to 32 weeks without pay. After the first six weeks the parents both now and in 1987 could share the rest of the weeks. Chapter 5 is based on this study.

Overall, the data in this first study consisted of three samples. First, all men who became fathers in the Norwegian municipality of Trondheim (the third largest urban area in Norway) were surveyed in 1987. The questionnaire was sent to 1,600 men, of whom 60 per cent responded. Only 0.9 per cent of those fathers (7) who had the right to share paid parental leave availed themselves of their right to do so, and they were all interviewed. A total of 2.7 per cent of the fathers took some unpaid parental leave so that altogether, 3.6 per cent of the fathers shared the parental leave with the mothers (Brandth and Kvande, 1989). Second, to obtain a broader basis of leave users, a questionnaire was sent to all men in Norway registered by the National Insurance Administration (Rikstrygdeverket) who had taken paid leave in 1987. This sample consisted of 260 men, and the response rate was 75 per cent. Data from this shows that fathers who took parental leave in the 1980s had a high level of education and were in the high to middle income range.

Finally, we conducted interviews with 10 couples, mothers and fathers, who became parents in 1987 and who had shared the parental leave period. Only seven fathers had shared the paid parental leave in Trondheim this year; they and their partners were all interviewed. Moreover, three couples who shared the unpaid leave period were interviewed. The interviews were held in 1988 with the mothers and fathers separately. As is evident, couples sharing parental leave in 1987 comprised a very small group – a minority of involved fathers.

The second main study was conducted about 10 years later, towards the end of the 1990s. The father's quota had been introduced just a few years earlier, and this was the first study in Norway to examine how fathers used and experienced an earmarked and non-transferable leave. Chapters 6, 9 and 10 use data from this study.

Data in this study consisted of a questionnaire sent to all men who became fathers in the same municipality as the first study. The survey was sent in 1996 to a sample consisting of 2,194 people, and the response rate was 62.8 per cent. A year later, interviews were conducted with 30 couples, 10 of whom had only used the father's quota, and 10 who had also shared the parental leave. It turned out that couples with a high and middle educational background dominated the sample. We therefore decided to interview 10 additional couples who had occupations that did not require a higher education. This supplied a broader social background to the total interview sample. The interview sample was drawn from the couples who had answered the questionnaire and who had agreed to being contacted.

The third and most recent study is an interview study of fathers only. The main part of the interviews was conducted in 2012 and 2013, and consisted of 40 interviews. The father's quota had existed for about 20 years, and at this time the leave system had become even more generous, the father's quota having expanded to 12 weeks and more fathers obtaining eligibility. Chapters 2, 3, 4, 7, 8 and 11 are based on this study. The interview sample was comprised of fathers who are Norwegian-born as well as having an immigrant background (20). As the fathers used the parental leave system in different ways, the size of the sample makes sub-samples possible. Thus, in Chapter 4 on flexible timing of the leave, the analysis examines the experiences of those fathers who used the father's quota flexibly. Likewise, Chapters 3 and 8 are based on the interviews with immigrant fathers only, while Chapter 6 is based on the fathers who used the whole father's quota consecutively while the mothers went back to work.

The fathers were recruited by contact with various work organizations, in addition to snowballing individual fathers. Extra effort was put into finding interviewees with those with a lower educational background. Two-thirds of the sample have a higher and middle education at Master's and Bachelor's levels. The occupational composition of the sample is, however, varied, comprising craftsmen, teachers, consultants, researchers, health, administrative and service staff. They work in many different forms of organizations. A majority of the sample is employed in private companies of various sizes, and 10 per cent are self-employed. The fathers and mothers had all been employed before the birth of the child. Most fathers were employed full time, and only a couple of students held part-time work. All of the fathers lived with the mother and child(ren). The children involved may be the first, second or third child. The interviewees lived in Trondheim, a city that was also the site for the two previous studies. Fathers most often take their leave after the mother, that is, starting when the child is aged from 9 to 12 months, and at the time of the interview, the oldest child was two-and-a-half years old, making fathers' leave experiences quite recent.

One chapter is based on an additional study. Chapter 13 employs interviews from a recent study of middle-managers in the engineering sector, and was conducted in 2017. Nine fathers were found through strategic selection according to three criteria. First, they were fathers who had a management position; second, they had used the father's quota; and third, they had children young enough for the fathers to remember the leave period in relative detail.

Index